# 江门长堤历史街区

CHANGDI HISTORICAL NEIGHBORHOOD IN JIANGMEN CITY

孙一民　张春阳　林健生　苏　平　骆　乐　编著
Sun Yimin, Zhang Chunyang, Lin Jiansheng, Su Ping, Luo Le

华南理工大学出版社
SOUTH CHINA UNIVERSITY OF TECHNOLOGY PRESS
·广州·

鸣谢：
江门市城乡规划局
华南理工大学亚热带建筑科学国家重点实验室

图0-1　长堤路历史照片
PICTURE0-1　HISTORICAL PICTURE OF CHANGDI ROAD

This book is sponsored by Jiangmen Urban Planning Bureau, and
State Key Laboratory of Subtropical Building Science,
South China University of Technology.

# 前言

江门是珠江三角洲西部的重要中心城市，久远的人类活动变迁与元末明初以来的经济社会发展，为这座风景秀美、交通门户地位显著的五邑之城带来了深厚的历史文化积淀。历史街区与历史建筑是体现江门历史文化城市特色的精髓所在，也是元末明初至今江门经济文化和社会生活变迁的载体与见证。其中，位于蓬江北岸的长堤历史街区集中体现了江门城市空间演变的基本脉络，同时也蕴含着江门多元且深厚的民俗文化和生活特色，是凝聚当地历史文化精华的核心所在。

长堤历史街区历史悠久，在江门城市发展过程中曾经是最为重要的城市中心区域，现今集合了各个历史时期的典型商业设施和居住建筑，形成了以墟顶、石湾直街和骑楼街区等为代表的重要片区。虽然经历了时代的变迁和社会的转变，部分历史建筑已经不复存在，但今天的长堤历史街区在整体上仍然保留着清代和民国时期的形态肌理和空间环境，并且保存了与陈白沙等历史名人史迹相关的建筑遗址。在珠三角地区，其历史风貌保存相对完整，作为自然环境和人文环境有机结合的代表区域，具有非常高的研究与保护价值，是岭南地区重要的传统文化遗产。

流连于江门优美的自然与人文风貌，细细查看历史遗迹的丰富留存，感受四通八达的交通汇集带来的多元文化交融，会让每一位历史街区保护规划的工作者都深深为此地着迷。编写本书时，编者团队多次前往江门历史街区进行拍摄调研，完成系统的考察和记录。穿梭在充满文化积淀的历史街区中，强烈感受着老江门独特的生活韵味和悠扬的文化气息。

本书侧重于江门长堤历史街区内现存的重要历史建筑和典型街巷空间环境的介绍，并对历史街区保护规划的研究和实践进行总结。根据各个历史时期的建设特点和现状，编者将现状历史街区分为四个风貌区：墟顶居住风貌区、石湾历史风貌区、华侨建筑风貌区和骑楼风貌区，并通过认真的现场调研勘察和后期的分类研究，整理出每个风貌区的保存现状和有价值的建筑影像信息。其中，华侨建筑风貌区融合在墟顶居住风貌区和石湾历史风貌区中，由于民国时期江门华侨归国投资兴建而得名，区内建筑是国内早期独栋别墅房地产开发建设的雏形，因此将其与另外两个风貌区区分开来。根据华南理工大学编制的江门历史街区建筑GIS数据库，通过建筑质量、建筑外观特色、建筑文化特色等建筑风貌的评定，筛选了二十余栋历史风貌建筑和四十余个街巷空间。读者在本书中可以看到江门在明清时期、民国时期和新中国成立后建设的，以及近年来改造的街区代表，包括骑楼建筑群集、中西风格合璧，曾有"小广州"之称的商业老区——长堤风貌街区；承载江门城市早年衣食住行、吃喝玩乐等丰富市民生活，并作为新中国成立初期政府所在地的常安路区；新中国成立前后作为江门及周边地区谈论时局、振兴文化的重要舆论阵地，文人趋之若鹜的莲平路街区；以及整体的空间格局和街巷脉络保留了传统岭南古村落空间形态特征的石湾直街等一批具有代表性的历史空间形态范例。

长堤历史街区内部至今仍然保留着清代和民国时期建筑群体和街区风貌，但除了常安路步行街和长堤风貌街等少部分地区外，街区内部大量历史悠久、风貌独特的建筑和街巷由于缺乏有效的保护和管理，其质量在逐步衰退，其价值也甚少为外界所了解。本书致力于记录和展示江门长堤历史街区内具有较高历史文化价值的建筑物以及形态和风貌保存较为完好的街巷空间，记录丰富而充满趣味的市井生活。通过对街巷等城市公共空间以及历史建筑的调查和研究，不仅可以展现江门历史街区的文化价值与历史价值，也能够发挥其在历史保护和文化复兴工作中的基础性作用，将江门长堤历史街区的原貌完整地呈现给广大读者朋友们，这也是本书编写的主要目的和意义所在。

作者

2015年12月

# PREFACE

Jiangmen, an important central city in the west part of Pearl River Delta, boasts rich historical and cultural heritages, beautiful landscapes and sophisticated transportation system, thanks to the human activities long time ago and social and economic development since the end of the Ming Dynasty and the beginning of the Qing Dynasty. Historical neighborhood and buildings are not only the essence of the city's historical and cultural heritage, but also physical carriers and witnesses of the city's social, economic and cultural development. Among these historical neighborhood and buildings, the Changdi Historical Neighborhood at the north bank of Pengjiang River is a core area displaying the evolution of the city's layout, accommodating its abundant and diversified folk culture and exemplifying its historical and cultural essence.

Since establishment, Changdi Historical Neighborhood has always been a significant urban area in Jiangmen that accommodates key commercial facilities and residential buildings in different times, and has been gradually divided into smaller important neighborhoods including Xuding District, Shiwan District and Qilou (Arcade Building) District. As time goes by, many historical buildings are gone, but Changdi Historical Neighborhood as a whole has maintained the urban texture and surrounding environment as in the periods of Qing Dynasty and the Republic of China. Historical sites related to famous celebrities like Chen Shabai were preserved. As an example that combines natural environment and rich cultural heritage, Changdi Historical Neighborhood stands as an important cultural heritage in Lingnan region worth studying and protecting.

The scholars were quite impressed as well and they immersed themselves in the beautiful natural and cultural landscape, visited the historical sites and felt the blend of culture brought by easy transportation. As the authors are writing this book, the team paid quite a few visits to the Changdi Historical Neighborhood, made systematic inspection and records, wandered in the historical districts rich in cultural elements and were impressed by the unique charm of lifestyle in Jiangmen and its cultural context.

This book introduces important historical buildings and typical streets and lanes in the Changdi Historical Neighborhood, and make a conclusion on researches and practices on the protection plans of the Neighborhood. Based on different styles of buildings in different times and their status quo, the authors further divide the Neighborhood into four districts, including Xuding Residential District, Shiwan Historical District, Modern Overseas Chinese

Architecture District and Qilou (Arcade Building) District, and document the status quo and valuable images of buildings in every district after field research and classification. Among the four districts, the Modern Overseas Chinese Architecture District, which was originally mixed within the Xuding District and Shiwan District, gained its name because the building of this district was funded by overseas Chinese back in the Republic of China era, and buildings in this district can be seen as an early form of property development of single houses in China, therefore the authors divide it as an independent district. According to the GIS database of Jiangmen Historical Neighborhood and Buildings edited by South China University of Technology, after reviewing and evaluating the construction quality, architectural and cultural features, 27 historical buildings and 42 streets and lanes were selected. Readers can see in this book examples of neighborhood that were built during the Ming and Qing dynasty, the Republic of China era and after the establishment of People's Republic of China and are still in use until today, including the old commercial district- Changdi Historical Neighborhood (nicknamed as Little Guangzhou), which features Qilou (arcade buildings) groups and western and eastern architectural styles; the Chang'an Lu District, which used to be the center of daily life and dining and entertainment for Jiangmen citizens, and once functioned as the location of city government in the early years of People's Republic of China; the Lianping Lu District, a popular place for intellectuals to discuss political affairs and rejuvenate local culture; and the Shiwanzhi Street where the overall spatial layout and streets and lanes in the ancient Lingnan villages were well preserved. All the mentioned above buildings and neighborhood are typical examples of how historical spaces are preserved.

The historical neighborhood still retains the buildings and streets of the Qing Dynasty and the Republic of China. Yet due to lack of effective protection and management, the quality of the most time-honored and unique buildings and streets is getting worse and its values are little known to the outside world (with the exception of Chang'an Pedestrian Street and Changdi Street). We are writing to record and display the historical buildings and well-preserved streets in the Changdi Historical Neighborhood as well as interesting folk life. Research and study on such public spaces as streets and lanes and historical buildings will not only reveal the cultural and historical values of streets and neighborhoods in Jiangmen city, but also build a foundation for preservation and renovation. This is why this book is published.

**Authors**
**Dec.2015**

# 目 录

## 1 长堤历史街区概述

### 1.1 长堤历史街区发展概述 003
1.1.1 长堤历史街区发展概况 003
1.1.2 长堤历史街区重要街巷发展概述 011

### 1.2 江门长堤历史街区的现状认知 017
1.2.1 层叠丰富的文化积淀 017
1.2.2 特色独具的待修缮历史风貌建筑 017
1.2.3 居商混合的用地结构 019
1.2.4 肌理致密的传统街巷 025
1.2.5 快速城市化带来的冲击和挑战 025

## 2 风貌建筑及街巷空间

### 2.1 近代华侨建筑风貌区 045
2.1.1 南芬里 10 号和 11 号 049
2.1.2 南芬里 24 号 055
2.1.3 南芬里 25 号 057
2.1.4 南芬里 30 号 059
2.1.5 南芬里 34 号 061
2.1.6 南芬里广场 063
2.1.7 龙聚里 3 号 067

|  |  |  |
|---|---|---|
| 2.1.8 | 龙聚里 5 号 | 069 |
| 2.1.9 | 龙聚里 35 号和 36 号 | 071 |
| 2.1.10 | 启明里 39~42 号 | 075 |
| 2.1.11 | 启明里 60 号和 61 号 | 077 |
| 2.1.12 | 启明里 69 号和 70 号 | 079 |
| 2.1.13 | 长庆里 25 号 | 081 |
| 2.1.14 | 明德坊 | 083 |
| 2.1.15 | 余庆里 | 086 |
| 2.1.16 | 宝和按当铺 | 095 |

| 2.2 | 骑楼风貌区 | 097 |
|---|---|---|
| 2.2.1 | 中华酒店 | 100 |
| 2.2.2 | 仓后路 44 号 | 105 |
| 2.2.3 | 书院路 2 号 | 107 |
| 2.2.4 | 钓台故址 | 111 |
| 2.2.5 | 中山纪念堂 | 115 |
| 2.2.6 | 莲塘南当铺 | 119 |
| 2.2.7 | 常安路 | 121 |
| 2.2.8 | 堤中路 | 125 |
| 2.2.9 | 莲平路 | 129 |
| 2.2.10 | 仓后路 | 133 |
| 2.2.11 | 兴宁路 | 137 |
| 2.2.12 | 众兴路 | 141 |
| 2.2.13 | 新市路 | 143 |
| 2.2.14 | 太平路 | 145 |
| 2.2.15 | 水街农贸市场（榄豉路、新椰路） | 147 |

| | | |
|---|---|---|
| 2.3 | 石湾历史风貌区 | 153 |
| | 2.3.1　新第里 1、2、3 号 | 157 |
| | 2.3.2　新第里 15 号 | 161 |
| | 2.3.3　石湾直街、新第里 | 163 |
| 2.4 | 墟顶居住风貌区 | 167 |
| | 2.4.1　墟顶街 | 171 |
| | 2.4.2　东南盛街 | 175 |
| | 2.4.3　京果街 | 179 |
| | 2.4.4　新盛街 | 181 |
| | 2.4.5　永安按当铺 | 183 |
| | 2.4.6　三十三级台阶 | 185 |

# 3　保护与复兴

| | | |
|---|---|---|
| 3.1 | 保护与复兴实施策略 | 189 |
| | 3.1.1　保护与复兴目标定位 | 189 |
| | 3.1.2　整体保护、渐进式的街区修复策略 | 191 |
| | 3.1.3　街区与地域文化复兴 | 191 |
| | 3.1.4　生态技术的应用 | 197 |
| | 3.1.5　保护与复兴的多方探索 | 197 |
| | 3.1.6　旧城开发资金筹措 | 203 |

|  |  |  |
|---|---|---|
| 3.2 | 历史街区的保护与更新 | 207 |
|  | 3.2.1　街巷体系和公共空间的发展 | 207 |
|  | 3.2.2　弘扬特色与场所再造 | 207 |
|  | 3.2.3　历史风貌建筑保护更新和新建筑发展 | 211 |
|  | 3.2.4　产业及人口结构调整 | 217 |
| 3.3 | 旧城复兴项目策划 | 225 |
|  | 3.3.1　保护项目 | 225 |
|  | 3.3.2　更新与升级项目 | 225 |
|  | 3.3.3　植入项目 | 227 |
|  | 3.3.4　环境设施改善 | 227 |

| | |
|---|---|
| **附录：江门长堤历史街区重要历史建筑名录** | 232 |
| **主要参考文献** | 250 |
| **图片来源** | 251 |
| **后记** | 252 |

# CONTENTS

1 **Profile of Changdi Historical Neighborhood**
   1.1  OVERVIEW OF CHANGDI HISTORICAL NEIGHBORHOOD    003
       1.1.1  History of Changdi Historical Neighborhood    003
       1.1.2  Overview of Important Streets and Lanes in Changdi Historical Neighborhood    011

   1.2  PERCEPTIONS ON THE STATUS QUO OF CHANGDI HISTORICAL NEIGHBORHOOD    017
       1.2.1  Rich Cultural Heritage    017
       1.2.2  Unrenovated Historical Buildings with Unique Architectural Styles    019
       1.2.3  Land layout and Structure for Commercial and Residential Purposes    019
       1.2.4  Traditional Alleys and Streets reflecting Dense Urban Texture    025
       1.2.5  Impacts and Challenges brought by Rapid Urbanization    025

2 **Historical Buildings and Lanes**
   2.1  MODERN OVERSEAS CHINESE BUILDINGS DISTRICT    045
       2.1.1  No.10 & No.11 of Nanfen Lane    049
       2.1.2  No. 24 of Nanfen Lane    055
       2.1.3  No.25 of Nanfen Lane    057
       2.1.4  No.30 of Nanfen Lane    059
       2.1.5  No.34 of Nanfen Lane    061
       2.1.6  Nanfen Lane Square    063
       2.1.7  No.3 of Longju Lane    067
       2.1.8  No.5 of Longju Lane    069
       2.1.9  No. 35 & NO.36 of Longju Lane    071

|  |  |  |
|---|---|---|
| 2.1.10 | No.39 - 42 of Qiming Lane | 075 |
| 2.1.11 | No.60 & No.61 of Qiming Lane | 077 |
| 2.1.12 | No.69 & No.70 of Qiming Lane | 079 |
| 2.1.13 | No.25 of Changqing Lane | 081 |
| 2.1.14 | Mingde Lane | 083 |
| 2.1.15 | Yuqing Lane | 086 |
| 2.1.16 | Baohe Pawnshop | 095 |
| **2.2** | **QILOU (ARCADE BUILDING) DISTRICT** | **097** |
| 2.2.1 | Zhonghua (China) Hotel | 100 |
| 2.2.2 | No.44 of Canghou Road | 105 |
| 2.2.3 | No. 2 of Shuyuan Road | 107 |
| 2.2.4 | Fomer Site of Fishing Terrace | 111 |
| 2.2.5 | Sun Yat-sen Memorial Hall | 115 |
| 2.2.6 | Liantangnan Pawnshop | 119 |
| 2.2.7 | Chang'an Road | 121 |
| 2.2.8 | Dizhong Road | 125 |
| 2.2.9 | Lianping Road | 129 |
| 2.2.10 | Canghou Road | 133 |
| 2.2.11 | Xingning Road | 137 |
| 2.2.12 | Zhongxing Road | 141 |
| 2.2.13 | Xinshi Road | 143 |
| 2.2.14 | Taiping Road | 145 |
| 2.2.15 | Water Street Farmer's Market (Lanchi Road and Xinye Road) | 147 |

|  |  |  |  |
|---|---|---|---|
| 2.3 | SHIWAN HISTORICAL DISTRICT | | 153 |
| | 2.3.1 | No.1 to No.3 of Xindi Lane | 157 |
| | 2.3.2 | No. 15 of Xindi Lane | 161 |
| | 2.3.3 | Shiwanzhi Street and Xindi Lane | 163 |
| 2.4 | XUDING RESIDENTIAL DISTRICT | | 167 |
| | 2.4.1 | Xuding Street | 171 |
| | 2.4.2 | Dongnansheng Street | 175 |
| | 2.4.3 | Nuts Street | 179 |
| | 2.4.4 | Xinsheng Street | 181 |
| | 2.4.5 | Yong'an pawnshop | 183 |
| | 2.4.6 | Thirty-three Stone Steps | 185 |

## 3 Protection and Regeneration

|  |  |  |  |
|---|---|---|---|
| 3.1 | STRATEGY FOR PRESERVATION AND RESTORATION | | 189 |
| | 3.1.1 | Preservation and Restoration Positioning | 189 |
| | 3.1.2 | Renovation for Phased Renewal and Overall Protection | 191 |
| | 3.1.3 | Blocks and Local Culture Renaissance | 191 |
| | 3.1.4 | Application of Eco-technology | 197 |
| | 3.1.5 | Efforts from Multiple Stakeholders | 197 |
| | 3.1.6 | Fundraising for the Urban Renewal Project | 203 |
| 3.2 | PROTECTION AND REGENERATION | | 207 |
| | 3.2.1 | The Development of Street System and Public Space | 207 |
| | 3.2.2 | Highlighting the Unique Style and Remaking of the Place | 207 |

|  |  | 3.2.3 | Protection & Renewal of Historical Buildings and Development of New Buildings | 213 |
|---|---|---|---|---|
|  |  | 3.2.4 | Industry and Population Restructuring | 217 |
|  | 3.3 | OLD TOWN RESTORATION PLAN |  | 225 |
|  |  | 3.3.1 | Conservation Projects | 225 |
|  |  | 3.3.2 | The Regeneration and Updating Projects | 225 |
|  |  | 3.3.3 | The Implant Projects | 227 |
|  |  | 3.3.4 | Improving the Environment | 227 |

| **APENDIX** | 232 |
|---|---|
| **MAIN REFERENCE** | 250 |
| **IMAGES SOURCE** | 251 |
| **EPILOGUE** | 253 |

# 1 长堤历史街区概述

Profile of Changdi Historical Neighborhood

图1-1-1 江门市在珠三角的区位
PICTURE1-1-1 POSITION OF JIANGMEN IN THE PEARL RIVER DELTA

# 1.1 长堤历史街区发展概述
## 1.1 OVERVIEW OF CHANGDI HISTORICAL NEIGHBORHOOD

江门市位于广东省中南部、珠江三角洲西部，东邻中山、珠海，西连阳江，北接佛山、云浮，南临南海，毗邻港澳（见图1-1-1）。江门，因地处西江与其支流——蓬江的汇合处，江南的烟墩山和江北的蓬莱山（旧名"狗山"）对峙如门，故名江门。江门作为五邑地区的枢纽，位居粤西地区和西南各省通往珠三角和粤港澳的交通要道，扼西江以及粤西沿海交通之门户，是珠江三角洲经济区的中心城市之一。从以蓬莱山（今江门一中所在地）、烟墩山（今江门十一中所在地附近）和凤凰山（今文化城所在地）为主的小岛陆域的形成，到新会冲积三角洲的出现，江门独特的区位条件和地理格局为其经济、社会、文化奠定了发展的沃土，人类活动的变迁也逐步改变着自然环境与城市空间的形态。

在江门的城市发展中，位于蓬江北岸的长堤历史街区集中体现了江门城市历史变迁的脉络，同时也蕴含着江门多元且深厚的城市文化和市民生活特色，是凝结地方历史文化的精华所在。

### 1.1.1 长堤历史街区发展概况

江门长堤历史街区位于江门市蓬江区，南接蓬江，西临胜利路，东至跃进路，北至建设路和蓬莱路。江门长堤历史街区核心区（见图1-1-2）是街区内历史风貌最为完整、历史建筑最为集中、保存状况最为完好的区域，是保护的重点区域之一。该区用地总面积37.4公顷，核心区内现存历史风貌建筑及环境占地面积26.56公顷，比例为71.75%。

江门长堤历史街区的发展起源于元末明初，江门的先辈在蓬江北岸的蓬莱山山腰上开辟了一个墟场，叫作"江门墟"。"江门墟"的建立使这里逐渐形成了墟集，这成为历史街区发展的雏形。当年的外海、白石、白沙、水南四乡村民多乘墟船来这里"趁墟"，登岸的水闸门口就刻有"江门"二字。

明朝时期，江门依托繁盛的河运已经成为当时新会规模最大的一个镇。明成化年间（1465—1487年）发展为"日日来鱼虾""商船夺港归"的热闹商贸集市。明朝后期，河流在蓬莱山山脚一带逐渐冲积成陆

Located in the central south of Guangdong Province and western part of Pearl River Delta, adjacent to Zhongshan and Zhuhai in the east, connecting to Yangjiang in the west, neighboring with Foshan and Yunfu in the north and bordering with Nanhai in the south (PICTURE1-1-1), Jiangmen city gained its name for being located at the junction of Xijiang River and its branch Pengjiang River, and also for a landscape in the shape of a "gate" together formed by the Yandun Mountain at the southern bank and the Penglai Mountain at the northern bank of the river. As the hub of Wuyi area, Jiangmen's role as a vital communication center connecting the western part of Guangdong Province and Southwest provinces with other cities to the Pearl River Delta, Hongkong and Macao, makes it the key gateway to Xijiang River and coastal areas in the western part of Guangdong Province, and it's one of economic centers to the Pearl River Delta. From small island area consisting of Penglai Mountain (where the No.1 Middle School of Jiangmen is located), Yandun Mountain (where the No. 11 Middle School of Jiangmen is located) and Fenghuang Mountain (where the Jiangmen Cultural City is located), to the emergence of Xinhui Alluvial Delta, the unique geographic location and layout of Jiangmen city laid solid foundation for its economic, social and cultural development, furthermore, traces of human activities also help to shape the natural environment and urban spatial layout.

During the development of Jiangmen city, the Changdi Historical Neighborhood at the northern bank of Pengjiang Rive, as the essence of local history and culture, epitomizes rich and diversified local cultural heritage and citizens daily life.

### 1.1.1 History of Changdi Historical Neighborhood

Changdi Historical Neighborhood locates in the Pengjiang District of Jiangmen city, connecting with Pengjiang River in the south, expanding to Shengli Road in the west, Yuejin Road in the east, Jianshe Road and Penglai Road in the north. The core area of the Neighborhood (PICTURE1-1-2), with the intact historical heritages, most historical buildings and best preserved conditions, is the focus of our protection work. This area covers a total of 36.02 hectares, among which 26.56 hectares are historical buildings and spaces, accounting for 73.73% of the total area.

The development of Changdi Historical Neighborhood can be dated back to late Yuan and Early Ming Dynasty, when the predecessors initiated a market place called Jiangmen Marketplace on the mountainside of Penglai

图1-1-2 江门历史街区范围
PICTURE1-1-2 AREA OF JIANGMEN HISTORIC DISTRICT

图1-1-3 江门西堤历史照片
PICTURE1-1-3 HISTORICAL PICTURE OF THE WEST EMBANKMENT OF CHANGDI

图1-1-4 蓬江沿岸历史照片
PICTURE1-1-4 HISTORICAL PICTURE OF PENGJIANG COAST

图1-1-5 蓬江沿岸历史照片
PICTURE1-1-5 HISTORICAL PICTURE OF PENGJIANG COAST

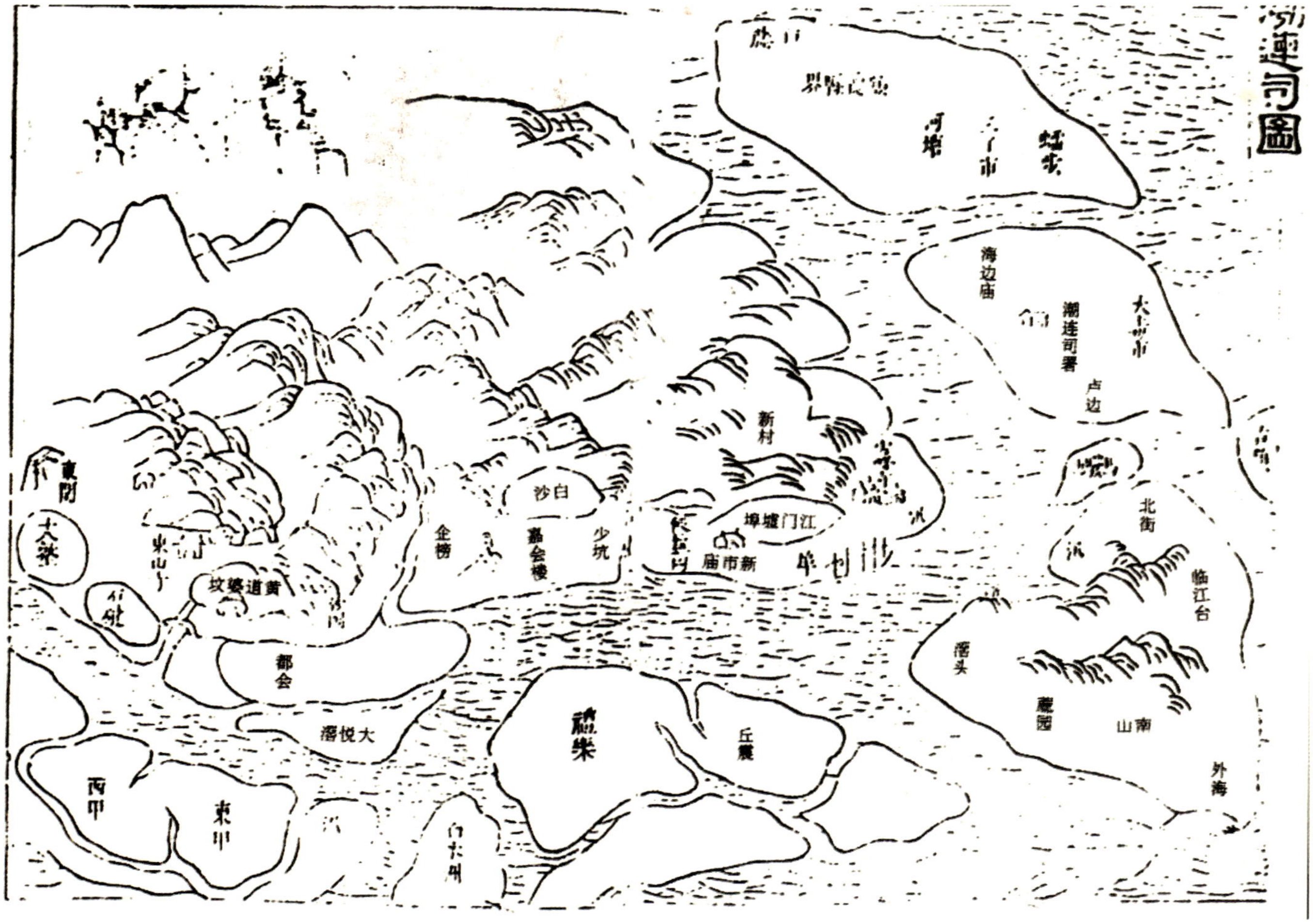

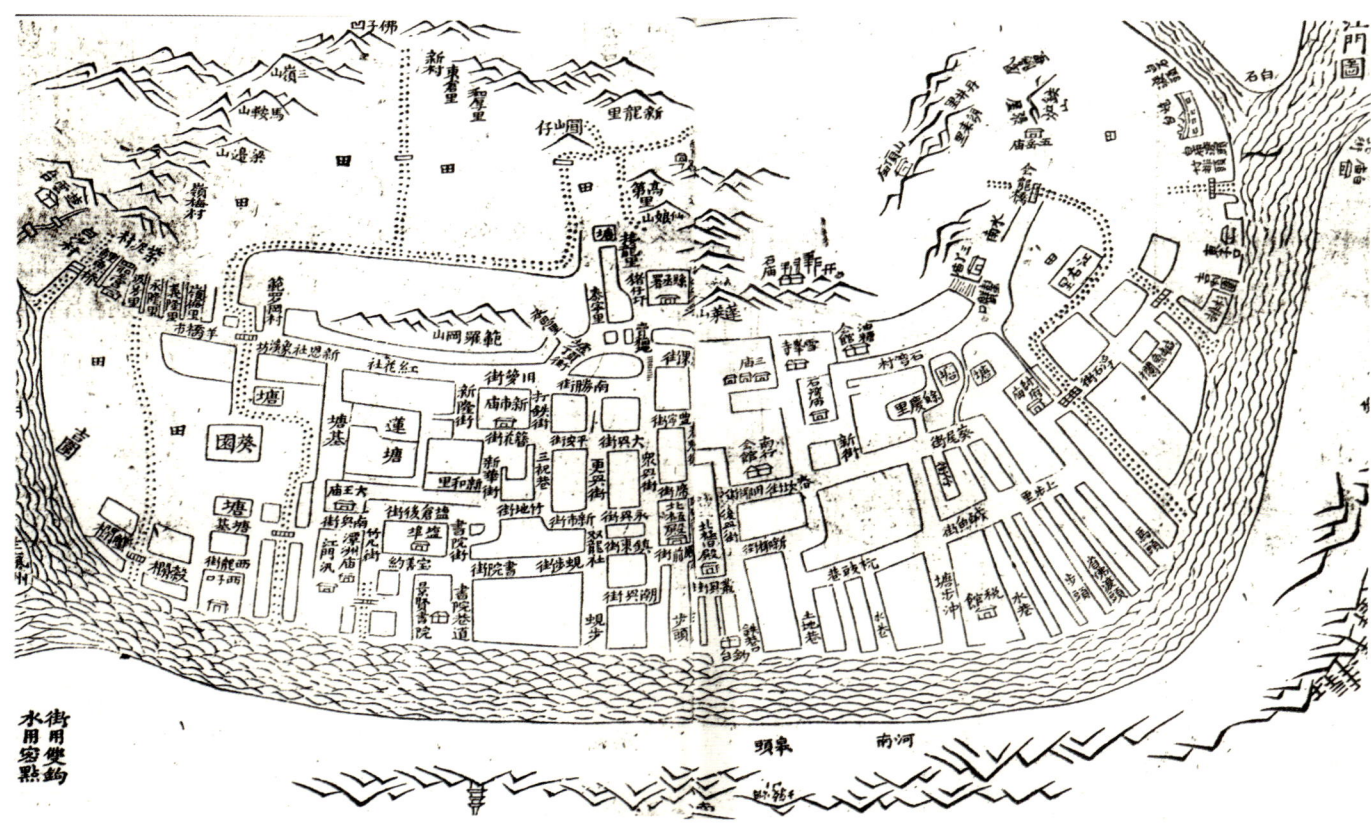

图1-1-6 潮连司图 [清康熙二十九年(1690年)]
PICTURE1-1-6 CHAO LIAN SI [KANGXI TWENTY-NINE (1690)]

图1-1-7 江门图 [清道光二十年(1840年)]
PICTURE1-1-7 JIANGMEN [DAOGUANG TWENTY (1840)]

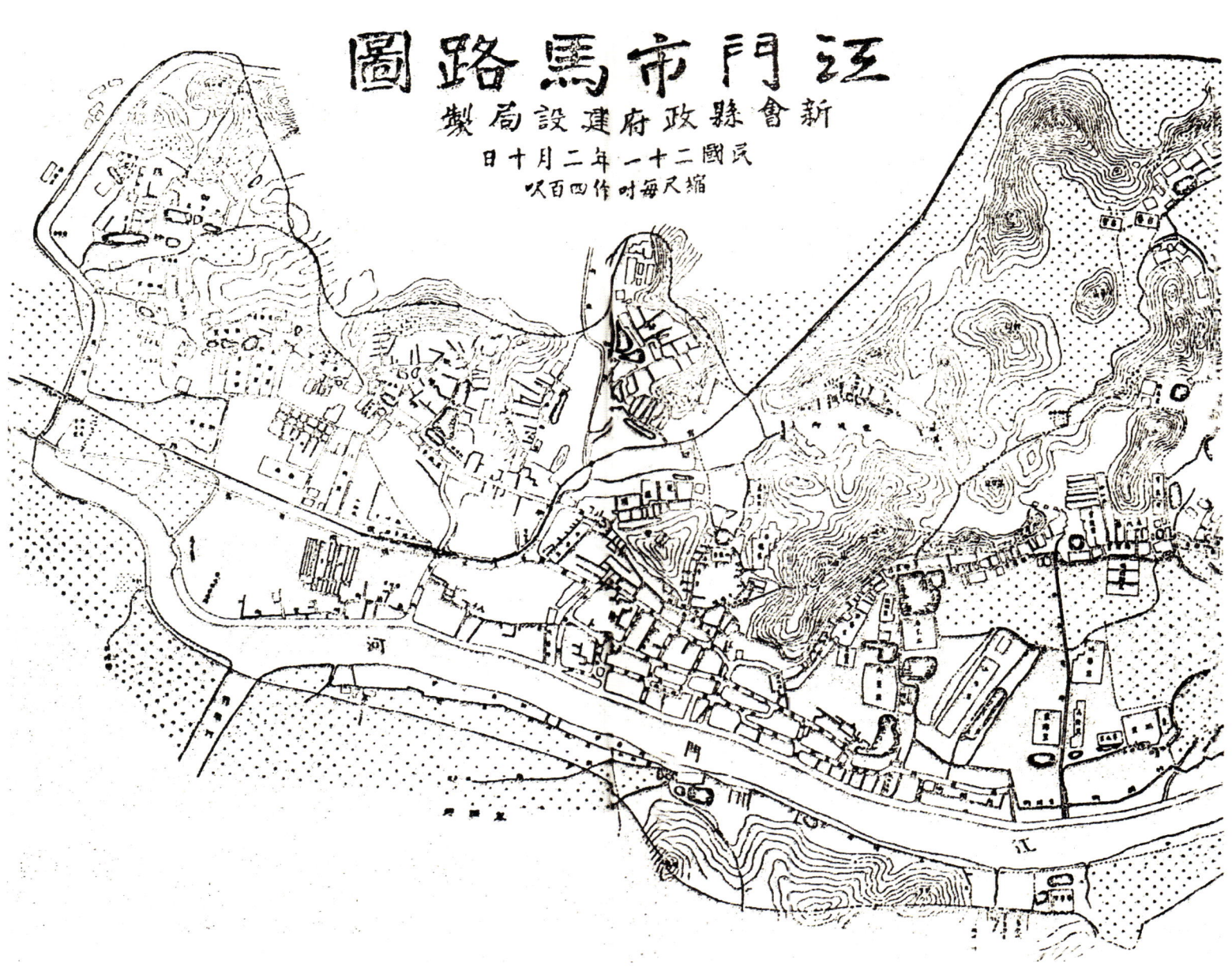

图1-1-8 江门市马路图[民国二十一年(1932年)]
PICTURE1-1-8 ROAD MAP OF JIANGMEN (1932)

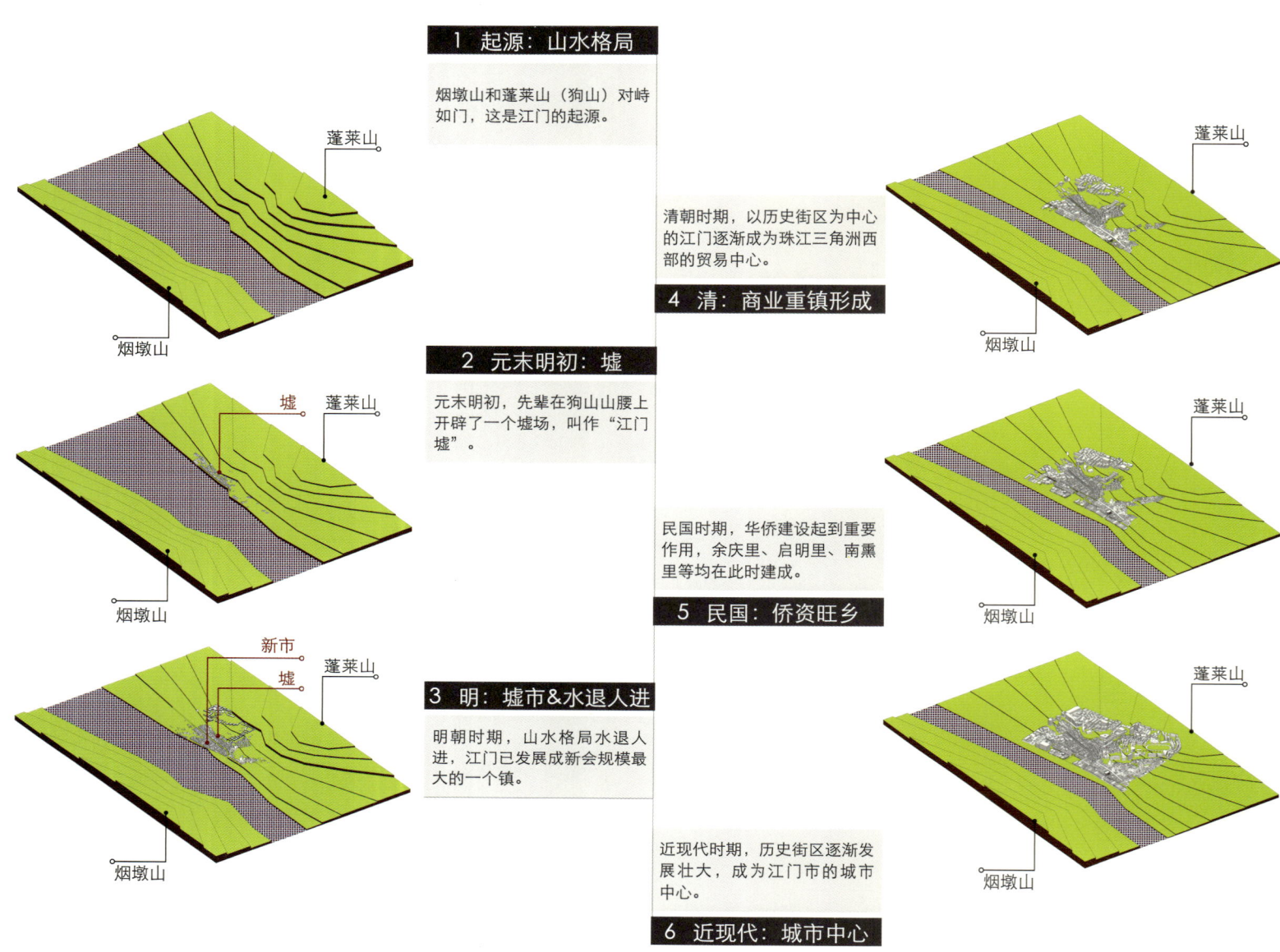

图1-1-9 历史街区发展演变
PICTURE1-1-9 THE TRANSFORMATION OF HISTORIC DISTRICT

地，江门的陆地开始进一步向河边延伸，形成一湾的河边高地。江门墟从一个旧墟逐步演化为一个包括商店、作坊等在内的"新市"。其后，新市继续向南、东南方向发展，建设范围继续扩展。17世纪初，江门墟因商贸而兴盛，西江中下游一带的商品多在此地集散。

清康熙元年（1661年）和清康熙三年（1664年），朝廷两次下令"迁界"，"江门墟"一度变为废墟。康熙八年（1669年）复界，居民重返"江门墟"。清康熙二十四年（1685年），粤海关在江门咸鱼街83号开设江门正税口，征收正税（货物税）。后经过一百多年的建设，逐渐成为珠江三角洲西部的贸易中心。

嘉庆年间（1796—1820年），设在常安涌边的江门讯升为千总衙署，人们在衙署营前开了些店铺做生意，常安涌两边逐渐兴旺起来。

到了道光年间（1821—1850年），江门与佛山、陈村、石龙并称广东四大商业重镇，历史街区的范围延伸到沙洲上，蓬江河边的长堤上有了比较集中的商铺，全镇建有40多条街道，商铺房舍鳞次栉比，客商云集，成为当时省内的大城镇之一。

根据清光绪二十八年（1902年）《中英续议通商行船条约》，于清光绪三十年（1904年）将江门辟为对外通商口岸并设置海关，为广东八大关之一。江门成为五邑乃至粤西地区的对外通商口岸，商贸更为活跃，迎来了新一轮发展。五邑华侨在工业、交通运输、房地产、商业和银信金融等方面的投资和开发，对江门市经济发展和市政建设作出了重大贡献。如在历史街区中，1913年建成的余庆里（见086页）、1914年建成的启明里（见075页）、1926年建成的南芬里（见049页），都是面向归侨、侨眷进行建设和销售的。

1949年10月23日，江门解放。之后，江门建制多次调整、升格，先后隶属于粤中行署、肇庆专区、佛山专区管辖。江门境域也随之扩展，经济发展日益加速。到1998年末，江门市辖新会、台山、开平、恩平、鹤山五个县级市（习称五邑）和江海、蓬江两个县级市辖区，人口378.9万人。江门市区，习称江门，是中共江门市委、市政府所在地，也是江门市经济、文化和交通的中心。

2000年至今，江门大力发展北新区，城市中心已经从江门长堤历史街区转移到北新区。中心区的北移，导致旧城中心区地位逐渐衰落，人口外迁、长堤历史街区居住人口逐渐老化、居住及商业环境质量

Mountain. The Jiangmen Marketplace gradually evolved to small fairs, known also as the early form of the historical neighborhood. Villagers from Waihai, Baishi, Baisha and Shuinan counties came to the fair by boats, and the water gate where they landed the bank carried lettering of Jiangmen.

During the Ming Dynasty, thanks to the prospered river transport, Jiangmen developed as the biggest town of Xinhui. Until Chenghua's reign (1465-1487), the district became a booming commercial market with busy boats buzzing around with fresh fish and shrimp everyday. In late Ming Dynasty, alluvial land was formed at the foot of Penglai Mountain (also called Goushan Mountain in the past), extending the land area of Jiangmen to riverside, thus an arch of riverside highland was formed. From then on, Jiangmen evolved from an old marketplace to a new urban district with stores and workshops. After years of development and extension to the south and southeast, by the early 17th century, Jiangmen Marketplace became so prospered that most commodities from the middle and lower reaches of Xijiang River were distributed in this area.

In the third year of Kangxi's reign in Qing Dynasty (the year of 1664), in order to defeat the anti-Qing rebels from the Ming Dynasty, the central government issued a decree to force residents in coastal areas to move toward inland and prohibited any commodity boat to exit the sea, making the Jiangmen area a deserted place for five years. In the eighth year of Kangxi's reign (1669), the central government withdrew the order, allowing uprooted residents to move back to their hometown. In the twenty-fourth year of Kangxi's reign (1685), the Canton Customs authority set up the Jiangmen Commodity Tax Office at No. 83 of Xianyu Street to levy tax on commodity trade. After a century of development, Jiangmen became a trading center in the western part of Pearl River Delta.

During emperor Jiaqing's reign (1796-1820), Jiangmen military camp located by the Chang'an stream was updated as Qianzong Government, attracting citizens to open shops near the government site and brought prosperity along the Chang'an stream.

By the emperor Daoguang's reign (1821-1850), Jiangmen became one of the four major commercial towns in Canton, together with Foshan, Chencun and Shilong, and the historical neighborhood extended to sandbank, gathering stores along the Pengjiang River bank. There were up to 40 streets and lanes in Jiangmen, where stores and residential houses were placed closely side by side and merchants were busy with their businesses, making the place one of the biggest towns in Canton.

In the twenty-eighth year of Guangxu's reign (1902), in the Mackay Treaty signed by the royal court and Britain, after two years, Jiangmen became a Treaty Port, and Jiangmen Customs Office, one of the eight Customs Offices in Canton back then, was set up. Since then, Jiangmen's business and trade further boomed and the area became a trading port for Wuyi, even western part of Canton to do business with foreigners. Overseas Chinese from the Wuyi area contributed a lot to the economic and urban development of Jiangmen by investing in industry,

图1-1-10 长堤风貌街
PICTURE 1-1-10 CHANGDI STREET

图1-1-11 长堤路历史照片
PICTURE 1-1-11 HISTORICAL PICTURE OF CHANGDI ROAD

图1-1-12 莲平路
PICTURE 1-1-12 LIANPING STREET

下降、街区内的建筑与城市空间环境缺乏有效保护、旧建筑年久失修、区内道路系统缺乏有效整合和管理等问题突出。虽然长堤历史街区存在上述问题，整体风貌受到一些新建设的破坏，但长堤历史街区文化积淀丰厚、历史建筑魅力犹存。长堤历史街区的发展充分反映了江门社会、经济、文化等方面的长期演变过程，形成了极具地域特色的空间形态特征。其中，融合自然山水格局的街巷体系成为城市空间发展的脉络骨架和肌理特质，在江门长堤历史街区的发展建设当中也起着维系性的关键作用。

## 1.1.2 长堤历史街区重要街巷发展概述

江门长堤历史街区的街巷体系按照建设时间顺序可以分成从明清时期沿袭至今的街区、民国时期建设的街区、新中国成立后新建和改建的街区三类。其中，从明清时期沿袭至今的街区道路名称基本沿用旧称，反映了当时热闹的集市情况，如京果街、卖鸡地、红花社等，都是根据当时街道经营的主要商品命名的；而清朝海禁解除后的路名，如更兴路、

transportation, real estate, commerce and financial institutes. For example, projects in historical neighborhood such as the Yuqing Lane built up in 1913 (page 086), Qiming Lane built up in 1914 (page 075) and Nanfen Lane built up in 1926 (page 049) were all constructed for and sold to returned overseas Chinese and their families.

Jiangmen was liberated on 23rd, October of 1949, after which the status of the city was adjusted and updated for many times, from under the jurisdiction of Yuezhong Government to be administered by Zhaoqing and Foshan successively. By the end of 1998, Jiangmen was home to 3.789 million population and its jurisdiction included five county-level cities, namely Xinhui, Taishan, Kaiping, Enping and Heshan (Known as Wuyi) and two county-level administrative regions-Jianghai and Pengjiang. The downtown of Jiangmen, where the CPC Jiangmen Committee and Jiangmen Government is located is the economic, cultural and transportation center of the city.

From 2000 till now, as the government focuses on the development of the Beixin District, the city center has been shifted from Changdi Historical Neighborhood to the Beixin District, which caused declined status of the old town as the city center, loss of population, degraded living and commercial environment in this part. Due to lack of effective protection, problems such as deteriorated buildings and unattended streets became significant. Although the surrounding environment of Changdi Historical Neighborhood were influenced by the rise of new buildings, the profound cultural heritage and charms of old buildings were maintained. The development of Changdi Historical Neighborhood, with its unique spatial features perfectly reflected the long-term social, economic and cultural evolution of Jiangmen. The spatial layout of streets and lanes with natural elements formed the basic structure and texture of urban spaces and played crucial role in the development of Changdi Historical Neighborhood.

### 1.1.2 Overview of Important Streets and Lanes in Changdi Historical Neighborhood

Streets and lanes in Changdi Historical Neighborhood can be classified to three types according to chronological order: streets built during Ming and Qing Dynasty, streets built during the Republic of China period, streets built or rebuilt after the establishment of People's Republic of China. Streets that were built during Ming and Qing Dynasty and are still in use today inherited their old names that indicate the prosperity of the marketplace in the past, for example, Nuts Street, Chicken Market, Red Flower Market, etc. were named after major commodities traded on the street; streets named after the revoking of the decree to remove citizens from coastal areas, such as Gengxing (regeneration) Road, Chang'an (eternal peace) Road reflected citizen's wishes for peace and stability. Some of the names were adjusted, for example, the old Shangbu Lane is called Shangbu Road now. Most neighborhood of the Republic of China era were built during the 1920s to 1930s, and they are still using old names and locating

图1-1-13 常安路
PICTURE1-1-13 CHANG'AN STREET

图1-1-14 石湾直街
PICTURE 1-1-14 SHIWANZHI STREET

常安路等，则反映了人民渴望和平的心愿；部分路名在使用过程中也有所改动，如原上步里所在地现被称为上步路。民国时期建设的街区主要集中在20世纪20—30年代，此时也翻新重筑了不少明清时期的道路，但仍使用原名，道路位置也基本与明清时期一致。新中国成立后新建的街区道路命名也大都与历史背景相关，如为了纪念解放战争胜利而建设的胜利路、"大跃进"时期修建的跃进路等，都体现了1949年后江门城市开发建设的时代特征。

根据对江门长堤历史街区街巷在建设年代、历史意义、保存程度等方面的综合评价，比较重要的街巷资源如下：

长堤风貌街（详见124页）：长堤风貌街位于蓬江河畔，东起蓬江大桥，西至胜利大桥，全长约1.5千米。长堤风貌街的建筑大部分在20世纪20年代和30年代建成。建筑风格中西结合，数百间骑楼各具特色，是江门的商业老区。鼎盛时期，这里商业、娱乐、物流等行业风生水起，高度繁荣，曾有"小广州"之称，也是目前广东省内乃至国内整体保存较完整的，且侨乡特色较为浓厚的历史文化风貌街区。2001年，长堤风貌街部分区域进行了改造整治，整体风貌宜人。

常安路（详见120页）：常安路与堤中路呈T字状交叉在一起。其优越的地理位置，使之成为江门古今繁荣之地。1925年，江门从新会划出成为省辖市，开始大规模的市政建设。民国十八年（1929年），市政促进委员会成立，从民间集资20余万元白银，用以修筑长堤、钓台路，扩宽13条马路。常安涌也在这时被填平，铺上水泥路面成为马路，常安路就此诞生。之后，人们在常安路两旁陆续建起了一些商铺、酒楼，百货店、洋货店、金饰店、西药店、文具店、镜画店、丝绸布匹店、茶庄、当铺等也纷纷开业，江门的商业中心逐渐从墟顶街、新市路、兴宁路转移到常安路来，常安路也成为江门的"太平（人民）南"（广州当时的商业中心）。当年，常安路属于衣食住行、吃喝玩乐的高雅消费场所，在常安路开设店铺的都是有钱人家，他们所穿的衣服都是时尚新潮的款式，美国货牛仔裤、原子皮带等都有售卖，只是价钱昂贵。新中国成立后，江门市人民政府就设在常安路，在此之前，省政府派出机构——粤中专员公署的办公地点也在这里，即现在的蓬莱商业城所处的位置。

莲平路（详见128页）：20世纪20年代开始，这里就是江门市最具规模的主干道，两旁商铺林立，繁荣兴旺。现在，莲平路上的商铺的外墙上隐隐约约

in the same place even after rebuilding and regeneration. Naming of the neighborhood and streets built after the establishment of People's Republic of China reflected the general historical background, for example, both the name of Shengli (victory) Road (to commemorate victory in the war of liberation), and Dayuejin (great leap forward) Road (built during the Great Leap Forward era) indicated features of the times after Jiangmen's liberation in 1949.

After evaluating the history, significance and preservation situation of neighborhood and streets in Changdi Historical Neighborhood, the following streets and lanes are selected:

Changdi Historical Street(page 124): located along the bank of Pengjiang River, the 1.5 kilometer long street starts from Pengjiang Bridge in the east and extends to Shengli Bridge in the west. Most buildings on the street were built in the 1920s and 1930s. This street used to be an old commercial area of Jiangmen, with architectures built in both Chinese and western styles, and arcade buildings designed with distinctive features. During its peak time, this street was highly prospered with dynamic commercial, entertainment and logistics activities, winning the nickname as Little Guangzhou. It is a famous historical neighborhood in Guangdong Province for the intact preservation of old buildings and strong cultural heritage as the hometown of overseas Chinese. After renewal projects to some parts of the street in 2001, Changdi Historical Street is now displaying its new charm to visitors.

Chang'an Road(page 120): Chang'an Road and Dizhong Road together form a T shape. The preferential location makes it a flourishing area of Jiangmen in both ancient and modern times. In 1925, when Jiangmen was separated from Xinhui and became an independent city directly governed by the province, the city started large-scale urban construction projects in the eighteenth year of the Republic of China (1929), the Urban Development Commission was established, and silver worth more 200,000 yuan were collected for the building of Changdi Road and Diaotai Road and the expansion of 13 other roads. It was then that the Chang'an street was filled with earth to build Chang'an Road, along which shops, restaurants, apartment stores, stores for imported goods, jewelry shops, pharmacies, stationers, galleries, silk & cloth stores, tea houses and pawnshops were opened, shifting the commercial center of Jiangmen from Xuding Street, Xinshi Road and Xingning Road to Chang'an Road. Back then, Chang'an Road was compared as the Renminnan Road (the commercial center of Guangzhou), where slap-up stores serving citizens daily necessities as well as their demand for feasting and entertainment were opened. Owners of those stores were very wealthy people dressed fashionably and sold high-priced jeans and belts imported from the US. After Jiangmen's liberation, Jiangmen People's Government was located on the Chang'an Road, and before the liberation, Central Canton Commissioner's Office was also on the Chang'an Road where the Pengjiang Shopping Center is standing now.

Lianping Road(page 128): as early as in the 1920s, Lianping Road has been the main street, boasting numerous

图1-1-15 青年广场
PICTURE 1-1-15  THE YOUTH SQUARE

图1-1-16 中山公园
PICTURE 1-1-16  ZHONGSHAN PARK

图1-1-17　远眺长堤路
PICTURE 1-1-17　BIRD-VIEW OF CHANGDI ROAD

能看到当年残留的斑驳的商铺名字。由于当年人流、物流等集聚，莲平路成为江门周边地区消息传播的聚集地。自1925年起，本地重要报社、通讯社，均在靠近新华路口一带的莲平路开设报馆。故此莲平路也成为此间的周边文人政客们激辩时局、指点江山和振兴文化、对外宣传的重要舆论阵地，周边文人均趋之若鹜。

石湾直街（详见163页）：石湾直街在城区街区东部，东北、西南走向。西南接大地塘通太平路，东北接新第里出跃进路，长194米，宽2～4米。石湾直街有居民约460人。这里本是明代始建的村落，因巷道弯曲，且多用条石（花岗岩）铺设，故称"石湾村"。后因市镇扩大，1935年经改造后改称"石湾直街"。虽然今日的石湾直街仅有少量的传统岭南民居建筑，但是其整体的空间格局和街巷脉络仍然承袭了传统岭南古村落的空间形态特征。

墟顶（原江门墟）（详见167页）：江门墟内各类货物有专门的销售划分区域，除了"猪仔墟""缸瓦地"外，还在京果街一带出售干果货物，在卖鸡地则销售鸡鸭鹅等家禽。这种功能布局形成了今天一个个有趣的街道名称，如安龙里"猪仔墟"是由于墟顶最初形成的时候，安龙里一带是卖活猪的墟集，故而得名。类似的还有泰宁里，旧名"缸瓦地"，是卖瓦缸瓦盆的地方。

除街巷空间外，街区内主要的开放广场空间还包括北部山体公园中的中山公园，以及近年来建设的青年广场、传统街巷内尺度宜人的启明里广场等街角公共开放空间。由于后期设计和建造管理上的一些问题，目前青年广场等开放空间的使用率较低，街角广场和建筑前广场等历史沿袭下来的开放空间虽然具有重要的场所价值，但是其在建设、维护和管理方面也仍然存在较多的不足，缺乏足够的投入。

prosperous stores. Now, the fainted store names from the past can still be seen on the external walls. The result of frequent flows of people and commodities is that Lianping Road became the source to spread information in Jiangmen area. Since 1925, important newspaper offices and news agencies all chose to establish their offices near Xinhua crossroad on Lianping Road, making the area an attractive propaganda base for intellectuals to discuss political situation, debate on current hot spot affairs and promote local culture.

Shiwanzhi Street(page163): located in the east part of the urban area, Shiwanzhi Street points the northeast-southwest direction. With a total length of 194 meters and width of 2~4 meters, the street accommodates about 466 residents and is linked to Daditang and Taiping Road in the southwest and Xindili and Yuejin Road in the northeast. The village was named Shiwan village because the roads in the village were mostly paved by granite stones. Because of the expansion of townships, the road was renamed Shiwanzhi Street in 1935 after renovations. Although only a few of traditional Lingnan Residential buildings are remained on Shiwanzhi Street today, the overall spatial and streets layout still inherited basic characteristics of Lingnan ancient villages.

Xuding (the old Jiangmen Marketplace) (page167): Jiangmen Marketplace was zoned for different commodities. For example, apart from Piggy Market and Clay Pots Market, Nuts Street was for dried fruits and nuts, and Chicken Street was for the selling of poultry such as chicken, duck and goose. Street names vividly indicate their functions in the past, for example, Piggy Market at Anlong Lane was named because the place was used for trading pigs in earlier times. Another example is Taining Lane, also known as Clay Pots Market, for selling clay wares in the past.

Apart from streets and lanes, open air spaces in the neighborhood also include Sun Yat-sen Park in the Mountain Park in the north, the newly built Youth Square, and well-designed Qiming Lane Square in traditional lanes. Due to improper design and management, the space utilization rate in Youth Square is relatively low. The value of other open spaces such as Jiejiao Square and Jianzhuqian Square is also impacted by insufficient management and investment.

图1-2-1 江门历史街区历史文化建筑分布图
PICTURE 1-2-1  DISTRIBUTION OF JIANGMEN HISTORIC ARCHITECTURE

● 现存历史点　　● 已经不存在的历史点

图1-2-2 蓬江沿岸历史照片
PICTURE1-2-2  HISTORICAL PICTURE OF PENGJIANG COAST

# 1.2 江门长堤历史街区的现状认知
## 1.2 PERCEPTIONS ON THE STATUS QUO OF CHANGDI HISTORICAL NEIGHBORHOOD

### 1.2.1 层叠丰富的文化积淀

江门的文化历史丰富多样，悠久的历史造就了这里深厚的文化积淀——庙会文化、戏剧曲艺文化、兴学重教文化、饮食文化和宗教文化等都是当地文化的代表。教育文化是促进江门市社会经济发展的重要社会动因，江门自古就有兴学重教的传统，明代思想家和教育家陈献章（陈白沙）先生就是杰出的代表。民间古歌谣唱道："白沙先生归故乡，我送先生路远长，但愿先生长福寿，年年教我学文章。"江门市是个岭南风情浓厚的地方，遍布大小街巷并反映着江门人生活特色的饮食文化，尤其是长堤历史街区内的酒楼茶肆和传统小吃独具特色。传统节日里人们携儿带孙上街，看舞龙、游花灯会、逛民俗庙会等是具有传统乡土气息的当地民俗文化的重要体现。粤剧曲艺文化在江门五邑地区也同样具有深沉、厚重而特别的历史积淀。

长堤历史街区内具有丰富的历史文化遗存，比如宝和按当铺旧址、中山纪念堂、启明里等。在台阶上的江门墟是江门的起源之地，旧时因为这里地势高，又濒于水，前人将这里辟为墟场。每逢墟期，小商小贩和农民可来趁墟买卖。20世纪20—30年代，五邑侨乡掀起"建房热"，华侨在江门历史街区建成了启明里等统一布局的居住社区，启明里也成为当年江门知名的华侨聚居点。当然，随着历史的变迁，有些著名的历史建筑已无迹可寻，如雪峰寺、景贤书院等。雪峰寺是江门市区有文献可稽的最古老的佛教寺院，毁于"文化大革命"时期，被毁前非常繁盛。尽管一些历史建筑已经不复存在，但现在的江门长堤历史街区仍然整体保留着清代和民国时期的建筑群体和街区环境，虽然时代变迁历经沧桑，历史街区内文化积淀依然层叠丰厚。

### 1.2.2 特色独具的待修缮历史风貌建筑

历史风貌建筑是构成历史街区城市意象的重要内容之一。江门长堤历史街区内的历史建筑文化资源主要是由祠堂、民居及其历史环境组成的，包括保存较为完整的石湾直街周边及墟顶周边传统建筑，

### 1.2.1 Rich Cultural Heritage

Rich and diversified cultural heritages were brewed in the time-honored history of Jiangmen city, and temple fairs, operas, tradition of respecting teaching and learning, plentiful diet culture and strong religious belief are all examples of local culture. Respecting teaching and encouraging learning is a long tradition in Jiangmen, whose social and economic development owed a lot to the importance attached to education. Chen Xianzhang (Chen Baisha), thinker and educator of the Ming Dynasty is a prominent figure in this regard. There is a folk song to prove the point: when Mr. Chen is going back to his hometown, I always go as far as I could to see him off, it is my sincere wish for his longevity and happiness, so that he can pass knowledge to me every year. Jiangmen features strong and profound Lingnan customs and culture. The city, especially the Changdi Historical Neighborhood, is plastered with restaurants, tea houses and traditional snacks, reflecting its unique diet culture. It is an important aspect of folk culture for citizens to take their families to go out for dragon parade, lantern displays and temple fairs on traditional festivals, and Canton Opera in Jiangmen of the Wuyi area is also a profound and special culture heritage.

The historical cultural heritages in Changdi Historical Neighborhood are very rich, including Baohe Pawnshop, Sun Yat-sen Memorial Hall and Qiming Lane. On top of 33 steps is the origin of Jiangmen-Xuding, also known as Jiangmen Marketplace. Because of its high-lying and water-facing position, it was selected as the location for a marketplace. Farmers and vendors can come here to do business during market days. During 1920s and 1930s, there was a boom to build houses by overseas Chinese in Wuyi area, and that's how the residential areas with similar layout such as Qiming Lane was built and became a well-known habitat community for overseas Chinese. As time goes by, some famous historical buildings are nowhere to be found, for example, Xuefeng Monastery and Jingxian Academy, etc., with the former being the oldest and a very popular Buddhism monastery documented in history, before being destroyed during the Cultural Revolution. Despite that some of the historical buildings are not here anymore after vicissitudes of the times, the overall architectural groups and streets surroundings back in the Qing Dynasty and Republic of China period are still maintained as a very rich cultural heritage of Jiangmen.

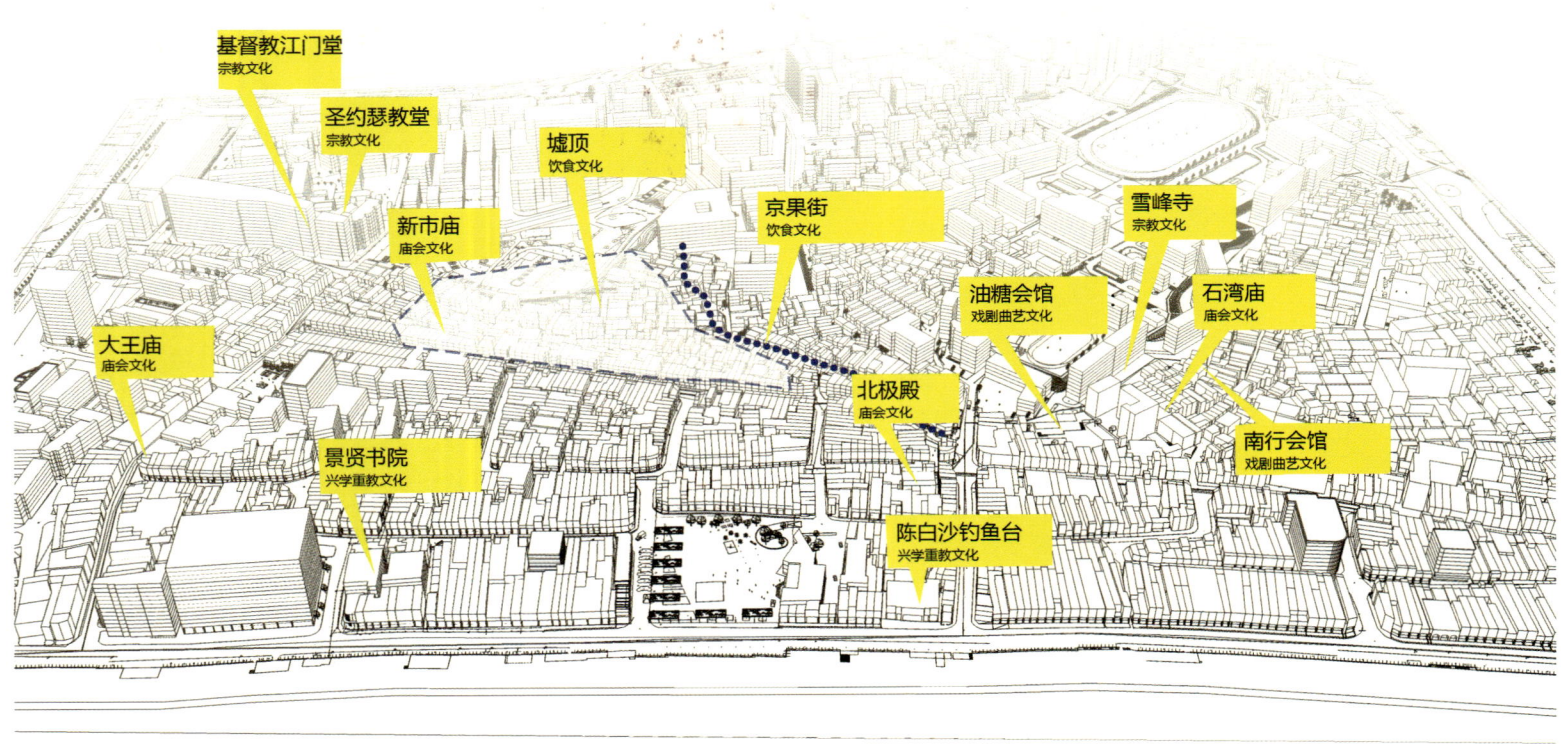

图1-2-3 江门历史街区历史非物质文化建筑分布图
PICTURE 1-2-3 DISTRIBUTION OF JIANGMEN HISTORIC INTANGIBLE CULTRURE ARCHITECTURE

图1-2-4 蓬江沿岸历史照片
PICTURE 1-2-4 HISTORICAL PICTURE OF PENGJIANG COAST

这是江门市重要的传统乡土建筑遗产的代表,其中具有地方特色、保存完整、形象精美、工艺高超的部分传统民居灰塑,也成为广府地区乡土建筑遗产风格的重要代表。此外,还有沿蓬江北岸大片保存完好、格局完整的骑楼建筑群以及侨乡文化和华侨投资影响下的侨乡建筑群落,如启明里和余庆里等。

长堤历史街区内建筑物风貌的分布呈现一定的片区特征。根据建筑年代,历史风貌建筑主要集中在骑楼街区、石湾直街和墟顶片区。这三个片区的建筑主要是清代后期及民国时期的,形成了整个历史街区的核心传统风貌区,其中启明里、余庆里等建筑群体现了较为独特的侨乡建筑风貌。历史街区内大部分建筑以1~3层为主,但骑楼街区内也夹杂有部分新建筑,对传统风貌产生了一定的影响。

在建筑结构方面,南部传统建筑片区以砖木建筑为主,20世纪二三十年代兴建的骑楼建筑距今已经有80余年,多以木桩基础为主,承载能力较低。街区内历史建筑的质量普遍不佳。虽然长堤风貌街在20世纪90年代曾经对外部立面进行过粉刷和修复,大部分外观质量较好,但内部基础以及结构受损仍然较为严重。其余骑楼街、石湾直街以及墟顶传统居住区部分的建筑质量基本都属于一般以及较差的等级。整个历史街区内砖木结构建筑由于年久失修,房屋内部破坏较严重,部分成了危房,相当部分建筑存在着不同程度的使用安全问题,亟待整修或重建。

### 1.2.3 居商混合的用地结构

历史街区内的现状建筑功能主要以居住和商业功能为主,大体格局上北部为现代居住建筑,南部沿河为旧城骑楼商业区及居住区。沿城市主干道胜利路设置有商业设施和公共服务设施。基地内有一块面积较大的教育用地,现为景贤中学校址。区内主要公共活动场所包括中山公园以及青年广场。常安路步行街是区内唯一的一条步行商业街,长约1千米,以服饰等零售经营为主。

石湾直街片区主要以传统居住建筑为主,空置建筑比例较高,沿石湾直街零星分布少量生活服务性商业。墟顶片区以传统居住建筑为主,居住人口也逐渐老化,商业服务设施主要分布在几栋多层建筑的底层。骑楼片区首层部分具有丰富的商业业态,但首层以上利用率不高,仅有少量用作仓储和居住,大部分闲置,片区内功能"混合"的建筑比例较高。骑楼街区用地的内部往往为加建的居住建筑,密度

### 1.2.2 Unrenovated Historical Buildings with Unique Architectural Styles

Historical buildings are one of the important elements to form a city's image. Historical resources in old buildings in Changdi Historical Neighborhood includes well-preserved traditional architectures including ancestral halls, residential houses and their surroundings around Shiwanzhi Street and Xuding Street, which stand as typical examples of traditional local architectural heritages. Well-preserved, delicate and consummate lime sculptures applied on traditional local buildings are also examples of the architectural style in Cantonese-speaking area. More examples include arcade buildings with intact exterior look and layout along the northern bank of Pengjiang River and buildings invested by overseas Chinese like Qiming Lane and Yuqing Lane.

Different district in Changdi Historical Neighborhood features distinct architectural styles. Qilou (arcade building) District, Shiwanzhi Street and Xuding District, built during late Qing Dynasty and Republic of China period, become the core area of traditional buildings of the whole Neighborhood, for owning the largest number of historical buildings. Style of Qiming Lane and Yuqing Lane reflect very unique features as the hometown of overseas Chinese. Most buildings in this area are one to three floored ones, however, the appearance of some new buildings have a certain impact on the overall traditional style.

In term of structures, most traditional buildings in the southern part are of brick-wood structure, therefore it is common that arcade buildings constructed during the 1920s and 1930s with wood ground foundation are of quite low subgrade bearing capacities. Although after renewal and painting projects in the Neighborhood in the 1990s, the exterior look of most buildings are nice, the foundation and interior structure are badly damaged. Conditions of other traditional buildings on the Qilou (arcade building) street, Shiwanzhi Street and Xuding Street are on or below medium level. The interior of brick-wood-structure buildings in the Neighborhood are in serious conditions due to lack of repair work, some of which even endanger residents' safety and need to be repaired or rebuilt as soon as possible.

### 1.2.3 Land layout and Structure for Commercial and Residential Purposes

Land layout in the Neighborhood is mainly for commercial and residential purposes, with modern residential buildings in the northern part and traditional commercial arcade building and residential buildings in the southern part along the river. Business facilities and public service facilities are also built along the main street-Shengli Road. For example, a quite big piece of land is designated for education use, where the Jingxian Middle School is located now; other public space includes Zhongshan Park and the Youth Square. Chang'an Road Pedestrian Street, with a total length of one kilometer and retailing stores

图1-2-5 蓬江沿岸历史照片
PICTURE1-2-5　HISTORICAL PICTURE OF PENGJIANG COAST

图1-2-6　龙聚里
PICTURE1-2-6　LONGJU LANE

图1-2-7　墟顶居住风貌区鸟瞰图
PICTURE1-2-7　BIRD-VIEW

图1-2-8 建筑风貌评价
PICTURE 1-2-8　ARCHITECTURAL STYLE EVALUATION

图1-2-9 启明里和新第里鸟瞰图
PICTURE 1-2-9　BIRD-VIEW OF QIMIN LANE AND XINDI LANE

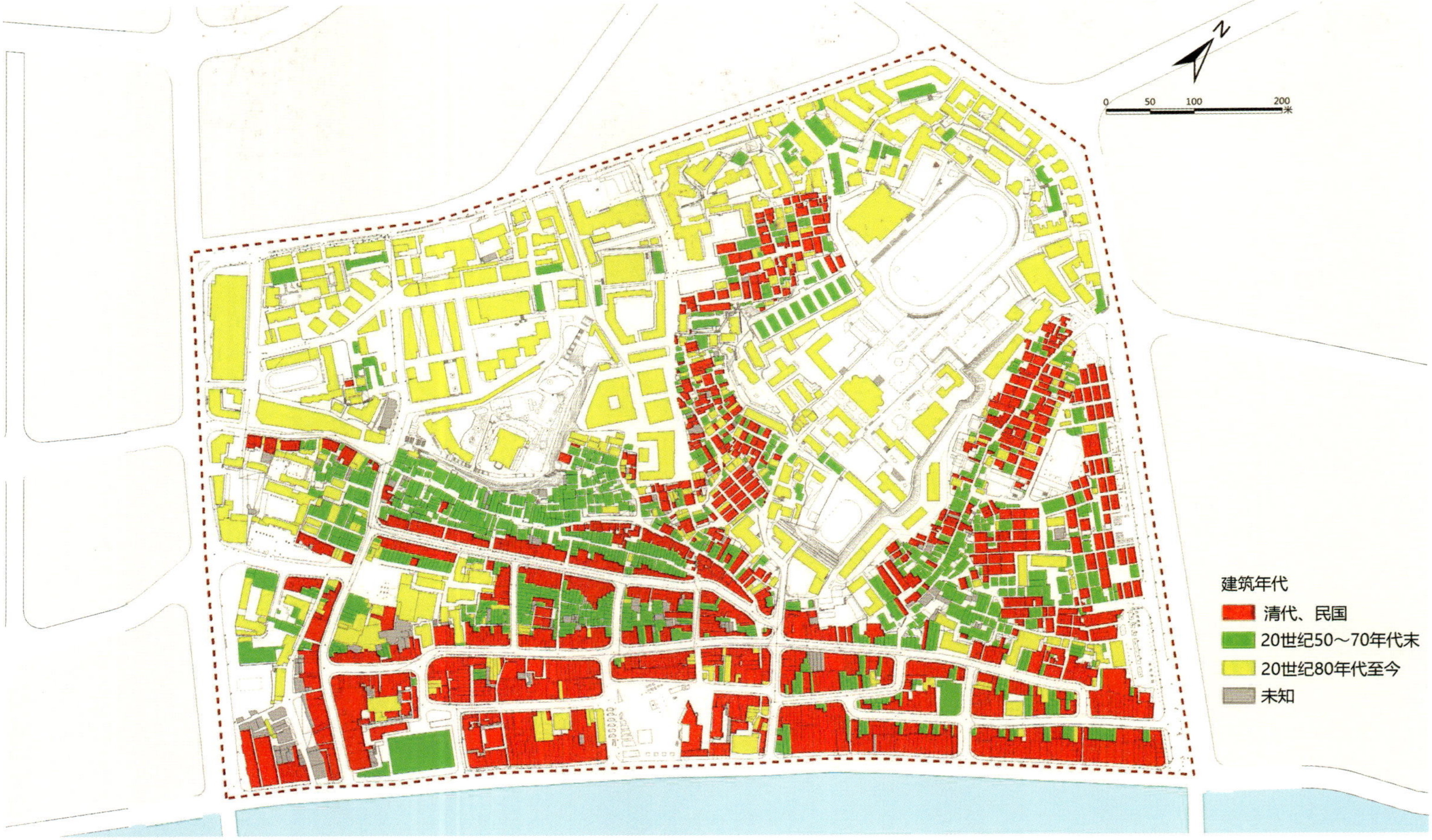

图1-2-10 建筑年代评价
PICTURE1-2-10 CONSTRUCTION TIME EVALUATION

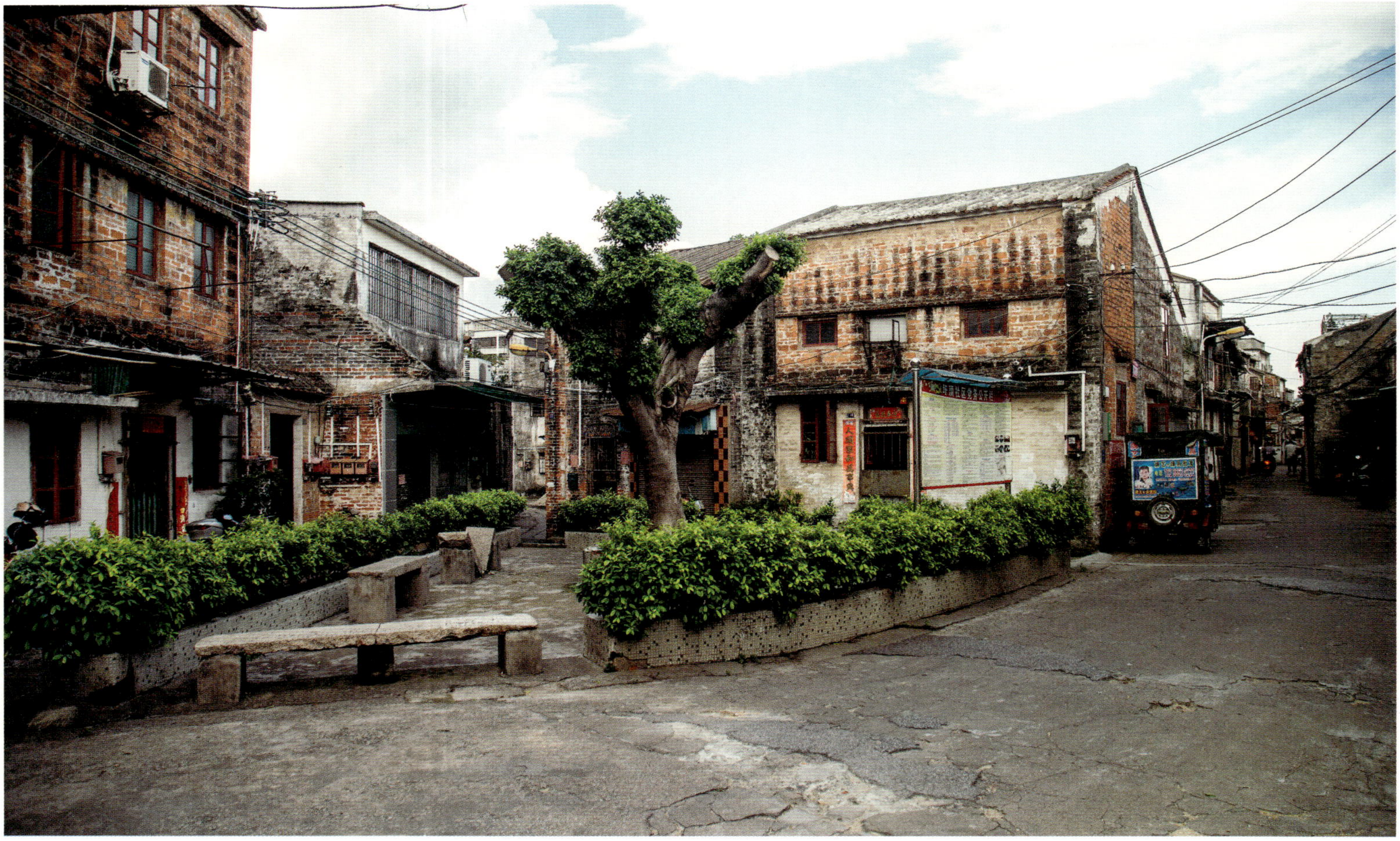

建筑年代
- 清代、民国
- 20世纪50～70年代末
- 20世纪80年代至今
- 未知

图 1-2-11 墟顶街
PICTURE 1-2-11 XUDING STREET

图1-2-12 建筑层数评价
PICTURE 1-2-12 FLOORS EVALUATION

图1-2-13 仓后路
PICTURE 1-2-13 CANGHOU ROAD

023

图1-2-14　原粤中专员公署（现蓬江商业城）
PICTURE 1-2-14　CANTON GOVERNMENT OFFICE (PENGJIANG COMMERCIAL CITY)

图1-2-15　明德坊建筑群
PICTURE 1-2-15　MINGDE FANG ARCHITECTURE

过高导致整体环境质量下降，形成"商包住"的形态。

街区内以商住用地以及二类居住用地为主，用地结构多样、混杂，同时公共绿地较为缺乏，骑楼片区以商住混合用地为主。

### 1.2.4 肌理致密的传统街巷

长堤历史街区地处蓬江旧城区，对外交通比较便利，地块四周有城市主干道胜利路、建设路和跃进路环绕，并通往城市北部。在历史街区内部，除了常安路步行街和石湾直街是步行道，3米以上道路基本上能行车，2～3米的街坊路人与摩托车混行。街区内部主要道路宽度为8～10米，主要道路网等级差异不大，内部东西向联系较强，南北向联系较弱。历史居住区内多为宽度为1～5米的内部街巷，路网密集，主次分明。街区内支路、街坊路密集，以人车混行为主，完整保留了传统的城市形态肌理。但由于缺乏规划和管理维护，部分路面状况不佳或存在断头路，造成了一定的交通问题。

### 1.2.5 快速城市化带来的冲击和挑战

快速的城市化进程给历史街区的持续发展带来了冲击和影响。近十余年来陆续兴建的大型建筑物破坏了老城区舒适的邻里尺度和完整的场所风貌。

街区内新建建筑主要分布在历史街区的北部，以及骑楼街区的局部地区。这些建筑虽然使用质量较好，但在高度、体量和形象等方面对历史街区的风貌具有一定的影响。如常安广场就是滨江长堤风貌街中最为突兀的一栋现代高层建筑，它的形态严重破坏了沿江天际线轮廓。墟顶中山公园东侧的几栋多层居住建筑对墟顶传统的低层建筑风貌造成严重的破坏。景贤中学所占据的蓬莱山上基本为多层现代建筑，与两侧的传统建筑也形成了较大的冲突。

城市扩张后中心区的北移，导致旧城中心区地位的衰落、经济发展的缓慢和居民的外迁，尤其是年轻劳动力都在外打工并逐步外迁，在历史街区里生活的主要是老年人和低收入群体。区域内的传统商业主要面向中低收入人群，仍然保持了一定的活力，但也存在着商业辐射力和竞争力不足的问题，缺乏高层次的服务产业。街区内的建筑与城市空间环境缺乏有效保护，大量历史建筑年久失修，以砖木结构为主的建筑安全性存在很大隐患。由于部分新建建筑缺乏有效的控制，导致城市形态肌理和历史风貌的破坏。区内道路系统也缺乏有效整合和管理，交通网络不畅。现状大部分建筑的权属为私房，

such as clothes shops, is the only high street in the district.

Most buildings in the Shiwanzhi District are for residential purposes, with high vacancy rate and a number of service institutes along the Shiwanzhi Street. Buildings in the Xuding District are also mainly residential houses, with an aging population and stores mostly distributed on the ground floor of several multi-floored buildings. As for the Qilou (arcade building) District, the first floors of buildings are occupied by diversified commercial activities, but other floors are mostly vacant, with only a few functioning for storage and accomodation. Most buildings are of multiple functions in the district. Because the residential houses were built later in the district, excessive density has deteriorated the whole environment and formed a layout where commercial and residential functions are mixed together.

The structure of land use in this Neighborhood is mixed and various, with most part being commercial land and R2 land, and very few public green land. In the Qilou (Arcade building) District, most buildings are for mixed commercial and residential use.

### 1.2.4 Traditional Alleys and Streets Reflecting Dense Urban Texture

Located in the old Pengjiang District, Changdi Historical Neighborhood is surrounded by the main street Shengli Road, Jianshe Road and Yuejin Road, and is well connected with the northern part of the city. Except two pedestrian streets Chang'an Road and Shiwanzhi Street, other streets in the Neighborhood can be used as driveways. For example, roads wider than 3 meters can be used as drive lanes, and road with a width of 2-3 meters can be used both by pedestrians and motorcycles. Most roads in the Neighborhood belong to similar classification, mainly 8-10 meters wide, and are better connected with each other in east to west direction than north to south direction. The densely but rationally distributed lanes in the residential area of the neighborhood are mainly 1~5 meters wide, on which both pedestrians and vehicles are able to travel. Basic urban texture is preserved in this area, but due to insufficient maintaining and management, some roads are in poor condition or even cut off, which cause traffic difficulties.

### 1.2.5 Impacts and Challenges Brought by Rapid Urbanization

Rapid urbanization process brought impact and challenges to the continuous development of traditional neighborhood. Large buildings developed in recent years ruined the comfortable scale and intact style of the neighborhood.

New buildings are mostly distributed in the northern part of the Neighborhood and some part of the Qilou District. In spite of the good quality, new buildings have some negative influence on the overall style of the

图1-2-16 石湾直街
PICTURE 1-2-16 SHIWANZHI STREET

图1-2-17 历史街区鸟瞰图
PICTURE 1-2-17 BIRD-VIEW OF HISTORICAL NEIGHBORHOOD

图1-2-18 历史街区鸟瞰图
PICTURE 1-2-18 BIRD-VIEW OF HISTOCIAL NEIGHBORHOOD

占历史街区建筑的半数以上。北部居住区的建筑年代较新，大多为1979年后新建的住宅，这些都为历史街区保护与改造带来一定难度。

随着对历史街区价值的重新认识，城市社会和城市经济的发展完善，从政府到民间都在呼吁开展历史街区的保护工作，这为整体保护和修整长堤历史街区带来了新的契机。城市经济水平和基础设施的发展提高了历史街区在江门乃至珠三角地区的地位，使地方政府在历史街区保护上有清晰认识和政策上的倾斜，为当地产业的重新繁荣和旅游等服务业的发展带来了新的可能。新的发展是历史街区落后面貌改变的重要机遇，但也可能对传统建筑乃至文化带来新的冲击，如何平衡开发和保护是历史街区发展的一个重要议题。

Neighborhood, due to different height, size and look. For example, the modern high-rise Chang'an Plaza seems very abrupt among other buildings along the Bingjiang Street, which seriously impacts the skyline along the river; unique features of some low-rise at the east of Sun Yat-sen Part in Xuding District are also influenced by several multi-floored buildings; Penglai Mountain where Jingxian Middle School is located is basically covered by multi-floored modern buildings, which do not match the styles of traditional features near the mountain.

The shift of city center to the north during urban expansion also caused the deterioration of economic development and loss of population, especially young generation that migrated to other cities, leaving only elders and low-income ones. Traditional businesses mainly serving the low-income group maintained certain vitality, however, weaknesses such as limited influence, low competitiveness and few high-level service industry in the neighborhood do exist. Due to insufficient protection, a large number of historical buildings are in urgent need of repairing, and serious safety hazards are threatening brick-wood structured buildings as well. Moreover, lacking of effective management also leads to damages to overall urban texture and historical heritages. Poor management and planning also cause a lot of traffic problems; more than half of buildings in the neighborhood are private houses, and most buildings in the norther district are modern ones built after 1979. All the problems mentioned above mean that the protection and regeneration work in Changdi Historical Neighborhood is not a easy job.

Reevaluation of historical neighborhood, development in social and economic undertakings, importance attached by government and nongovernmental sectors all bring new opportunities for the protection and renewing work of Changdi Historical Neighborhood. As economic develops and city infrastructure improves, the status of historical neighborhood is promoted so that their value is clearly recognized to win more government support. Reflourishing of local economic and prosperity of service industry, such as tourism not only brings new possibilities and new opportunities to renew historical neighborhood, but also brings new impact to traditional buildings and local culture. Therefore, an important topic in the development and renewal of historical neighborhood is how to strike a balance.

图1-2-19　余庆里鸟瞰
PICTURE 1-2-19　BIRD-VIEW OF YUQING LANE

图1-2-20　历史街区鸟瞰图
PICTURE 1-2-20　BIRD-VIEW OF HISTOCIAL NEIBOURHOOD

图1-2-21 历史街区鸟瞰图
PICTURE 1-2-21　BIRD-VIEW OF HISTOCIAL NEIBOURHOOD

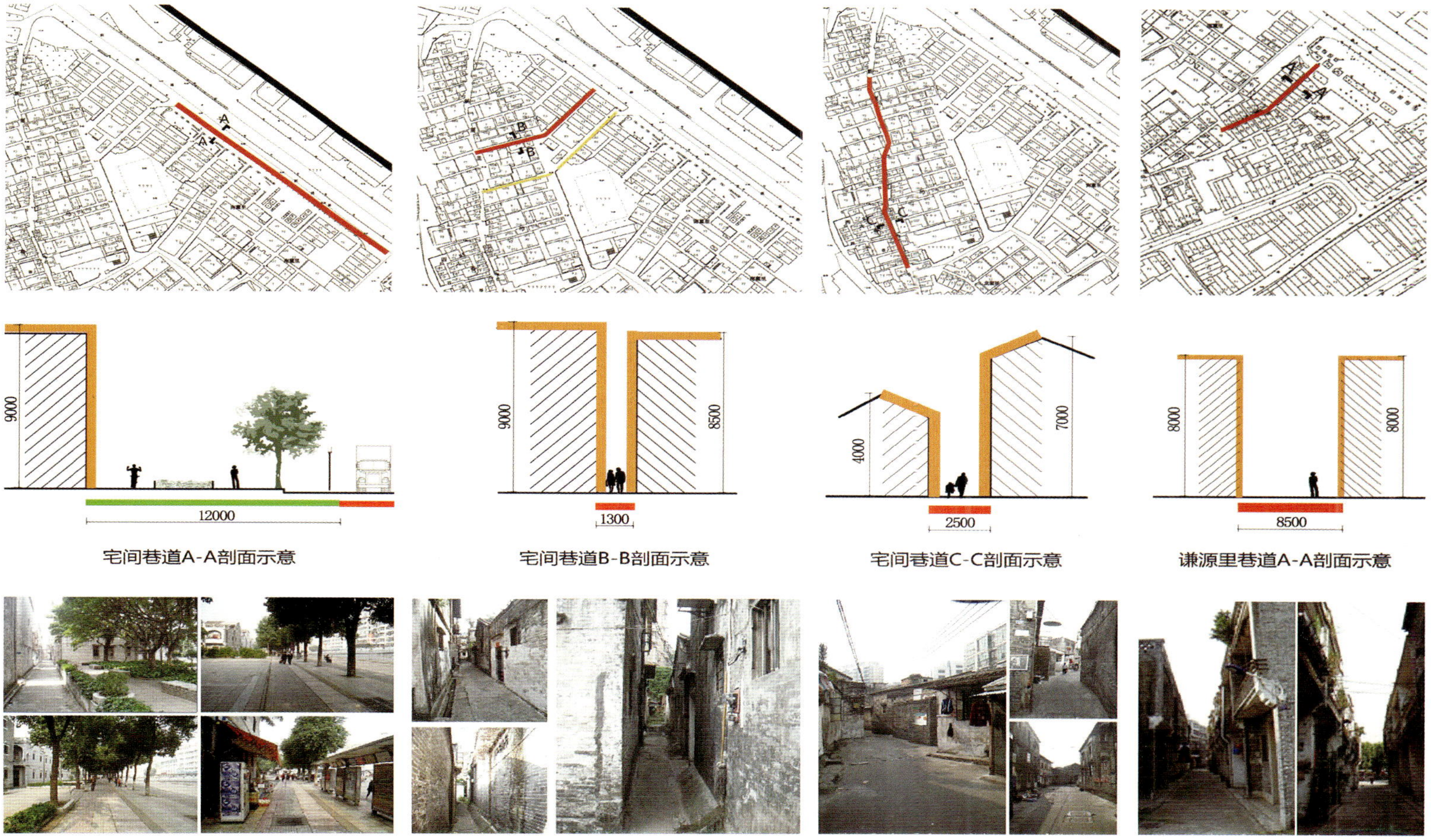

宅间巷道A-A剖面示意　　宅间巷道B-B剖面示意　　宅间巷道C-C剖面示意　　谦源里巷道A-A剖面示意

图1-2-22 街巷剖面示意图
PICTURE 1-2-22　SECTION OF THE STREEIS

图1-2-23 骑楼街书院路
PICTURE 1-2-23 ARCADE STREET IN SHUYUAN ROAD

图1-2-24 骑楼街上步路
PICTURE 1-2-24 ARCADE STREET IN SHANGBU ROAD

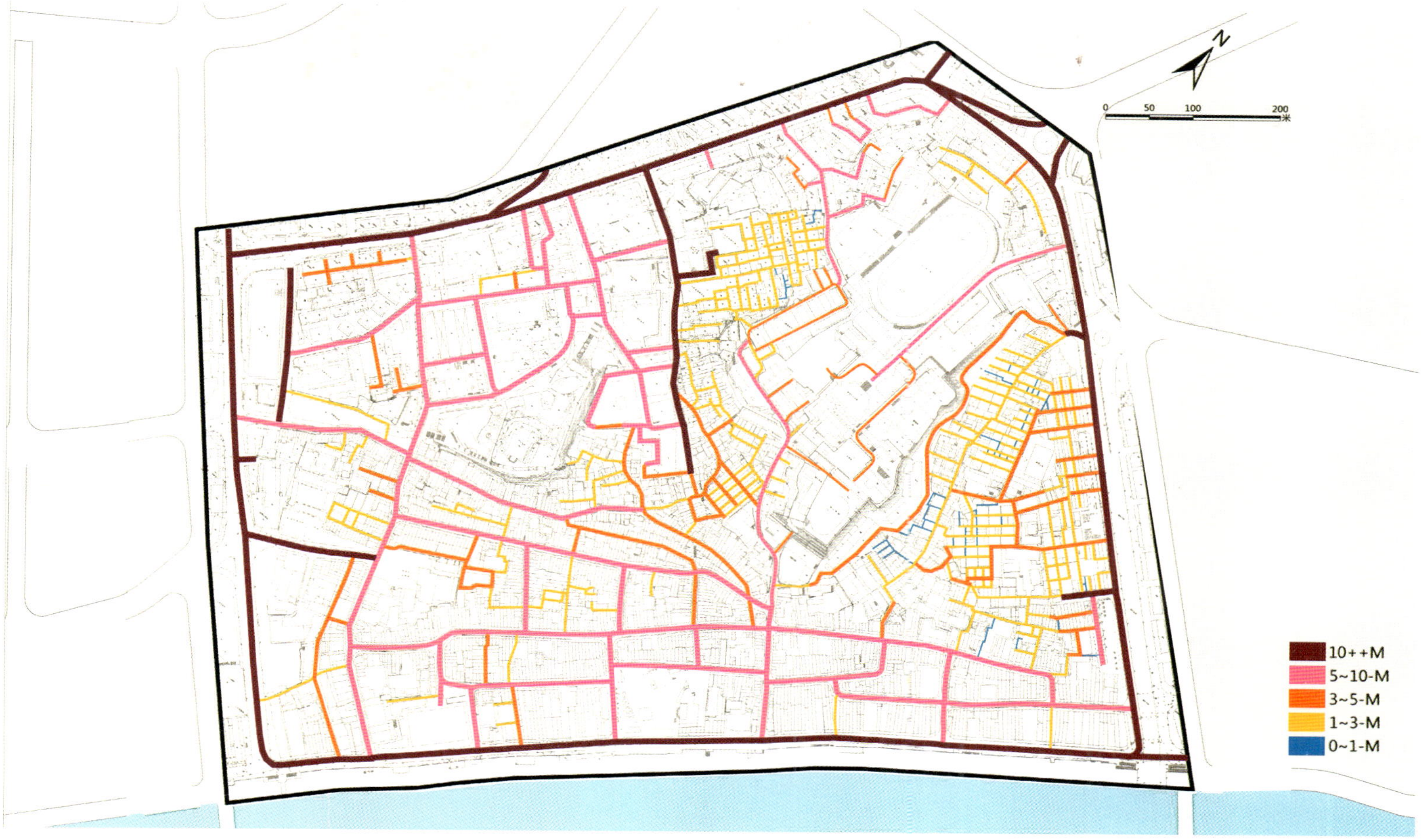

图1-2-25 现状道路宽度示意图
PICTURE 2-2-25　EXISTING ROAD WIDTH

图1-2-26 骑楼街堤中路
PICTURE 1-2-26　ARCADE STREET IN DIZHONG ROAD

图1-2-27 新第里1、2、3号入口局部
PICTURE 1-2-27 PORTION OF THE ENTRANCE OF NO.1 TO NO.3 TO XINDI LANE

图1-2-28  启明里39-42号外观局部
PICTURE 1-2-28  PORTION OF NO.39-42 OF QIMING LANE

图1-2-29  墟顶居住风貌区鸟瞰图
PICTURE 1-2-29  BIRD-VIEW

# 2 风貌建筑及街巷空间

Historical Buildings and Lanes

图2-0-1 长堤路现状
PICTURE 2-0-1 STATUS PICTURE OF CHANGDI ROAD

图2-0-2 历史街区现状局部鸟瞰图
PICTURE 2-0-2 BIRD-VIEW OF JIANGMEN HISTORIC DISTRICT

长堤历史街区背靠蓬莱山，南面蓬江，形成了独特的山水格局。历史上江门"水退人进"的发展变迁，使历史街区从陆地向河边延伸，形成一湾高地，从旧墟市变成商贸发达的"新市"。在历史长河中，该地区逐渐形成了具有不同年代特征、密集分布的传统街巷空间，拥有着具有独特地域特色的历史风貌建筑。江门长堤历史街区年代久远，一直是江门重要的城市区域，集合了各个时期重要的商业和文化设施，并逐步形成了墟顶、石湾和骑楼街区等重要片区。时光荏苒，岁月无声，尽管很多历史建筑已经不复存在，但现在的江门长堤历史街区仍然整体保留着清代和民国时期建筑群体和街区环境，保存了与陈白沙等历史名人史迹相关的遗址。江门长堤历史街区的历史风貌保存完整性在珠三角地区极具代表性，它作为名人文化、历史文化遗产地、历史自然环境结合的代表，蕴涵了丰富的历史文化价值，是岭南地区重要的传统文化遗产。

城市格局、历史风貌建筑、传统街巷、历史遗迹和历史环境等都是历史街区的物质载体。江门长堤历史街区历经多个时期的发展演变，具有丰富的多样性和广泛的包容性特点。根据各个历史时期的建设特点和现状情况，可将现状历史街区分为四个风貌区：墟顶居住风貌区、石湾历史风貌区、近代华侨建筑风貌区和骑楼风貌区。其中墟顶居住风貌区为原江门墟所在地，历史最为悠久，至今仍保留着传统的空间格局及墟顶街、京果街、灯笼街、打铁街、卖鸡地等与墟市贸易活动相关的传统街巷名称，还有三十三级台阶、三桁瓦、钓台遗址等重要的历史遗迹。石湾历史风貌区可追溯的历史稍晚于墟顶，最负盛名的石湾直街原为当地有名的商业街，现状保留了石湾直街蜿蜒狭窄的街巷空间及一部分历史风貌建筑，并能探寻到石湾庙、雪峰寺等历史建筑的遗址。骑楼风貌区为历史街区内规模最大、保存最为完整的传统风貌区，共包括19条主要骑楼街，空间格局保存完整，绵延数公里长的道路两侧集中保留了大量精美的骑楼建筑和连续的城市街廓。近代华侨建筑风貌区为民国期间华侨投资兴建地产而得名，区内建筑布局规整有序，形式精美，反映了特定历史时期具有独特性的城市建设格局。

历史风貌建筑是江门长堤历史街区的重要组成部分，江门长堤历史街区共有历史风貌建筑2000余栋，规模之大，分布之集中，为江门乃至粤西地区所罕见。与风貌区划对应，历史风貌建筑也可以分为四种类型：墟顶居住建筑、石湾历史风貌建筑、近代

Changdi Historical Neighborhood presents a unique landscape by situating beside the Penglai Mountain and facing the Peng River in the south. Historically, with the change in the river course, the river receded and people moved forward. The historical neighborhood was expanded from the land to the riverside and formed the waterfront highland. An old market city became a new flourishing commercial city. Since establishment, Changdi Historical Neighborhood has always been a significant urban area in Jiangmen that gathers key commercial and cultural facilities in different times and has been gradually divided into smaller important neighborhoods including Xuding District, Shiwan District and Qilou (Arcade Building) District. As time goes by, many historical buildings are gone, but Changdi Historical Neighborhood as a whole has maintained its architecture complex and surrounding environment as in the periods of Ming Dynasty and the Republic of China. Related historical sites of famous celebrities like Chen Baisha have been preserved. With intact buildings and landscape, it is highly typical in the Pearl River Delta. As an example that combines historical and cultural heritage, celebrity culture with historical natural environment, Changdi Historical Neighborhood stands as an important heritage of traditional culture in Lingnan area with enriched historical and cultural value.

City layout, historical buildings, traditional streets, historical sites and environment are important physical carriers of a historical neighborhood. Developed and evolved in different periods, Changdi Historical Neighborhood features diversity and inclusiveness. The Neighborhood can be further divided into four districts based on different styles of buildings in different times and their status quo including Xuding Residential District, Shiwan Historical District, Modern Overseas Chinese Architecture District and Qilou (Arcade Building) District, of which, Xuding Residential District is the oldest where the then Jiangmen Marketplace was located. It has maintained the past layout and the names of the streets that indicate relevant trading activities in the marketplace like Xuding Street, Nuts Street, Lantern Street, Blacksmith Street, Chicken Market etc. It has also preserved important historical sites like Thirty-three Stone Steps, Sanhengwa Kitchen Knife Shop and Fishing Terrace. Shiwan Historical District is formed slightly later than Xuding Residential District. The most famous Shiwanzhi Street was a main commercial street and has preserved the zigzagging lanes as well as part of the historical buildings where Shiwan Temple and Xuefeng Temple can be found. Qilou (Arcade Building) District is the most well-preserved traditional district of the largest scale. It has 19 main arcade building streets with intact spatial layout and a large number of exquisite arcade buildings and continuous city outline. Modern Overseas Chinese Architecture District is named after the investors who built the properties. This district features structured and orderly layout with fine architecture, a reflection of the unique city layout in specific periods of time.

Historical buildings are an important component of Changdi Historical Neighborhood. With more than 2000

图2-0-3 长堤路历史照片
PICTURE 2-0-3 HISTORICAL PICTURE OF CHANGDI ROAD

图2-0-4 蓬江大桥历史照片
PICTURE 2-0-4 HISTORICAL PICTURE OF PENGJIANG BRIDGE

华侨建筑和骑楼历史建筑。其中，墟顶居住建筑多以居住为主，主要是低层和多层建筑；石湾历史风貌建筑以低层居住为主，部分建筑为商住混合之用；近代华侨建筑为近代华侨所建，具有统一的规划布局，立面形式中西合璧；骑楼历史建筑集中分布于南部骑楼街片区，以多层、商住混合功能为主，形式丰富、式样精美。现状保留的历史建筑多为民国所建，少量为清代所建。其中有宝和按当铺、永安按当铺和钓台三处市级文物保护单位，还有大量独具历史风貌特色，但尚未列入文物保护单位的历史建筑。

通过建筑风貌、建筑层数、建筑外观质量、建筑性质、建筑结构、建筑年代等方面的评价，结合不同评价方面的不同权重属性，本书对江门历史街区内的历史建筑文化资源进行了综合的价值评定。其中，启明里建筑群、余庆里建筑群、骑楼片区部分区域整体建筑风貌较好，建筑价值较高。其它类别的历史建筑也同样具有其特定的历史意义和价值，也应予以采取相应的保护和修缮措施。

为清晰完整地展现江门长堤历史街区风貌，本书以风貌区为单元，分别在各个风貌区内介绍其总体概况、历史建筑、街巷空间和历史遗迹。长堤历史街区共有3528栋建筑（包括历史建筑和新建建筑），其中，在核心保护区内有3128栋建筑。这3128栋建筑中有100栋（见附录232～233页）风貌保存优良，具有很高的历史研究价值，本书精选二十余栋质量较好的历史建筑做单栋建筑介绍，并对包含1080栋骑楼建筑的骑楼街区做整体介绍。通过大量影像和图纸资料，为读者展现江门长堤历史街区的独特魅力。

historical buildings located in the same area, the scale of Changdi is rarely seen in Jiangmen or even in West Guangdong region. In line with the aforementioned four districts, historical buildings can also be divided into four types: Xuding residential buildings, Shiwan historical buildings, modern overseas Chinese buildings and arcade buildings. Buildings in Xuding District, mostly low-rise and multiple-floored, are mainly for residential purposes. Buildings in Shiwan District are also mainly low-rise and for residence, but some are for both commercial and residential purposes. Buildings in Modern Overseas Chinese District are well-planned and built with both Chinese and western features. Arcade buildings are mainly located in the south Qilou District. With multiple floors and mixed commercial and residential functions, it has different styles with exquisite forms. Most preserved buildings were built in the Republic of China, and few were from Qing Dynasty. Baohe Pawnshop, Yong'an Pawnshop and Fishing Terrace are designated as Municipal Cultural Preservation Sites, yet there are a large number of buildings with unique historical features that are not included into the list.

This book offers a comprehensive evaluation of the historical, architectural culture resources in the historical neighborhoods of Jiangmen. It assesses the buildings' architectural style, layers, appearance quality, type, structure and the year they were built and weighs the different attributes. The buildings in Qiming Lane, Yuqing Lane and Qilou area are generally well preserved with high architectural value. Some other buildings are of historical significance as well and should be maintained and restored.

In order to depict a clear and complete picture of the Changdi Historical Neighborhood, this book will introduce the overall situation, historical buildings, streets and lanes and other historical sites in every district. Changdi Historical Neighborhood has 3528 buildings, of which 3128 are located in the core protection area. 100 buildings (page232-233 in the attachment) of the 3128 are well preserved and of high value for historical studies. This book will present 28 well-preserved buildings one by one and the Qilou (Arcade Building) District with 1080 arcade buildings as a whole. With plenty of images, drawings and pictures, this book expects to showcase the unique charm of the Changdi Historical Neighborhood to the readers.

图2-0-5 历史街区现状局部鸟瞰图
PICTURE 2-0-5 BIRD-VIEW OF JIANGMEN HISTORIC DISTRICT

图2-0-6 长堤历史街区建筑风貌图
PICTURE 2-0-6  DISTRICT OF CHANGDI HISTORICAL NEIGHBORHOOD

图2-1-1 启明里历史风貌建筑
PICTURE 2-1-1 HISTORICAL BUILDING IN QIMING LI

# 2.1 近代华侨建筑风貌区
## 2.1 MODERN OVERSEAS CHINESE BUILDINGS DISTRICT

民国初年，继广州之后，江门地区县城拆除城垣，开辟马路，建设新城市。江门拥有较强经济实力，又通过深受西方文化影响的华侨将西方城市规划思想和建筑形式引入江门的城市建设中，从而揭开中西规划和建筑文化在江门侨乡融合的历史篇章。

近代华侨建筑风貌区因民国初期江门华侨或政府投资兴建而得名。区内建筑为江门早期开发建设的房地产。该区具体包括启明里、南芬里、龙聚里、明德坊和余庆里共五个里坊，面积约 2.74 公顷。其中启明里和南芬里内建筑多为双开间两层建筑，正面有大量欧式风格线脚、柱式、山花和拱券样式，以"眼镜楼"最为出名。明德坊曾为民国期间政府员工宿舍。余庆里前身为新会县丞署，民国二年（1913 年），由商会投资，将其改建成民房，为江门早期的房地产开发项目。五个里坊的建筑布局规整、规划严谨，建筑立面造型精美，反映了近代江门房地产开发建设的特点和风貌。

In the early days of the Republic of China, Jiangmen has followed the suit of Guangzhou to have dismantled city walls and began to build roads for a new city. With a strong economy and the introduction of western urban planning theories and architecture forms into Jiangmen's urban construction by those westernized overseas Chinese, Jiangmen has opened a new chapter of the integration of Chinese and western planning and architecture culture in this hometown of overseas Chinese.

Modern Overseas Chinese Buildings District is named after those overseas Chinese investors or the government that constructed the buildings during the Republic of China. Those buildings represent the early properties development in Jiangmen. This District covers an area of 2.74 hectares including Qiming Lane, Nanfen Lane, Longju Lane, Mingde Lane and Yuqing Lane. There are mostly double-floored two-section buildings with European style lines and corners, pillars, pediments and arches on the facade in Qiming Lane and Nanfen Lane, of which, Glass Tower stands as the most famous example. Mingde Lane provided accommodation for government employees back in the Republic of China. Yuqing Lane was the former site of the Xinhui County Assistant Director and was then transformed into civil houses with the investment of commerce chambers and was among the real estate projects in Jiangmen in the early times. The aforementioned five lanes are well planned with a structured layout and an exquisite modeling of the facade, a reflection of the features and characteristics of real estate development in Jiangmen in modern times.

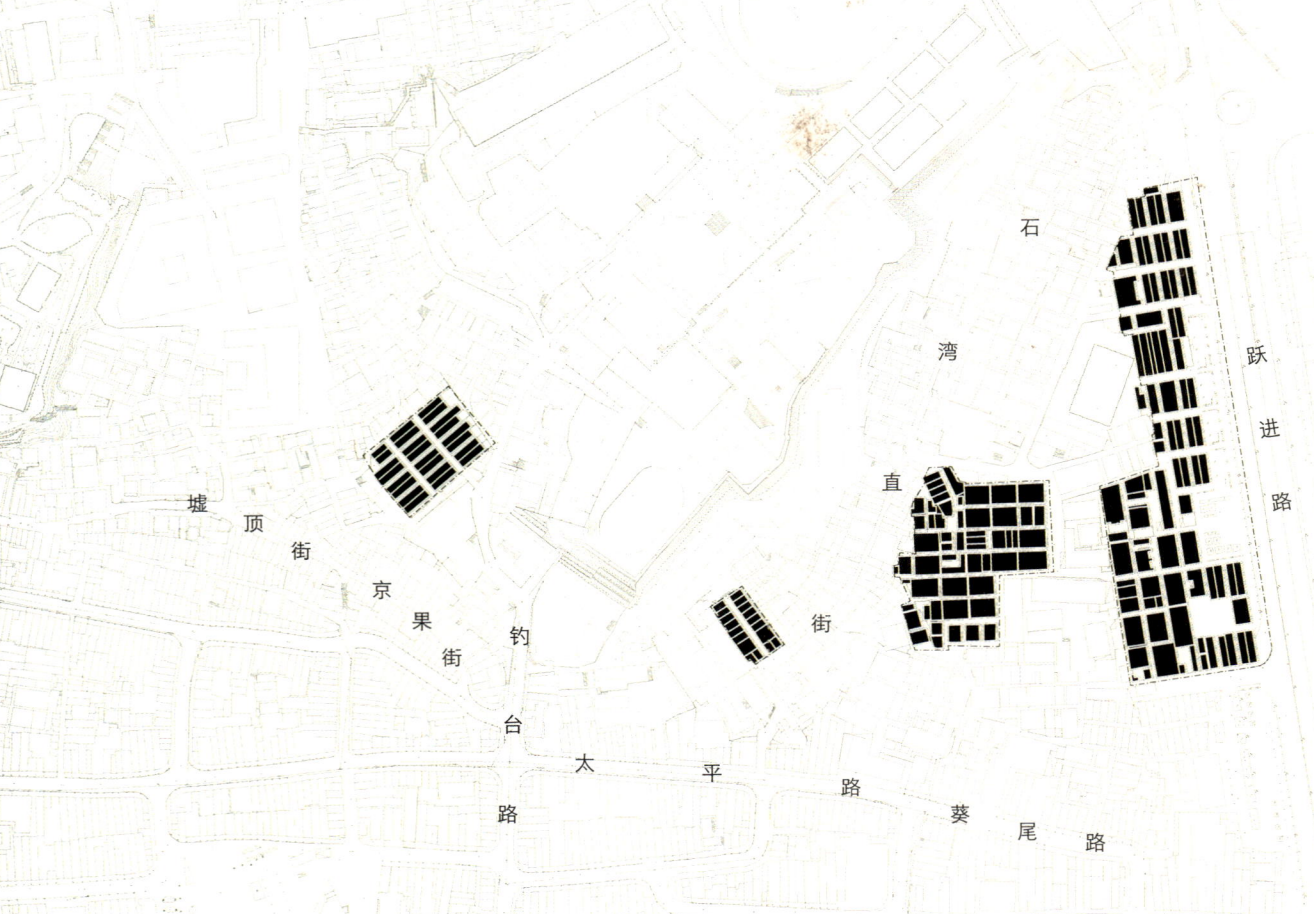

图2-1-2 区位图
PICTURE 2-1-2　LOCATION

■ 近代华侨建筑风貌区

图2-1-3 余庆里街道内景
PICTURE 2-1-3　THE ROAD IN THE YU QING LANE

图2-1-4 龙聚里36号
PICTURE 2-1-4 NO.36 LONG JU LANE

图2-1-5 龙聚里3号
PICTURE 2-1-5 NO.3 LONG JU LANE

图2-1-6 启明里39、42号
PICTURE 2-1-6 NO.39 42 QI MING LANE

图2-1-7 · 南芬里10号、11号正立面
PICTURE 2-1-7　FACADE OF NO.10 & 11 OF NANFEN LANE

## 2.1.1 南芬里 10 号和 11 号

南芬里 10 号和 11 号位于石湾片区的东部，跃进路以西。建筑为两开间二层砖混结构建筑，建造时间为民国初期，两开间占地面积分别是 82.5 平方米和 82.4 平方米。建筑保存状况良好，为南洋式风格。建筑外墙为青砖砌筑，立面保留了大量彩画装饰，三角形山花保存完整，上书"旺庐"和"润庐"四字。山花上有镂空的洞口，减小台风风压，充分适应岭南湿热气候，又使得建筑轻盈通透。二层阳台均有石米材质的多立克柱式和铸铁铁艺栏杆，一层为木质趟栊门，石质门套镶以石米门框，展现了江门华侨近代居住建筑的风貌，建筑整体古朴精美。

## 2.1.1 No.10 & No.11 of Nanfen Lane

Located in the east of Shiwan District and to the west of Yuejin Road, No. 10 and No. 11 of Nanfen Lane are double-floored brick-concrete structures with two sections in width. It was built roughly during the beginning of the Republic of China. The two sections cover 82.5m² and 82.4m² respectively. In good shape, the two buildings have Southeast Asia styles. The external walls of the buildings were constructed with plain bricks and a lot of plaster decorations can still be seen on the facade. The triangular pediment is well preserved with four characters Wang Lu and Run Lu written on it. The pediment with a hollow hole reduces typhoon wind pressure to adapt to the hot and humid climate in Southern China, and the building is light and transparent. The second floor balconies have chicken girt Doric order pillars and iron-cast handrails and the first floor has a wooden bar sliding door with the chicken girt frame embedded in stone. The building is primitive, simple, yet exquisite, a reflection of the features of the buildings for modern overseas Chinese in Jiangmen.

图2-1-8 区位图与平面轮廓图
PICTURE 2-1-8 LOCATION AND THE OUTLINE

图2-1-9 南芬里10号、11号外观
PICTURE 2-1-9 APPEARENCE OF NO.10&11 OF NANFEN LANE

图2-1-10 二楼阳台放大局部
PICTURE 2-1-10 BALCONY

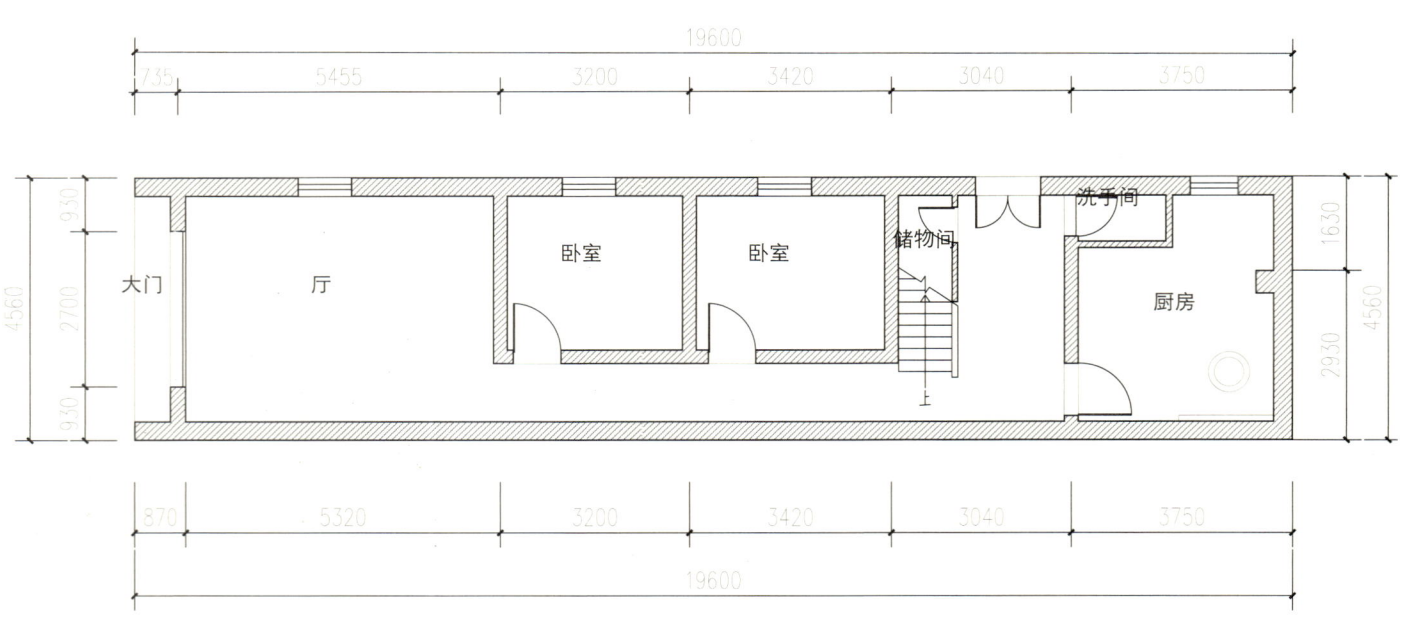

图2-1-11 南芬里11号首层平面图
PICTURE 2-1-11 THE FIRST FLOOR

图2-1-12 二楼阳台放大局部
PICTURE 2-1-12 BALCONY

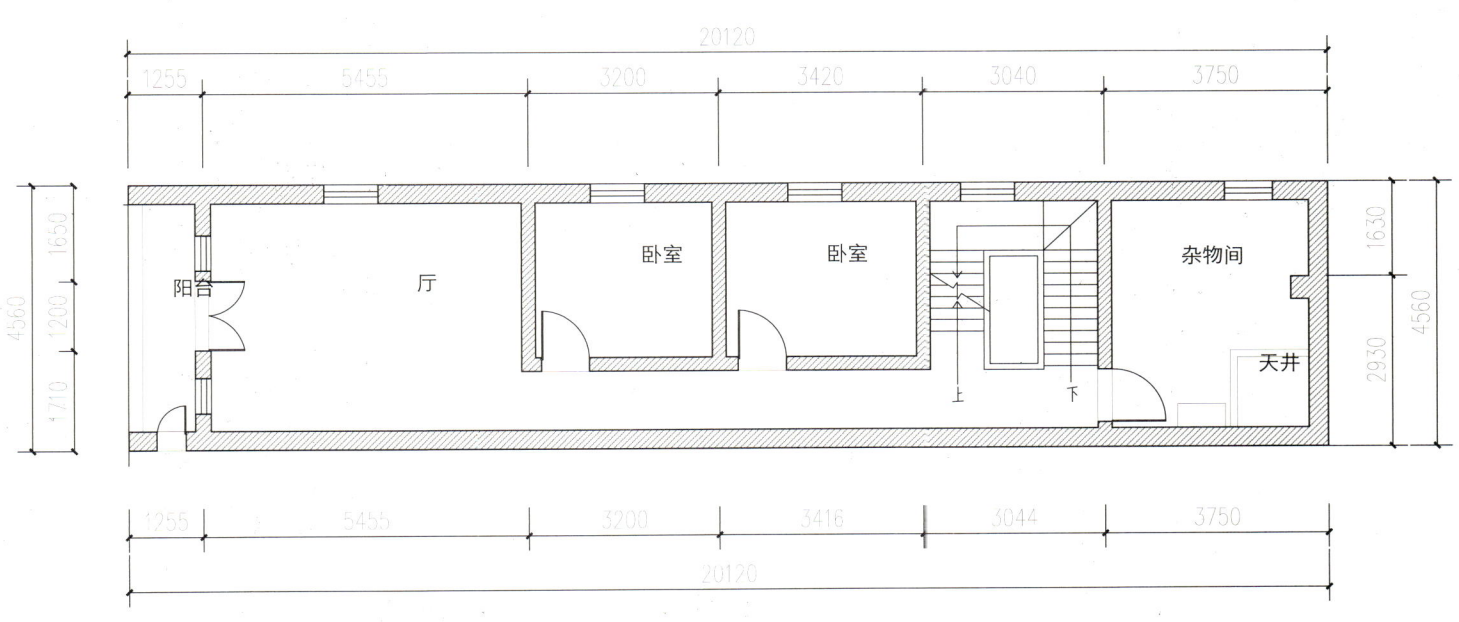

图2-1-13 南芬里11号二层平面图
PICTURE 2-1-13 THE SECOND FLOOR

051

图2-1-14 墙壁彩画
PICTURE 2-1-14　TEMPERA ON THE WALL

图2-1-15 墙壁彩画
PICTURE 2-1-15　TEMPERA ON THE WALL

图2-1-16 二楼阳台彩画
PICTURE 2-1-16　TEMPERA ON THE SECOND FLOOR BALCONY

图2-1-17　南芬里11号屋顶层平面图
PICTURE 2-1-17　THE ROOF FLOOR

图2-1-18　二楼阳台彩画
PICTURE 2-1-18　TEMPERA ON THE SECOND FLOOR BALCONY

图2-1-19 南芬里24号外观图
PICTURE 2-1-19 APPEARENCE OF NO.24 NANFEN LANE

## 2.1.2 南芬里 24 号

南芬里 24 号位于石湾片区的东部，跃进路以西，为一开间的二层砖混结构建筑，建造时间为民国初期，占地面积为 75.2 平方米。建筑保存状况良好，为仿巴洛克式样。建筑外墙为青砖砌筑，立面保留了部分彩画装饰，曲线形山花保存完整，上书"蘭室"二字。建筑二层阳台上砖石砌成的栏杆有金属花纹的装饰，一层入口已根据屋主使用需要改换成卷帘铁闸。房屋现为下商上住用途，下层商铺为南芬里棋牌馆。

## 2.1.2 No. 24 of Nanfen Lane

Located in the east of Shiwan District and to the west of Yuejin Road, No. 24 of Nanfen Lane is a double-floored brick-concrete structure with one section in width. It was built roughly during the beginning of the Republic of China with a total area of 75.2m². In good condition, the building imitates Baroque styles. The external walls were constructed with plain bricks and some of the plaster decorations are retained on the facade. The curved pediment is well preserved with two characters Lan Shi written on it. The brick-stoned handrails of the second floor balcony have been carved with metal decorations and the entrance on the first floor has been changed into roller blind iron gate according to the demands of the house owner. The building is now for mixed use where the second floor is for residence and the first for commercial use as a chess room in Nanfen Lane.

图2-1-20 区位图与平面轮廓图
PICTURE 2-1-20 LOCATION AND OUTLINE

图2-1-21 南芬里25号外观图
PICTURE 2-1-21 APPEARENCE OF NO.25 NANFEN LANE

图2-1-22 南芬里25号外观图
PICTURE 2-1-22 APPEARENCE OF NO.25 NANFEN LANE

### 2.1.3 南芬里 25 号

南芬里 25 号位于石湾片区的东部，为一开间的二层砖混结构建筑，建造时间为民国初期，建筑占地面积为 85.5 平方米。建筑保存状况良好，南洋式风格。建筑外墙为青砖砌筑，屋顶山墙山花保存完整，上书"壁卢"二字。三角形山花上有镂空的洞口，减小台风风压，充分适应了岭南湿热气候，又使得建筑轻盈通透。建筑二层阳台有石米材质的爱奥尼柱式，一层为木质趟栊门和石质门套，建筑现在依旧用作居住。

### 2.1.3 No.25 of Nanfen Lane

Located in the east of Shiwan District, No. 25 of Nanfen Lane is a double-floored brick-concrete structure with one section. It was built roughly during the beginning of the Republic of China with a total area of 85.5m². In good condition, the building is Southeast Asia styles. The external walls were constructed with plain bricks and the roof gable and pediment are well preserved with two characters Bi Lu written on it. Triangular pediment with a hollow hole reduces typhoon wind pressure to adapt to the hot and humid climate in Southern China, and the building is light and transparent. The second floor balcony has chicken girt Ionic order pillars and the first floor has a wooden bar sliding door embedded in stone. The building is primitive, simple, yet grand and is still for residential purposes nowadays.

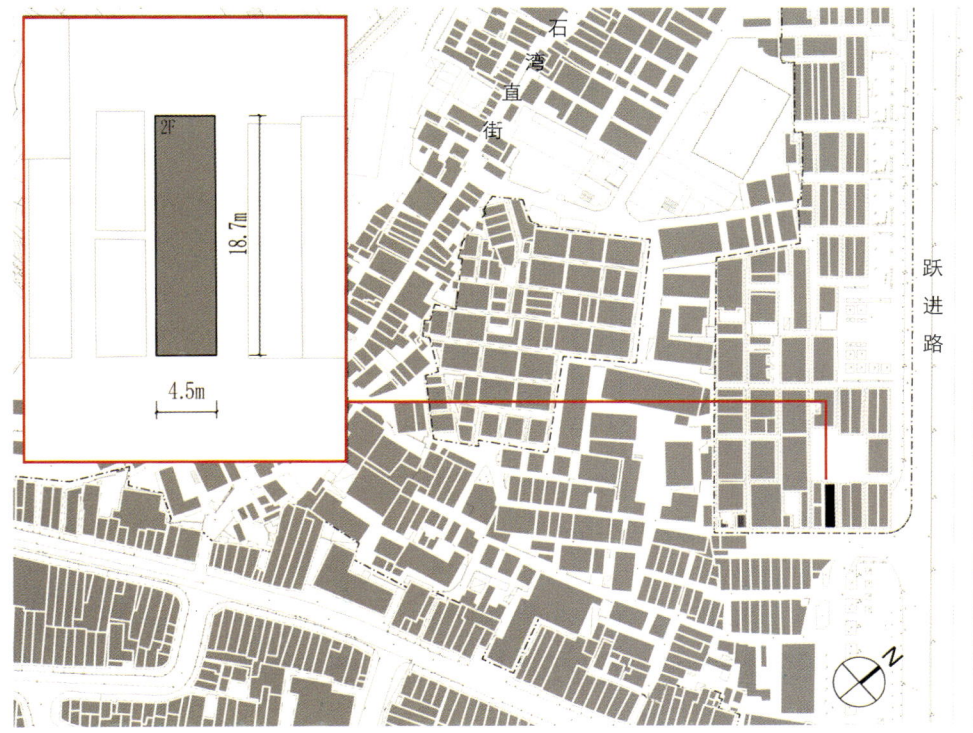

图2-1-23 区位图与平面轮廓图
PICTURE 2-1-23 LOCATION AND OUTLINE

图2-1-24 南芬里25号外观图
PICTURE 2-1-24 APPEARANCE OF NO.25 NANFEN LANE

图2-1-25　南芬里30号外观图
PICTURE 2-1-25　APPEARENCE OF NO.30 NANFEN LANE

## 2.1.4 南芬里 30 号

南芬里 30 号位于石湾片区的东部，为一开间的二层砖混结构建筑，建造时间为民国初期，建筑占地面积为 174.7 平方米。建筑保存状况良好，为典型的中西结合式样。建筑外墙为青砖砌筑，建筑二层阳台均有石米材质的爱奥尼柱式，栏杆为琉璃材质宝瓶栏杆，一层为木质趟栊门和石质门套。建筑现在依旧用作居住。

### 2.1.4 No.30 of Nanfen Lane

Located in the east of Shiwan District, No. 30 of Nanfen Lane is a double-floored brick-concrete structure with one section in width. It was built roughly during the Republic of China with a total area of 174.7m². In good condition, the building combines Chinese and western styles. The external walls were constructed with plain bricks. The second floor balcony has chicken girt Ionic order pillars and glass-made vase-shaped handrails, and the first floor has a wooden bar sliding door embedded in stone. The building is primitive, simple, yet grand and is still for residential purposes nowadays.

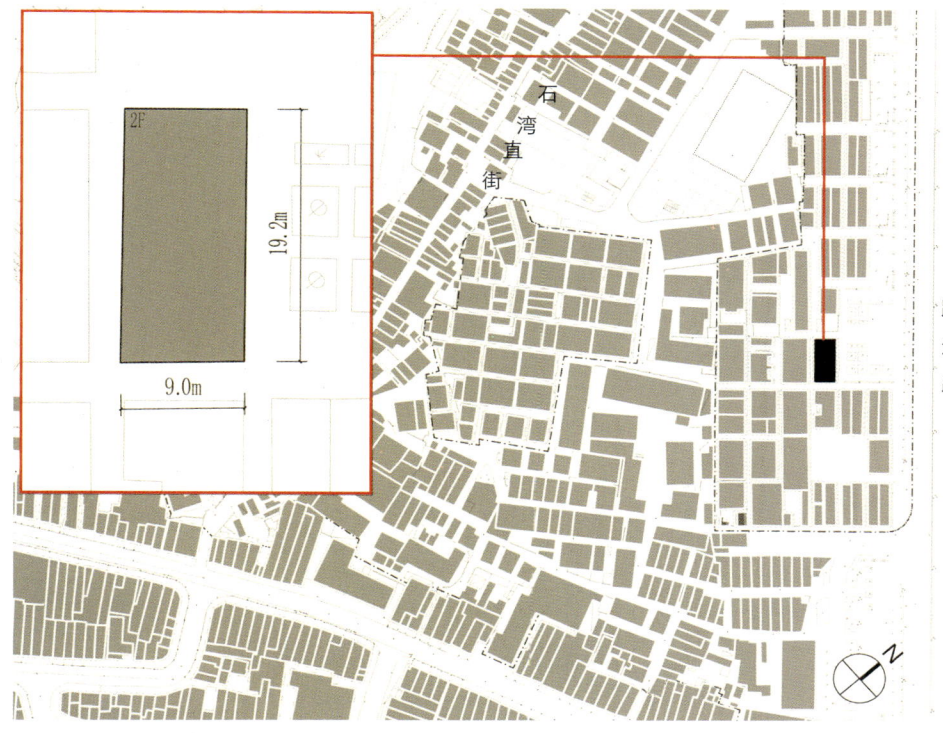

图2-1-26　区位图与平面轮廓图
PICTURE 2-1-26　LOCATION AND OUTLINE

图2-1-27　外观放大局部
PICTURE 2-1-27　PORTION OF THE FACADE

图2-1-28 南芬里34号外观图
PICTURE 2-1-28 APPEARENCE OF NO.34 NANFEN LANE

## 2.1.5 南芬里 34 号

南芬里34号位于石湾片区的东部，南芬里建筑群里，为三开间的二层砖混结构建筑，建造时间为民国初期，建筑占地面积为200.6平方米。建筑保存状况良好，建筑外墙为青砖砌筑。建筑保留了雕花栏杆、科林斯柱式以及拱券。建筑一层门洞已被封实，二层阳台的石米雕花栏杆以及科林斯柱式、拱券雕饰精美。整个建筑反映了当时岭南华侨建筑对西方建筑风格的大胆尝试。

## 2.1.5 No.34 of Nanfen Lane

Located in the east of Shiwan District and within the Nanfen Lane building complex, No. 34 of Nanfen Lane is a double-floored brick-concrete structure with three sections in width. It was built roughly during the Republic of China with a total area of 200.6m². In good condition, the external walls were constructed with plain bricks and most of the meticulously carved handrails and Corinthian order pillars are preserved with the arches remaining intact. The entrance of the first floor has been sealed, while the second floor balcony has chicken girt and beautifully carved handrails and exquisite Corinthian order pillars and arches. The building represents a bold attempt of the overseas Chinese in Southern China to imitate the western architecture.

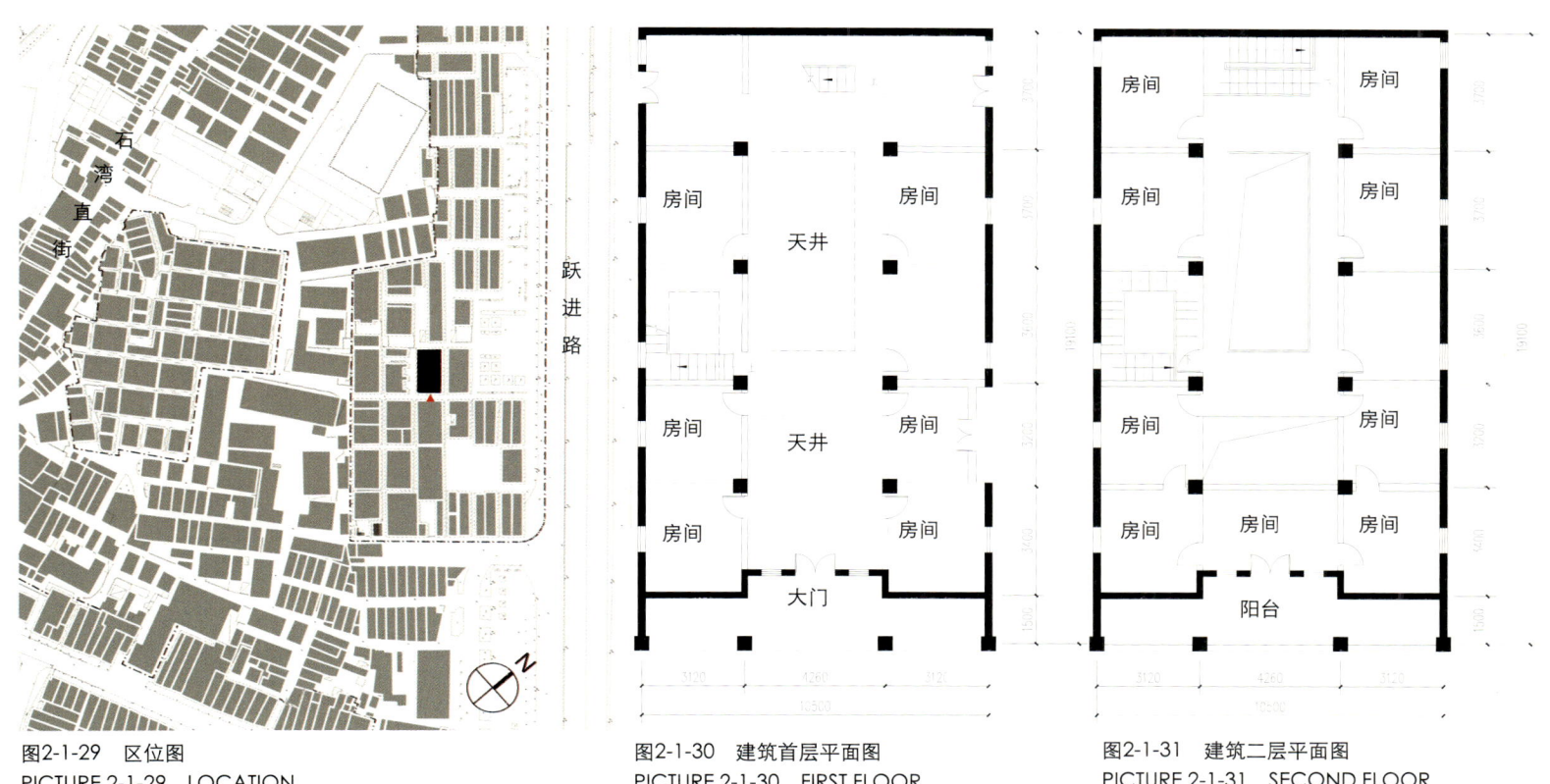

图2-1-29 区位图  
PICTURE 2-1-29 LOCATION

图2-1-30 建筑首层平面图  
PICTURE 2-1-30 FIRST FLOOR

图2-1-31 建筑二层平面图  
PICTURE 2-1-31 SECOND FLOOR

图2-1-32　广场外景
PICTURE 2-1-32　THE SQUARE

图2-1-33　广场外景
PICTURE 2-1-33　THE SQUARE

图2-1-34　广场外围道路
PICTURE 2-1-34　THE ROAD OUTSIDE THE SQUARE

## 2.1.6 南芬里广场

南芬里广场位于近代华侨建筑风貌区的东侧，跃进路以西，为历史保护街区内一长条形街旁的绿地，北侧、西侧和南侧被民国时期民居所包围，环境安静优美，吸引大量居民前来休憩。广场周围的建筑多数于民国初期建设而成，中西结合式样。建筑外墙为青砖砌筑。目前建筑的功能有作旅馆、商店、居住之用等。

## 2.1.6 Nanfen Lane Square

Located in the east side of the modern real estate district and to the west of Yuejin Road, Nanfen Lane Square is a piece of green land within the Historical Neighborhood. Surrounded by residential houses built in the Republic of China in its north, west and south, Nanfen Lane Square attracts a lot of local citizens to spend their leisure time with quiet and beautiful environment. Buildings surrounding the Square were mostly built in the beginning of the Republic of China with Chinese and western styles. The external walls were constructed with plain bricks. The buildings are now both used for commercial purpose as hotels and shops and for residential purpose.

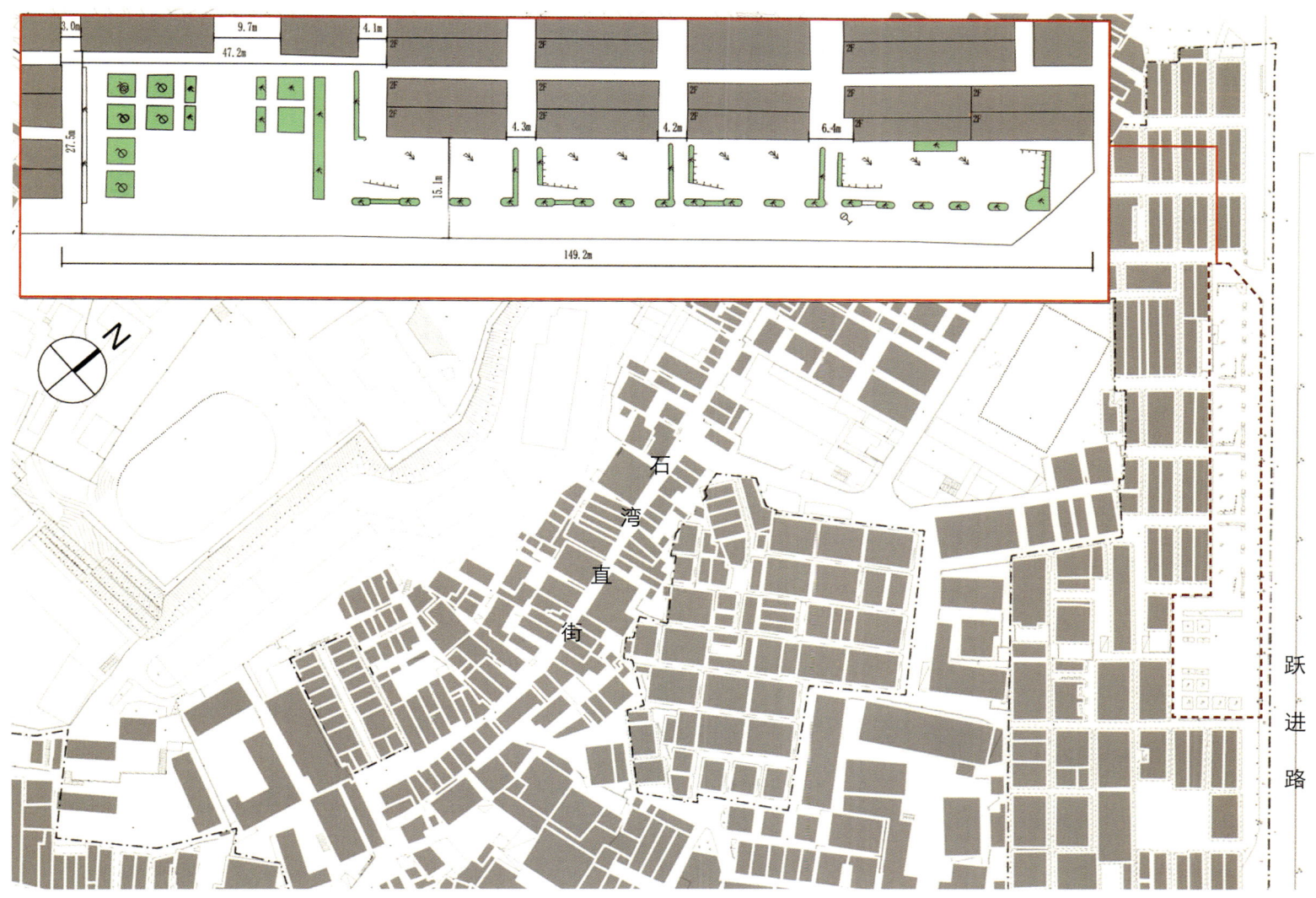

图2-1-35　区位图与平面轮廓图
PICTURE 2-1-35　LOCATION AND OUTLINE

图2-1-36 周边建筑放大局部
PICTURE 2-1-36　PORTION OF THE FACADE OF THE SURROUNDING ARCHITECTURE

图2-1-37 周边建筑入口局部
PICTURE 2-1-37　ENTRANCE OF THE SURROUNDING ARCHITECTURE

图2-1-38 周边建筑入口局部
PICTURE 2-1-38　ENTRANCE OF THE SURROUNDING ARCHITECTURE

图2-1-39 周边街巷
PICTURE 2-1-39 SURROUNDING ALLEY

图2-1-40 龙聚里3号外观图
PICTURE 2-1-40 APPEARENCE OF NO.3 LONGJU LANE

## 2.1.7 龙聚里3号

龙聚里3号位于石湾片区的东部，为一开间，主体二层、局部三层的砖混结构建筑，建造时间为民国初期，建筑占地面积为98.1平方米。建筑保存状况良好，建筑外墙为青砖砌筑，立面保留了部分彩画装饰以及山墙灰塑，山花为曲线形，繁复多样。建筑二层有石米材质的多立克柱式、拱券以及铁制的雕花栏杆，一层装有趟栊门。建筑现在依旧作居住用途。

## 2.1.7 No.3 of Longju Lane

Located in the east of Shiwan District, No. 3 of Longju Lane is a double-floored and partly three-floored brick-concrete structure with one section, covering a total area of 98.1m². It was built in the beginning of the Republic of China. In good condition, the external walls were constructed with plain bricks and part of the color painting decorations and plaster decorations are retained. The curved pediments are well preserved with complicated forms. The second floor has chicken girt Doric order pillars, arches and iron-made and beautifully carved handrails, and the first floor has a bar sliding door. The building still provides accommodation nowadays.

图2-1-41 区位图与平面轮廓图
PICTURE 2-1-41 LOCATION AND OUTLINE

图2-1-42 龙聚里3号外观图
PICTURE 2-1-42 APPEARENCE OF NO.3 LONGJU LANE

图2-1-43 龙聚里5号外观图
PICTURE 2-1-43 APPEARENCE OF NO.5 LONGJULANE

## 2.1.8 龙聚里5号

龙聚里5号位于石湾片区的东部,胜利路以西,为二开间二层砖混结构建筑,建造时间为民国初期,建筑占地面积为121.8平方米。建筑保存状况中等,建筑外观为青砖砌筑,山花为曲线形。建筑二层阳台铁制栏杆已换成砖造。建筑仍为居住用途。建筑主人在阳台上种植花草,生长茂盛的植物与古民居相映成趣。

## 2.1.8 No.5 of Longju Lane

Located in the east of Shiwan District and to the west of Shengli Road, No. 5 of Longju Lane is a double-floored brick-concrete structure with two sections in width, covering a total area of 121.8m². It was built in the beginning of the Republic of China. In moderate condition, the external walls of the building were constructed with plain bricks and the curved pediments on the rooftop are well preserved. The iron-made handrails on the second floor balcony have been replaced by bricks. The building still provides accommodation and the owner has grown some plants on the balcony, adding delight to the ancient building.

图2-1-44 区位图与平面轮廓图
PICTURE 2-1-44 LOCATION AND OUTLINE

图2-1-45 龙聚里5号外观图
PICTURE 2-1-45 APPEARENCE OF N0.5 LONGJU LANE

图2-1-46 龙聚里36号外观图
PICTURE 2-1-46 APPEARENCE OF NO.36 LONGJU LANE

## 2.1.9 龙聚里 35 号和 36 号

龙聚里 35 号和 36 号位于石湾片区的东部，胜利路以西，均为三开间二层砖混结构建筑，建造时间为民国时期，建筑占地面积分别为 163.9 平方米和 179.7 平方米。建筑保存状况良好，建筑外墙为青砖砌筑，立面保留了大量彩画以及灰塑装饰，36 号建筑屋顶山花保留完整，为砖石材质，搭配绿色琉璃宝瓶状栏杆。大多数窗户依旧为木制窗户，有石材为框，窗户上方的雕塑彩画保存完整。一层入口为趟栊门，镶有石米门框，房屋现在依旧作居住用途。

## 2.1.9 No. 35 & NO.36 of Longju Lane

Located in the east of Shiwan District and to the west of Shengli Road, No. 35 and No. 36 of Longju Lane are a double-floored brick-concrete structure with three sections in width, covering 163.9m² and 179.7m² respectively. It was built in the beginning of the Republic of China. In good condition, the external walls were constructed with plain bricks and lots of the color painting decorations and plaster decorations are retained and the brick-stoned pediments of NO.36 are well preserved. The masonry-made handrails are glass-made vase-shaped. Most of the windows are wooden and embedded in stone frames with complete forms of sculptures and color paintings on them. The first floor has a bar sliding door embedded in a chicken girt frame. The building still provides accommodation nowadays.

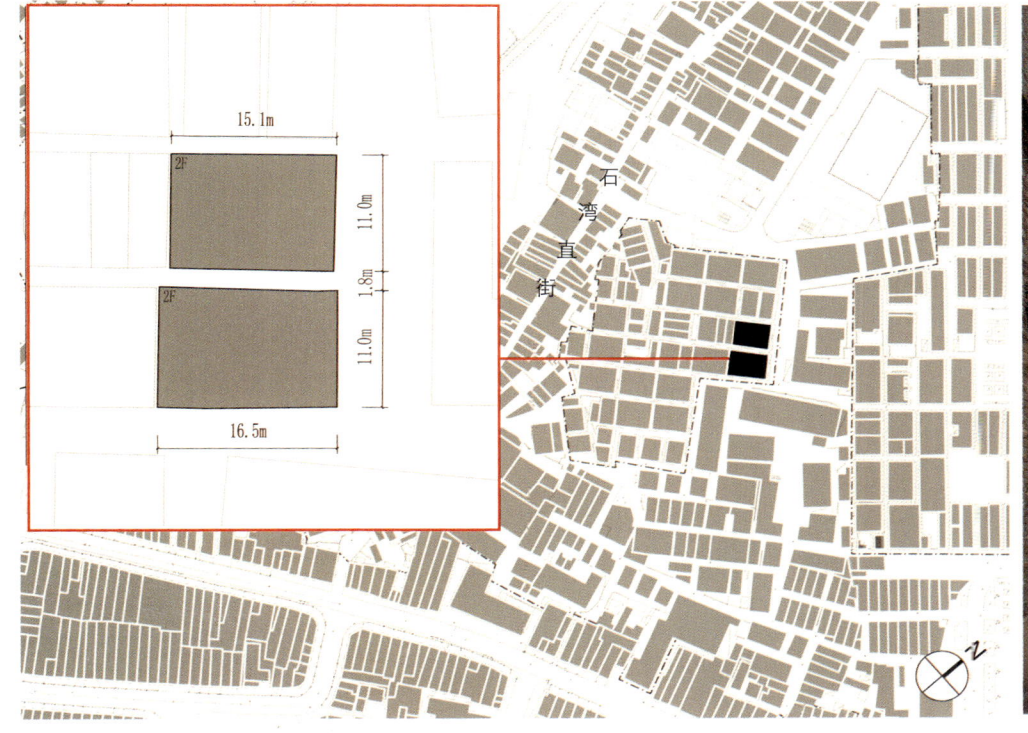

图2-1-47　区位图与平面轮廓图
PICTURE 2-1-47　LOCATION AND OUTLINE

图2-1-48　周围环境
PICTURE 2-1-48　THE SURROUNDINGS

图2-1-49　二楼阳台局部
PICTURE 2-1-49　PORTION OF THE BALCONY OF THE SECOND FLOOR

图2-1-50　一楼入口局部
PICTURE 2-1-50　PORTION OF THE ENTRANCE OF THE FIRST FLOOR

图2-1-51　二楼窗户局部
PICTURE 2-1-51　PORTION OF THE WINDOW OF THE SECOND FLOOR

图2-1-52　建筑西立面
PICTURE 2-1-52　WEST FACADE THE ARCHITECTURE

图2-1-53 启明里39～42号外观图
PICTURE 2-1-53 APPEARENCE OF NO.39～42 QI'MING LANE

## 2.1.10 启明里 39～42 号

启明里39～42号位于石湾片区的东部，跃进路以西，为两组两开间三层砖混结构建筑，建造时间为民国时期，建筑占地面积分别为213平方米和224平方米，两建筑中间有连廊。建筑保存状况良好，建筑外墙为青砖砌筑，立面大面积长满苔藓，屋顶山花为三角形形态。建筑二层阳台有烧瓷栏杆以及石米材质的爱奥尼柱式以及拱券，一层入口依旧保留着木质趟栊门以及石米门框，房屋至今仍作居住用途。

## 2.1.10 No.39-42 of Qiming Lane

Located in the east of Shiwan District and to the west of Yuejin Road, No. 39 to No. 42 of Qiming Lane are two sets of three-floored brick-concrete structures connected by a corridor and each with two sections, covering 213m² and 224m² respectively. They were built in the beginning of the Republic of China. In good condition, the external walls were constructed with plain bricks and the triangle-shaped rooftop pediments are well preserved with moss covering a large part of the facade. The second floor balconies have enamel handrails and chicken girt Ionic order pillars and arches. The first floor has a wooden bar sliding door embedded in a chicken girt frame. The buildings still provides accommodation nowadays.

图2-1-54 区位图与平面轮廓图
PICTURE 2-1-54 LOCATION AND OUTLINE

图2-1-55 启明里39-42号外观图
PICTURE 2-1-55 APPEARENCE OF NO.39-40 QIMING LANE

图2-1-56 启明里60号和61号外观
PICTURE 2-1-56 APPEARENCE OF NO.60 &61 QIMING LANE

## 2.1.11 启明里 60 号和 61 号

启明里 60 号和 61 号位于石湾片区的东部、跃进路以西，分别为一开间二层的砖混结构建筑，占地面积分别为 74.1 平方米和 76.7 平方米，建筑建造时间为民国时期。建筑保存状况良好，建筑外墙为青砖砌筑，并进行过一定的粉刷装修，立面装饰、屋顶山花保存完整。建筑二层阳台有绿色琉璃宝瓶状栏杆，与很多附近的民居一样保留有石米材质的塔司干柱式和拱券，一层入口依旧保留有木质的趟栊门以及石米门框，房屋至今仍作居住用途。

## 2.1.11 No.60 & No.61 of Qiming Lane

Located in the east of Shiwan District and to the west of Yuejin Road, No. 60 and No. 61 of Qiming Lane are double-floored brick-concrete structure with two sections in width, covering 74.1m² and 76.7m² respectively. They were built in the beginning of the Republic of China. In good condition, the external walls were constructed with plain bricks and have undergone some whitewashing and renovation. Decorations on the facade and the rooftop pediments are well preserved. The second floor balcony has green glass-made vase-shaped handrails, and has retained chicken girt Tuscan order pillars and circular arches like nearby buildings. The first floor has a wooden bar sliding door embedded in a chicken girt frame. The buildings still provides accommodation nowadays.

图2-1-57 区位图与平面轮廓图
PICTURE 2-1-57 LOCATION AND OUTLINE

图2-1-58 启明里60号和61号外观
PICTURE 2-1-58 APPEARENCE OF NO.60&61 QIMING LANE

PICTURE 2-1-59　APPEARANCE OF NO.70 QIMING LANE

## 2.1.12 启明里 69 号和 70 号

启明里 69 号和 70 号位于石湾片区的东部、跃进路以西，为二开间二层砖混结构建筑，占地面积均为 73.2 平方米，建造时间为民国时期。建筑保存状况中等，建筑外墙为青砖砌筑，山花保存完整。建筑一层墙面粉刷为白色，二层阳台有绿色琉璃宝瓶状栏杆，爱奥尼柱式，拱券保存完整，一层入口保留具有岭南特色的木质趟栊门，虽然年久失修，但是不减岭南侨乡民居的风貌。房屋至今仍在使用当中。

## 2.1.12 No.69 & No.70 of Qiming Lane

Located in the east of Shiwan District and to the west of Yuejin Road, No. 69 and No. 70 of Qiming Lane both are double-floored brick-concrete structure with two sections, each covering 73.2m² respectively. They were built in the beginning of the Republic of China. In moderate condition, the external walls were constructed with plain bricks and the pediments are well preserved. The walls on the first floor were painted white and the second floor balcony has green glass-made vase-shaped handrails and Ionic order pillars and the arch is well retained. The first floor has a wooden bar sliding door with Lingnan characteristics. Although the building looks a little dilapidated, it still has the features as a typical residential building for overseas Chinese in south China. The buildings are still in use.

图2-1-60 区位图与平面轮廓图
PICTURE 2-1-60 LOCATION AND OUTLINE

图2-1-61 启明里69号和70号外观图
PICTURE 2-1-61 APPEARENCE OF NO.69&70 QIMING LANE

图2-1-62 长庆里25号外观图
PICTURE 2-1-62 APPEARENCE OF NO.25 CHANGQING LANE

## 2.1.13 长庆里 25 号

长庆里 25 号位于石湾片区的东部，跃进路以西，是一座二层砖混结构建筑，建筑占地面积为 96.8 平方米，建造时间为民国时期。建筑保存状况良好，建筑为中西结合式样。建筑外墙为青砖砌筑，屋顶山墙保存完整，但山花上的字迹已无法辨别，侧立面部分墙面发黑受潮情况严重。建筑二层阳台有石米材质的栏杆，一层入口朝东北方向，有木制趟栊门。房屋现在仍有人居住。

## 2.1.13 No.25 of Changqing Lane

Located in the east of Shiwan district and to the west of Yuejin Road, No. 25 of Changqing Lane is a double-floored brick concrete structure, covering 96.8m². It was built in the beginning of the Republic of China. In good condition, the building has moderate appearance by combining Chinese and western styles. The external walls are constructed with plain bricks and the rooftop pediment is well preserved, yet the characters written on it can hardly be recognized. The walls on the side facade have turned dark because of heavy dampness. The second floor balcony has chicken girt handrails and the first floor has a wooden bar sliding door facing the northeast direction. The building still provides accommodation nowadays.

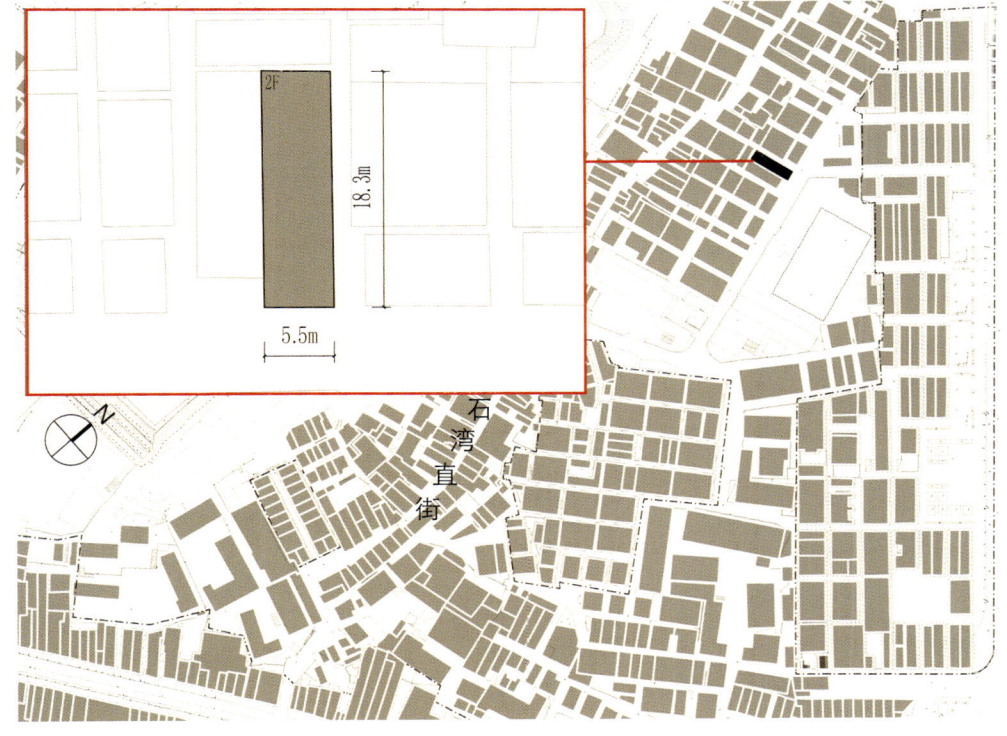

图2-1-63 区位图与平面轮廓图
PICTURE 2-1-63 LOCATION AND OUTLINE

图2-1-64 长庆里25号外观图
PICTURE 2-1-64 APPEARENCE OF NO.25 CHANGQING LANE

图2-1-65　明德坊鸟瞰图
PICTURE 2-1-65　BIRD-VIEW OF MINGDE LANE

## 2.1.14 明德坊

明德坊位于近代华侨建筑风貌区的西南部，石湾直街以西，由18栋建筑分列两排组成，建造时间为民国初期。整个建筑组群长39.63米，宽18.97米，建筑占地面积为751.78平方米，大部分为砖木结构。建筑群体风貌保存良好，大部分房屋已经没有人居住。巷道用花岗岩条石铺设，两旁的建筑依旧保留趟栊门和木质窗、铁制栏杆、山墙壁画。

## 2.1.14 Mingde Lane

Located in the Modern Overseas Chinese Buildings District and to the west of Shiwanzhi Street, Mingde Lane consists of 18 buildings in two rows. Built in the beginning of the Republic of China, the building complex is 39.63 meters long and 18.97 meters wide and covers a total area of 751.78m². Most of the buildings are of brick, timber and concrete structure and has double-floors. The complex is in good shape while the buildings are moderately preserved. The buildings are of traditional folk houses styles. The lane paths are paved by granite stone strips. The bar sliding doors, wooden windows, iron handrails and gable fresco have been retained in the buildings on both sides of the lanes.

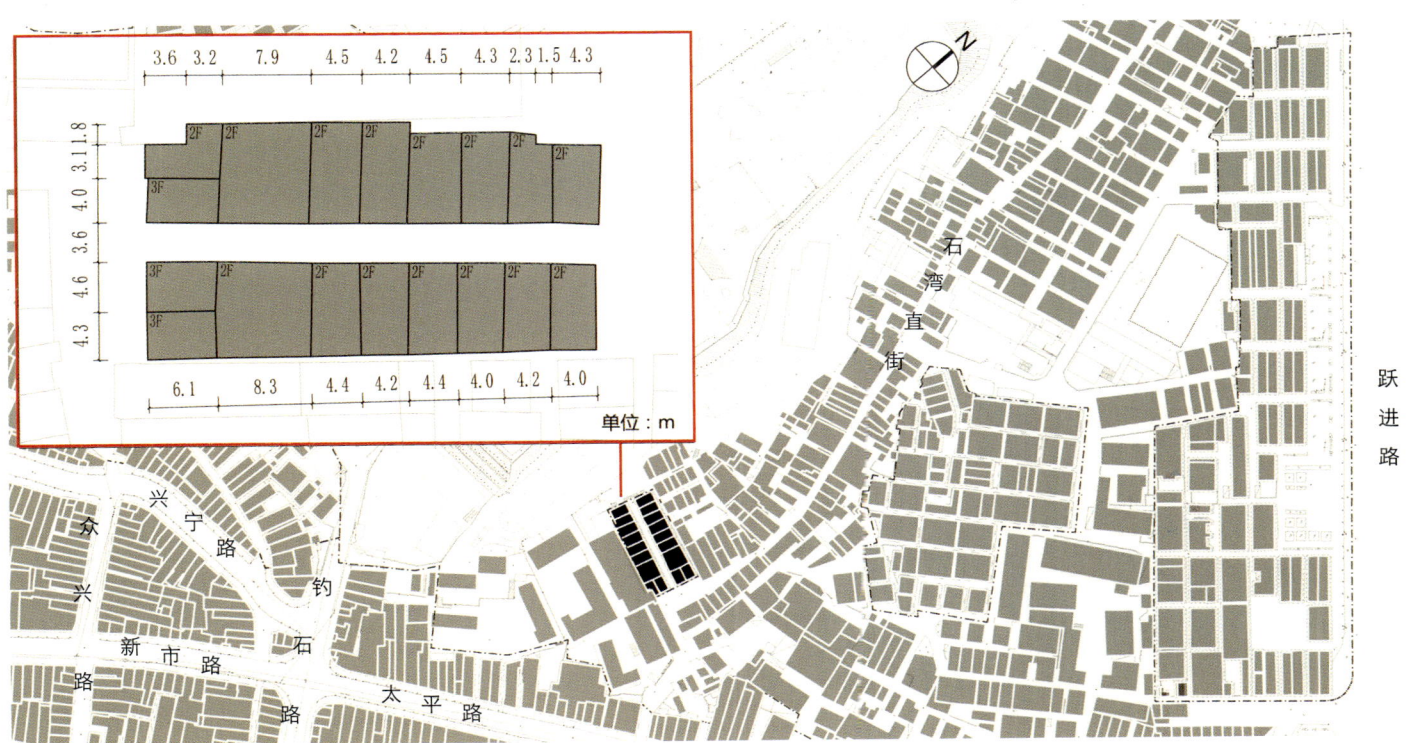

图2-1-66 区位图与平面轮廓图
PICTURE 2-1-66 LOCATION AND OUTLINE

图2-1-67 明德坊街道内景
PICTURE 2-1-67 INSIDE MINGDE LANE

图2-1-68　明德坊入口处
PICTURE 2-1-68　THE ENTRANCE OF MINGDE LANE

图2-1-69　从入口看街道内
PICTURE 2-1-69　THE VIEW FROM OUTSIDE THE ENTRANCE

图2-1-70　明德坊街道内景
PICTURE 2-1-70　INSIDE MINGDE LANE

## 2.1.15 余庆里

余庆里位于近代华侨住宅风貌区的西片区，建于民国初期，为清代江门县衙门遗址，由24栋两层建筑组成。整个建筑组群长63.25米，宽38.78米，建筑占地面积为2452.8平方米。大部分建筑为混合结构。建筑群风貌保存良好。建筑屋顶为中国传统坡屋顶。部分建筑保存情况良好，并仍保留有铁栏杆、木质趟栊门和墙面彩画。2013年时仍有28户人家居住于此。

## 2.1.15 Yuqing Lane

Located in the western area of the Modern Overseas Chinese Buildings District, Yuqing Lane was built during the Republic of China. Composed of 24 double-floored buildings, it is the former site of Jiangmen county government. The building complex is 63.25 meters long and 38.78 meters wide, covering a total area of 2452.8m². Most of the buildings have mixed structures. The building complex is in good condition with its features and structures well preserved. The roofs are traditional sloped roofs. Part of the buildings in good shape have maintained the iron handrails, wooden bar sliding doors and colored paintings. There are 28 households living here nowadays.

图2-1-71 余庆里街道内景
PICTURE 2-1-71 YUQING LANE

图2-1-72 余庆里街道内景
PICTURE 2-1-72 YUQING LANE

图2-1-73 区位图与平面轮廓图
PICTURE 2-1-73 LOCATION AND OUTLINE

图2-1-74 余庆里
PICTURE 2-1-74 YUQING LANE

图2-1-75 余庆里街道
PICTURE 2-1-75 ALLEY OF YUQING LANE

图2-1-76 区位图与平面轮廓图
PICTURE 2-1-76 LOCATION AND OUTLINE

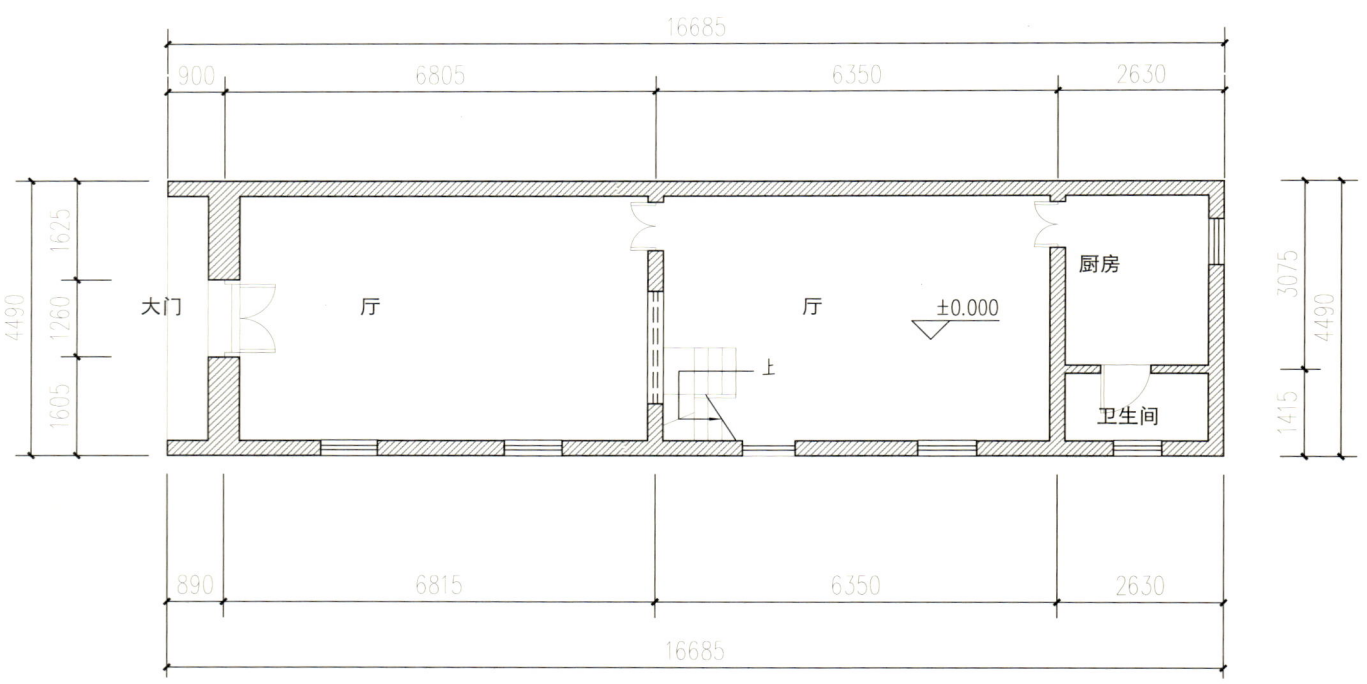

图2-1-77 余庆里17号首层平面图
PICTURE 2-1-77 FIRST PLAN

图2-1-78 余庆里鸟瞰
PICTURE 2-1-78　BIRD-VIEW OF YUQING LANE

图2-1-79 余庆里街道内景
PICTURE 2-1-79 YUQING LANE

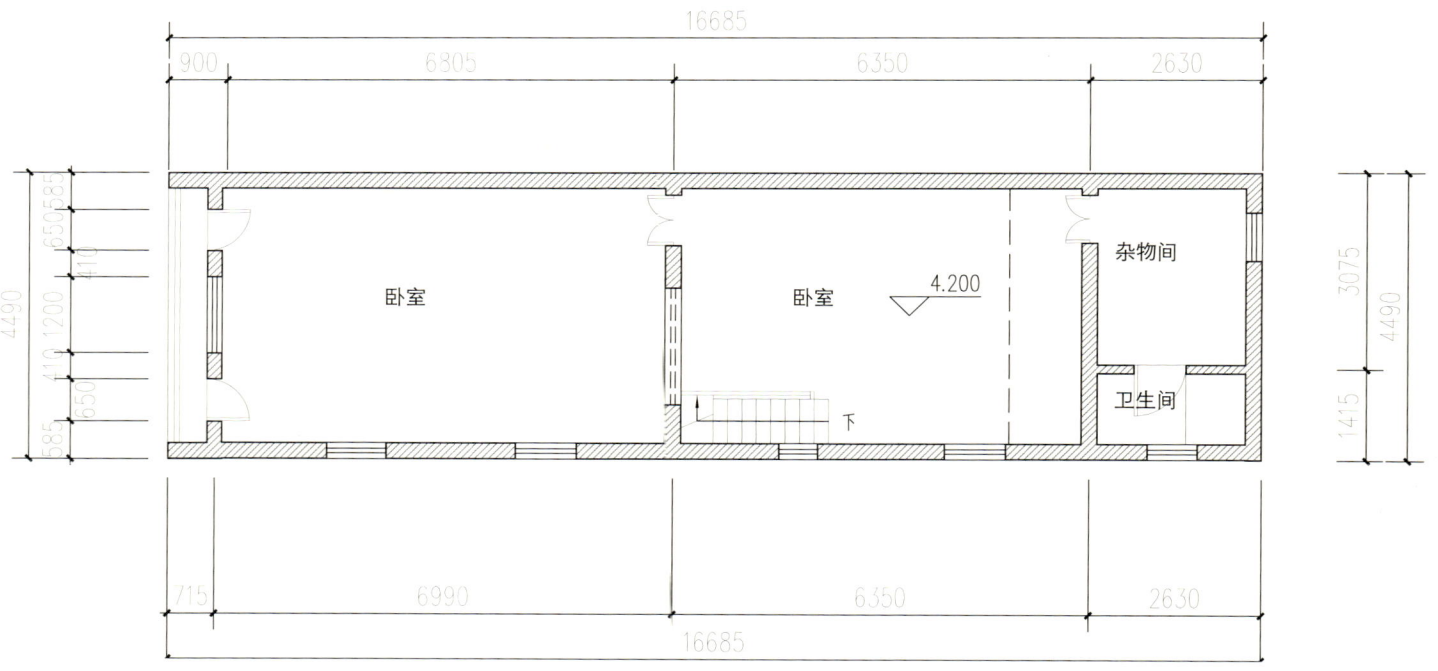

图2-1-80 余庆里17号二层平面图
PICTURE 2-1-80 SECOND FLOOR

图2-1-81 余庆里鸟瞰
PICTURE 2-1-81　BIRD-VIEW YUQING LANE

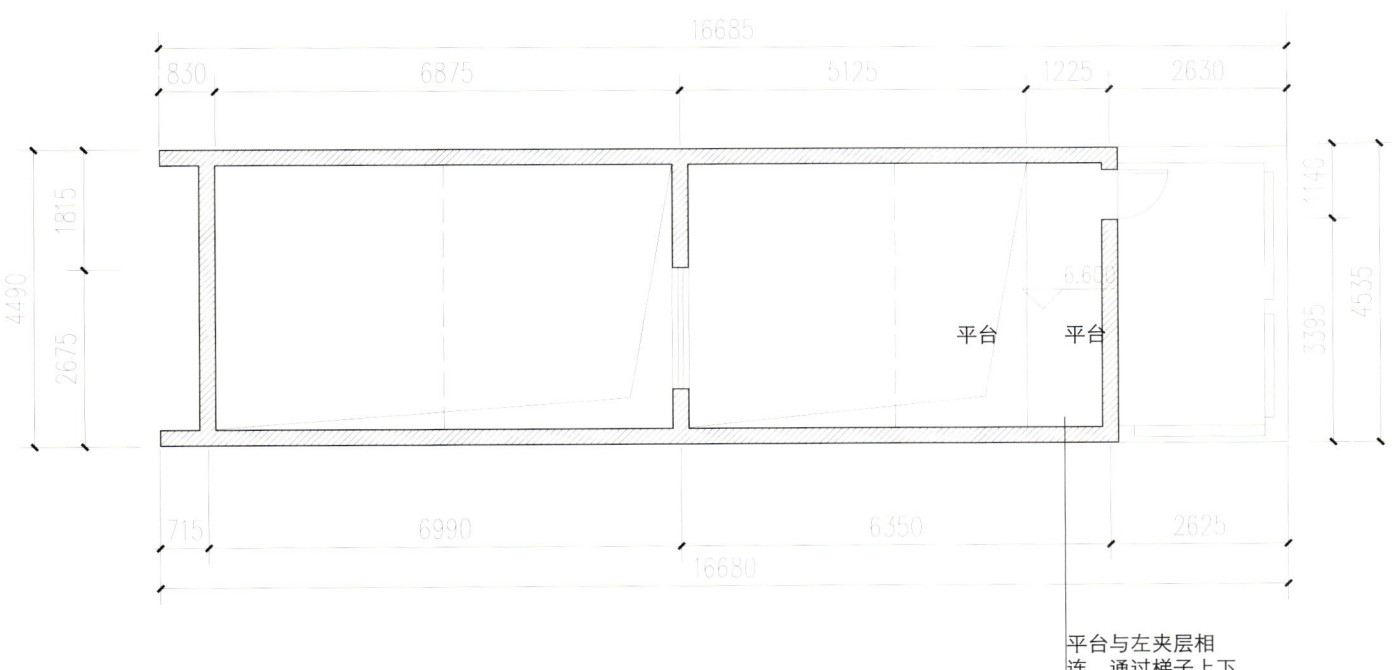

图2-1-82 余庆里17号屋顶层平面图
PICTURE 2-1-82　ROOF FLOOR

图2-1-83 宝和按当铺正立面
PICTURE 2-1-83 FACADE

## 2.1.16 宝和按当铺

宝和按当铺位于跃进路堤中路路口，建于民国时期，为江门市级文物保护单位。建筑坐西北向东南，东西长12.5米，南北宽10.4米，建筑占地面积为130平方米。建筑分为四层，高约14.5米，下面三层为花岗岩砌筑，上面一层为青砖砌筑，屋顶为单檐布瓦顶，东西两侧为锅耳山墙，上下四层均有防御性射击孔洞，与位于墟顶的永安按当铺旧址极为相似，均是民国期间江门十二家当铺之一。

## 2.1.16 Baohe Pawnshop

Located at the intersection of Yuejin Road and Dizhong Road, Baohe Pawnshop was built during the Republic of China and is now a Municipal Cultural Preservation Site. It sits against the northwest and faces the southeast with a length of 12.5 meters and a width of 10.4 meters, covering a total area of 130m². The building has four floors with a height of 14.5 meters. The three floors down were constructed with granite stones and the top floor with plain bricks. The roof top is of single eave and grey tiles with panhandle-shaped gables on the east and west sides. All floors have defensive shooting holes, very similar to the Yong'an Pawnshop in Xuding District. Both of them are among the 12 pawnshops in the Republic of China.

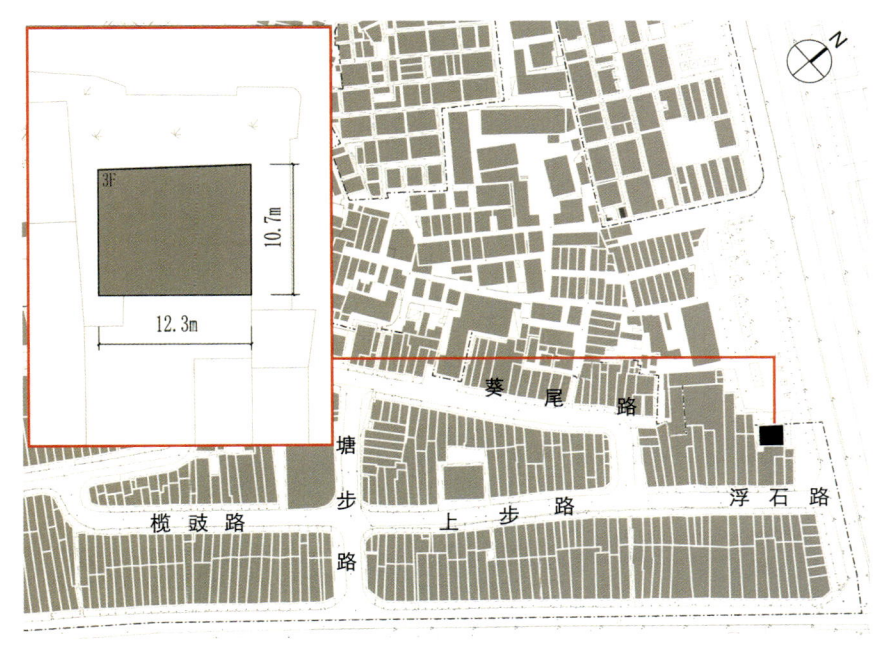

图2-1-84 区位图与平面轮廓图
PICTURE 2-1-84 LOCATION AND OUTLINE

图2-1-85 宝和当铺外观图
PICTURE 2-1-85 APPEARENCE OF BAOHE PAWNSHOP

## 2.2　骑楼风貌区
## 2.2　QILOU (ARCADE BUILDING) DISTRICT

骑楼风貌区位于江门历史街区的南部，南接堤中路、堤东路和蓬江，西邻胜利路，东至跃进路，包括常安路、莲平路、兴宁路、仓后路、新市路、太平路、书院路、堤中路、堤东路等 19 条骑楼街，总长度超过 5 公里，总面积约 22 公顷。

骑楼风貌区的历史最早可追溯至清末，清光绪二十八年（1902 年），江门被辟为通商口岸，吸引了许多海外华侨和各地商贾前来投资经商，长堤一带"华洋杂处，商旅辐辏"，更是一派繁荣兴旺；民国十四年（1925 年），广东省国民政府批准江门为省辖市，在民国十八年（1929 年）至民国二十年（1931 年）间，江门进行了大规模的市政建设和房屋建设。其中很大部分建筑是按照海外华侨带回来的各国建筑图样结合当地特色设计兴建的，这些楼房建筑样式相仿，形成连续的建筑架空层步行空间和沿街铺面，统称做"骑楼"。自此，一批中西结合的建筑物陆续在长堤滨江地区建成，经过半个多世纪的文化融合，最终形成了今天的骑楼风貌区。

骑楼风貌区保留了 1000 余栋骑楼建筑，多为民国时期所建，式样丰富，外观精美，其中在各个街角路口的骑楼形式处理独具匠心，充分体现了江门人民的建设才智。骑楼风貌区内现状仍有大量商户，业态丰富，极具活力。

Located in the south of the Changdi Historical Neighborhood, Qilou (Arcade Building) district is to the north of Dizhong Road, Didong Road and Pengjiang River, to the east of Shengli Road, to the west of Yuejin Road. Composed of 19 arcade building streets including Chang'an Road, Lianping Road, Xingning Road, Canghou Road, Xinshi Road, Taiping Road, Shuyuan Road, Dizhong Road, Didong Road, etc, the District covers a total area of 22 hectares with a total street length of 5 kilometers.

Qilou (Arcade Building) District can be dated back to the end of Qing Dynasty. In 1902 (the 28th year of Emperor Guangxu of Qing Dynasty), Jiangmen was designated as a trading port, attracting overseas Chinese and businessmen from all over the country to invest and do business here. Changdi was booming and prosperous with Chinese and foreign businessmen gathering and trading here. In 1925 (the 14th year of the Republic of China), the then Guangdong Provincial Government approved Jiangmen to be a city directly under the administration of the province Between 1929 and 1931, Jiangmen had undergone a large scale of public facilities and house construction. Most of the buildings were constructed based on foreign architecture patterns brought back by overseas Chinese in combination with local features. These buildings look similar and form a continuous walking space and provide roadside shops along the street. They are called the arcade buildings. Since then, buildings of both Chinese and western styles have been constructed along the riverbanks of Changdi, and has formed today's Qilou (Arcade Building) District after more than 50 years of cultural fusion.

Over 1000 arcade buildings still remain in the District. Most of them were built in the Republic of China with diversified forms and exquisite appearances. Those on the intersections of roads are carefully designed, showcasing the construction wisdom of Jiangmen locals. There are still a large number of businessmen engaging in diversified forms of trades, bringing vitality to the District.

图2-2-1 区位图
PICTURE 2-2-1  LOCATION

图2-2-2 常安街景
PICTURE 2-2-2  CHANG`AN ROAD

图2-2-3 常安街景
PICTURE 2-2-3  CHANG`AN ROAD

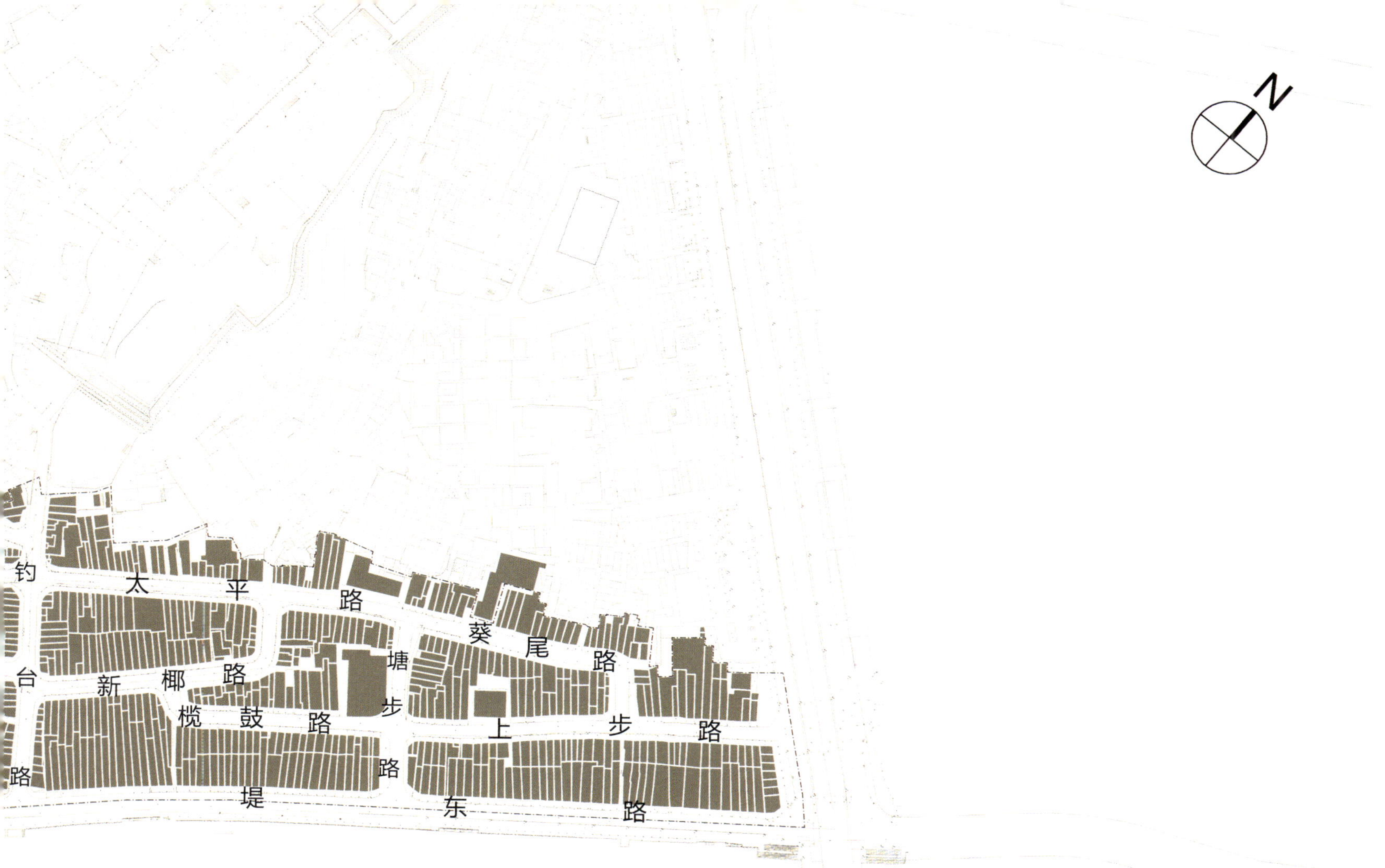

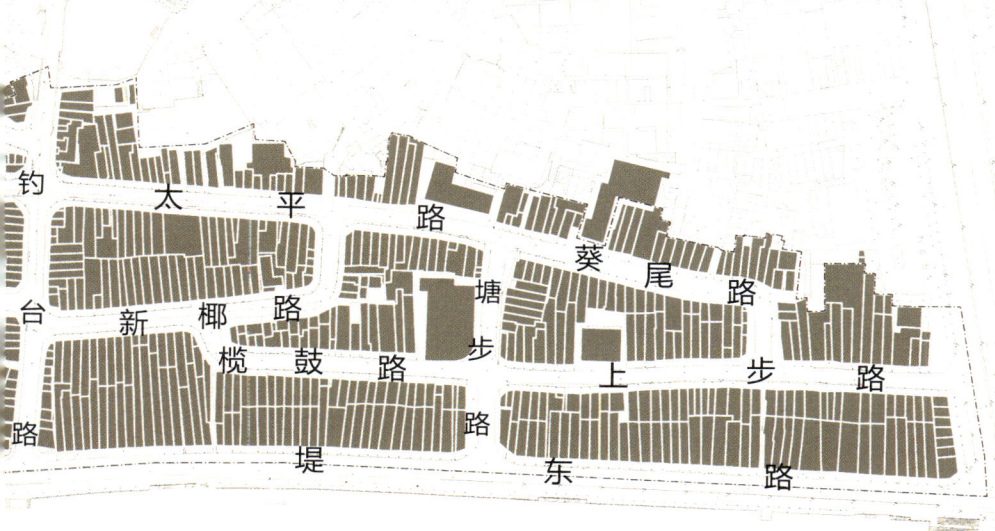

图2-2-4 太平路街景
PICTURE 2-2-4　TAIPING ROAD

图2-2-5 莲平路街景
PICTURE 2-2-5　LIANPING ROAD

图2-2-6 莲平路街景
PICTURE 2-2-6　LIANPING ROAD

## 2.2.1 中华酒店

中华酒店位于骑楼风貌区的西边，堤中路西北侧，为三开间三层砖混结构建筑，建筑占地面积为803.47平方米。建筑始建于1929年，保存状况良好，立面经过一定的改造，"中华酒店"四个字保存完好，现内部为"COCO连锁酒店"。中华酒店高三层，三开间，首层退入，形成中部开间两层通高的高拱券设计，二、三层窗户为拱形券柱式，窗户为满洲窗，三层挑出一米阳台，阳台外立面上分三部分，使用行、楷书分别书写酒店名称和广告语。

在中华酒店整体外部设计中，柱式的设计借鉴罗马叠柱式。一楼屋顶下左右梁上各刻有"民国十八年"和"潘秀记建筑"的字样。

## 2.2.1 Zhonghua (China) Hotel

Located in the west of the Arcade Building District and to the northeast of Dizhong Road, China Hotel is a three-floored brick-concrete structure with three sections in width, covering a total area of 803.47m². It was built in 1929. In moderate condition, the facade of the building has undergone some renovations and the four characters Zhong Hua Jiu Dian (China Hotel) are well preserved. Now the building is for the use of COCO Hotel. China Hotel is a typical arcade building with the first floor retreating. The middle section adopt high arch design and the windows in the second and third floors are arches with pillars. The windows are of Manchuria style. The balcony on the third floor is one meter in width and the facade outside of the balcony is divided into three sections with the hotel name and other advertisements written on them in standard or running scripts.

In its external designs, China Hotel adopts the Roman style piling pillars. On the one side of the pillar is carved "the 18th year of the Republic of China", and the other side " Pan Xiuji Architecture".

图2-2-7　中华酒店外观图
PICTURE 2-2-7　APPEARENCE OF ZHONGHUA HOTEL

图2-2-8 酒店楼梯
PICTURE 2-2-8 THE STAIRS

图2-2-9 区位图与平面轮廓图
PICTURE 2-2-9 LOCATION AND OUTLINE

图2-2-10 酒店入口
PICTURE 2-2-10 THE ENTRANCE

图2-2-11 中华酒店外观图
PICTURE 2-2-11 APPEARENCE

图2-2-12 仓后路44号外观图
PICTURE 2-2-12 APPEARENCE

## 2.2.2 仓后路 44 号

仓后路 44 号位于骑楼风貌区中部，仓后路与新华路路口北侧，是一座三层高的骑楼建筑，建筑占地面积 65.9 平方米。建筑保存状况良好，首层为商铺，有科林斯柱式做支撑，二楼和三楼的石米制阳台、石膏雕花保存完整，部分粉刷，建筑立面主要由红砖和米黄色粉刷墙面组成。建筑造型颇具特色。

## 2.2.2 No.44 of Canghou Road

Located in the middle of Arcade Building District and to the north of the intersections of Cangho Road and Xinhua Road, No. 44 of Canghou Road is a three-floored arcade building, covering a total area of 65.9m². In good condition, the first floor adopts Corinthian Order pillars and is used for commercial purpose. The second and third floor chicken girt balconies and plaster carvings are well preserved and partly painted. The facade of the building are mostly made of red bricks and painted beige. The building is very unique in its modeling.

图2-2-13 区位图与平面轮廓图
PICTURE 2-2-13 LOCATION AND OUTLINE

图2-2-14 仓后路44号外观图
PICTURE 2-2-14 APPEARENCE OF NO.44 CANGHOU ROAD

图2-2-15 外观图
PICTURE 2-2-15 APPEARENCE

### 2.2.3 书院路 2 号

书院路 2 号位于骑楼风貌街中部，书院路东侧路口与更兴路相交处，是一座三层高的骑楼建筑，建筑面积为 560 平方米。建筑保存状况良好，首层为商铺，有西洋柱式做支撑，二楼阳台有爱奥尼柱式，三楼的混凝土制阳台、栏杆和屋顶的石膏雕花保存完整。建筑立面主要由红色和米黄色粉刷墙面组成。建筑曾经作为远东大旅馆。目前为历史街区保护研究工作坊。

### 2.2.3 No. 2 of Shuyuan Road

Located in the middle of the Arcade Building District and at the east of the intersection of Shuyuan Road and Gengxing Road, No. 2 of Shuyuan Road is a three-floored arcade building, covering a total area of 560m². In good condition, the first floor adopts western style pillars and is used for commercial purposes. The second floor balcony has Ionic Order pillars. The third floor concrete balcony, handrails and the rooftop plaster carvings are well preserved. The facade of the building is mostly painted red and beige. The building was the Far East Hotel and is using for a workshop on protection of historical neighborhoods.

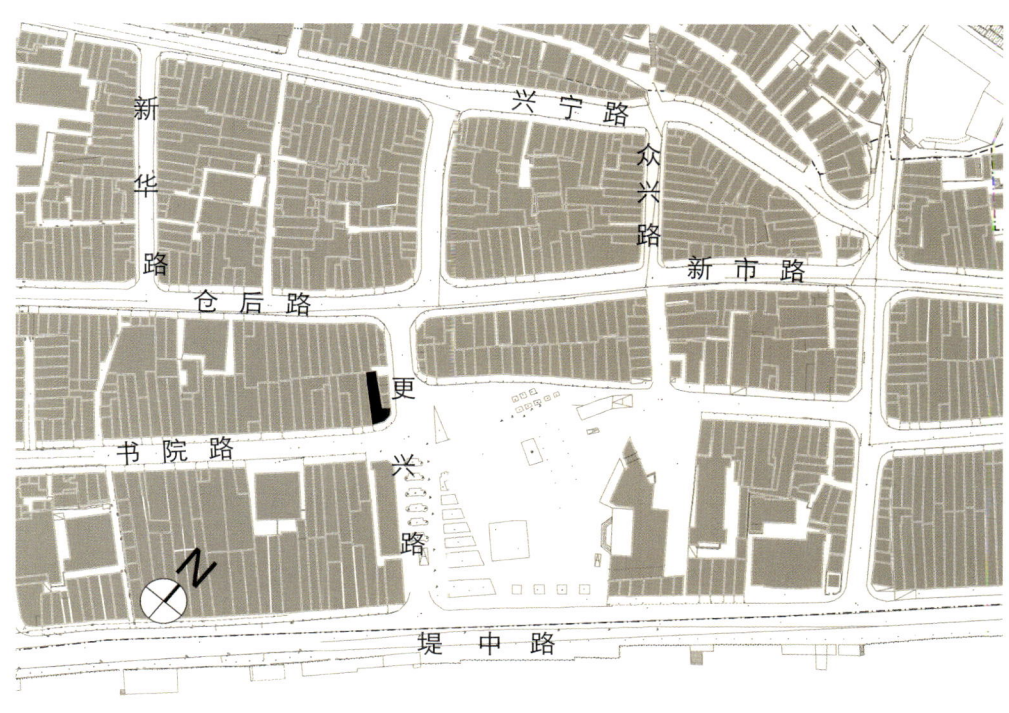

图2-2-16　区位图
PICTURE 2-2-16　LOCATION

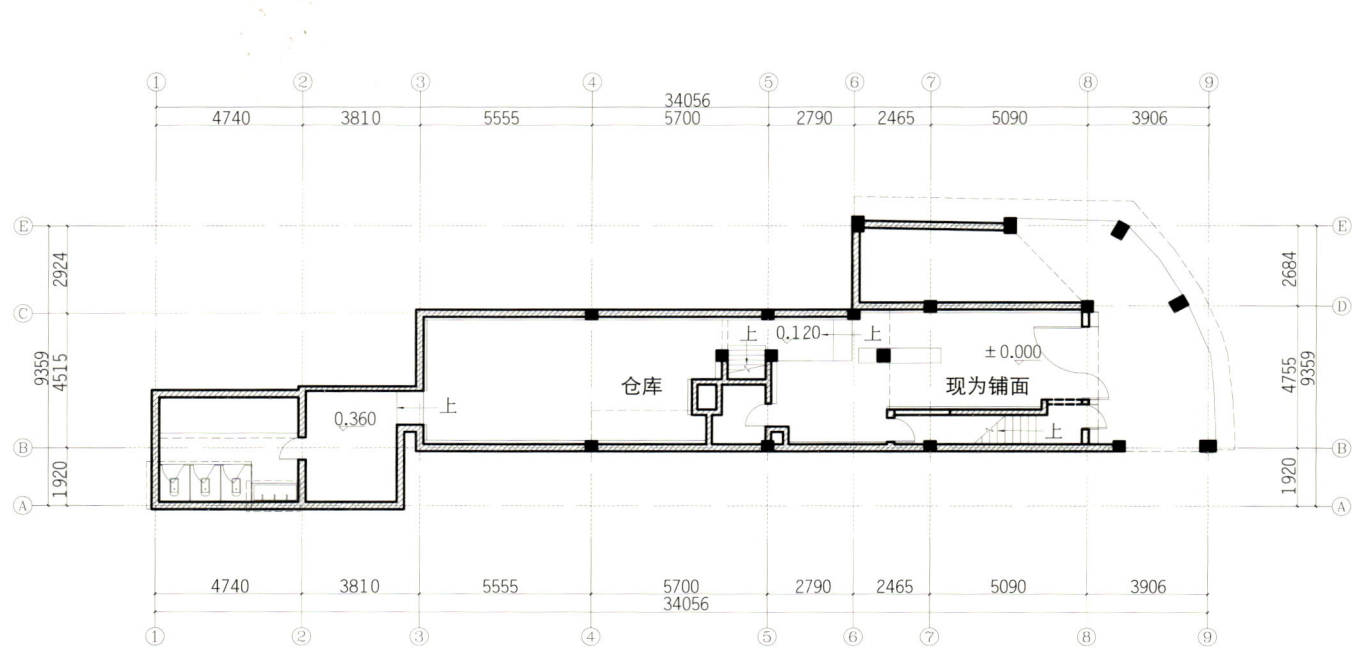

图2-2-17 首层平面图
PICTURE 2-2-17   FIRST FLOOR

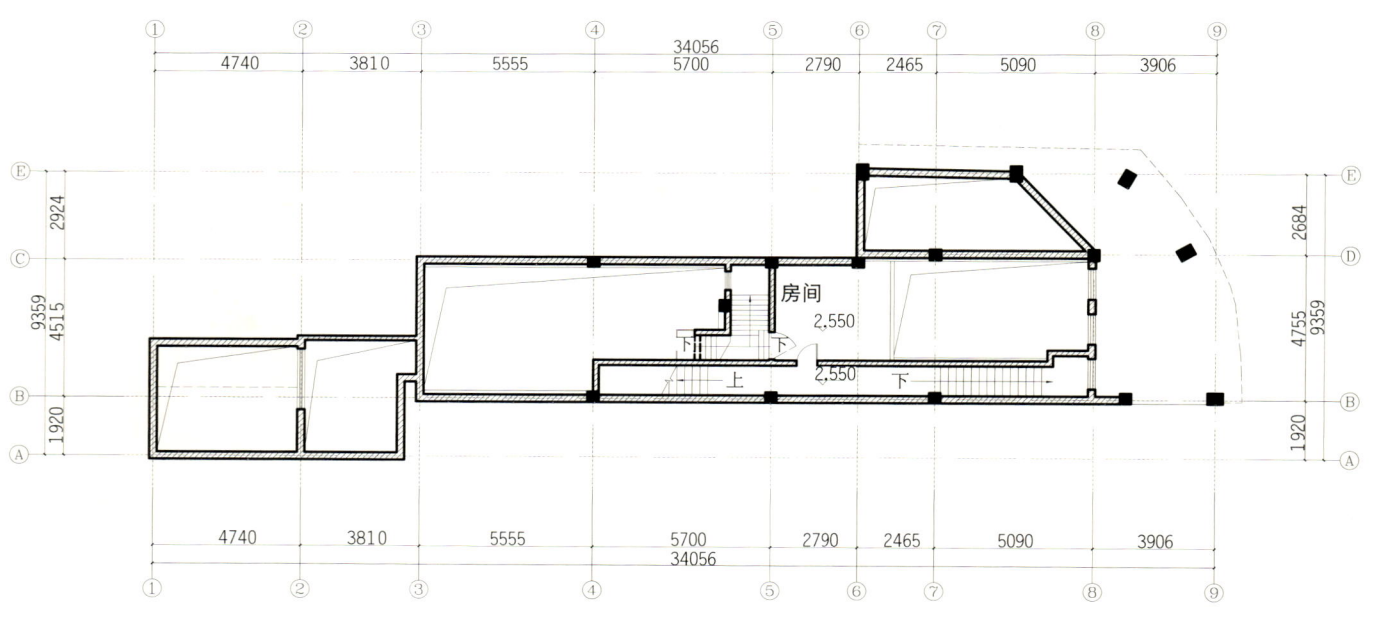

图2-2-18 夹层平面图
PICTURE 2-2-18   MEZZANINE

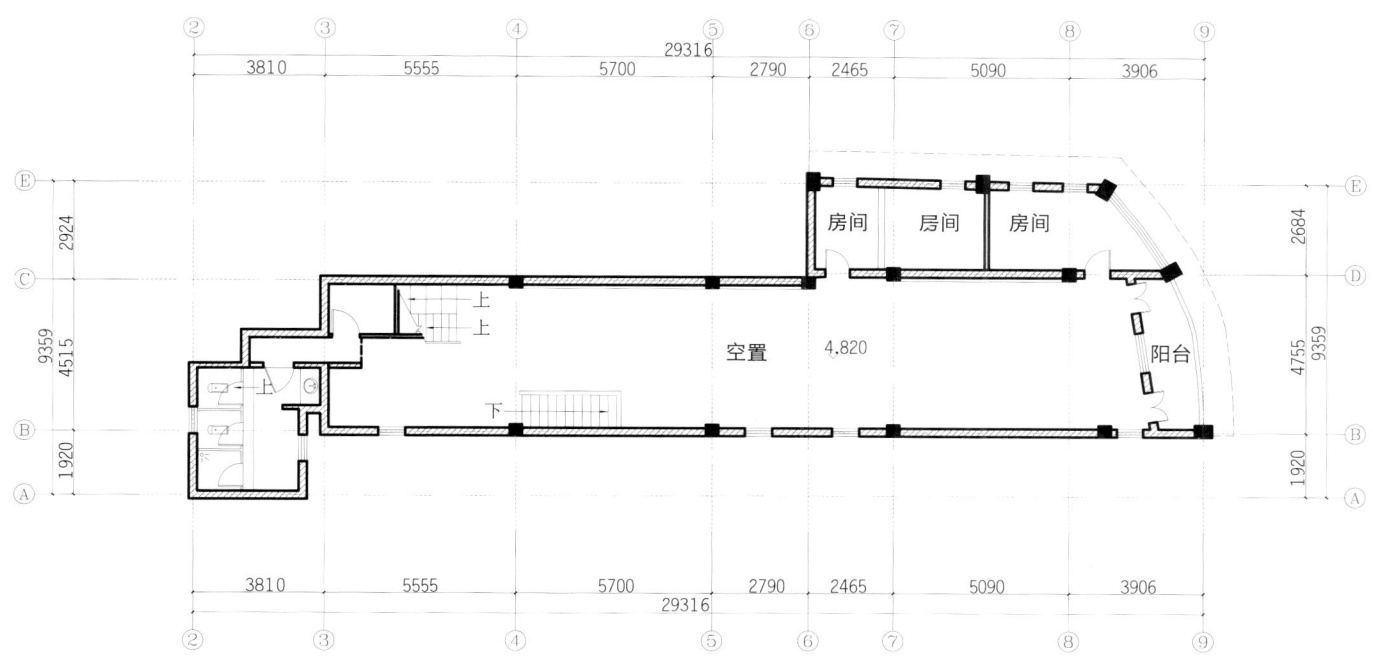

图2-2-19　二层平面图
PICTURE 2-2-19　SECOND FLOOR

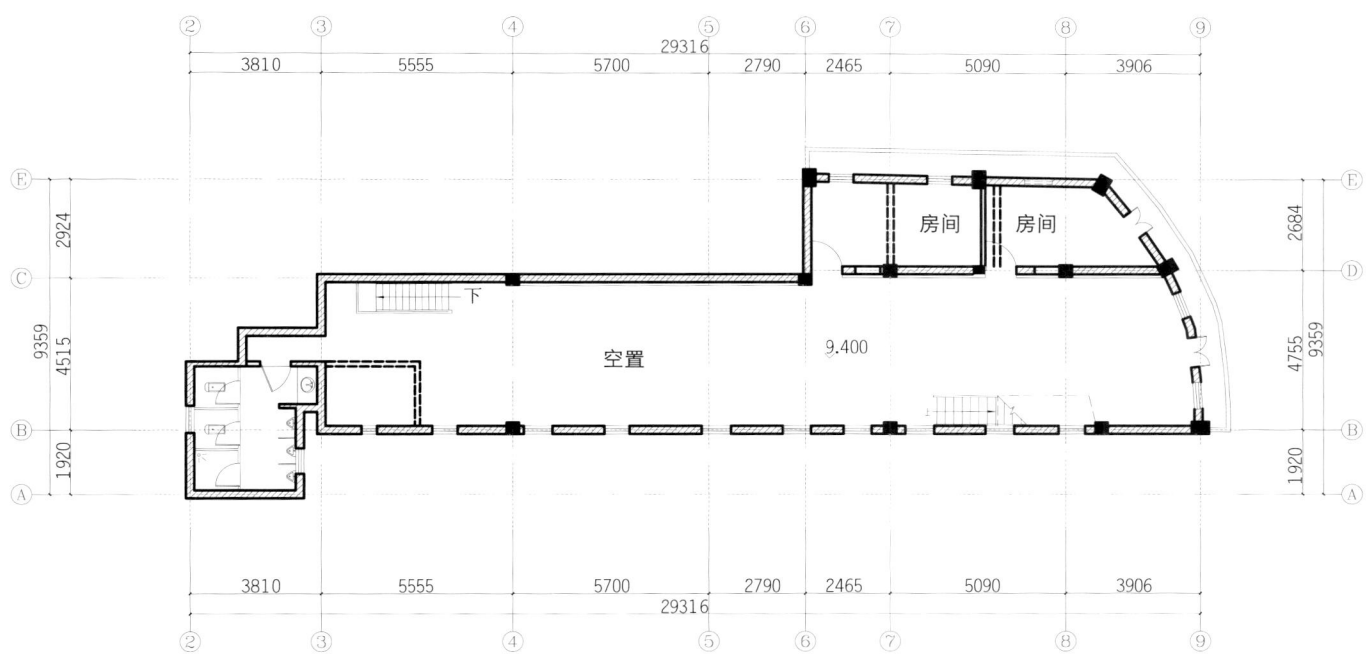

图2-2-20　三层平面图
PICTURE 2-2-20　THIRD FLOOR

图 2-2-21 钓台故址内部
PICTURE 2-2-21 MAIN ROOM OF THE ARCHITECTURE

## 2.2.4 钓台故址

钓台故址位于骑楼保护区的南面，堤中路以北，建于光绪十二年（1886年），为一座三进深院落，面宽6.56米，进深7.14米，占地面积为48平方米。建筑保存状况一般，故居原为一座三进深院落，现存第三进建筑为面宽进深各三开间、四柱穿斗式梁架结构，青砖砌墙，单檐布瓦硬山顶建筑。钓台为陈白沙所建，用作讲学及垂钓，故又名钓鱼台，是研究陈白沙与江门历史的重要史迹。

## 2.2.4 Former Site of Fishing Terrace

Located in the south of the Arcade Building District and to the north of Dizhong Road, the Fishing Terrace was built in 1886 and has three sections in length, covering 48m², with a width of 6.56 meters and a length of 7.14 meters. In moderate shape, the existing third section of the building is three bay in width and three halls in depth supported by four pillars. The external walls were built with plain bricks and the building has single-eave roofs with concealed-eave gables and grey tiles. The Fishing Terrace was named so because it was built by Chen Baisha for teaching how to fish. It is an important historical site to study Chen Baisha and the history of Jiangmen.

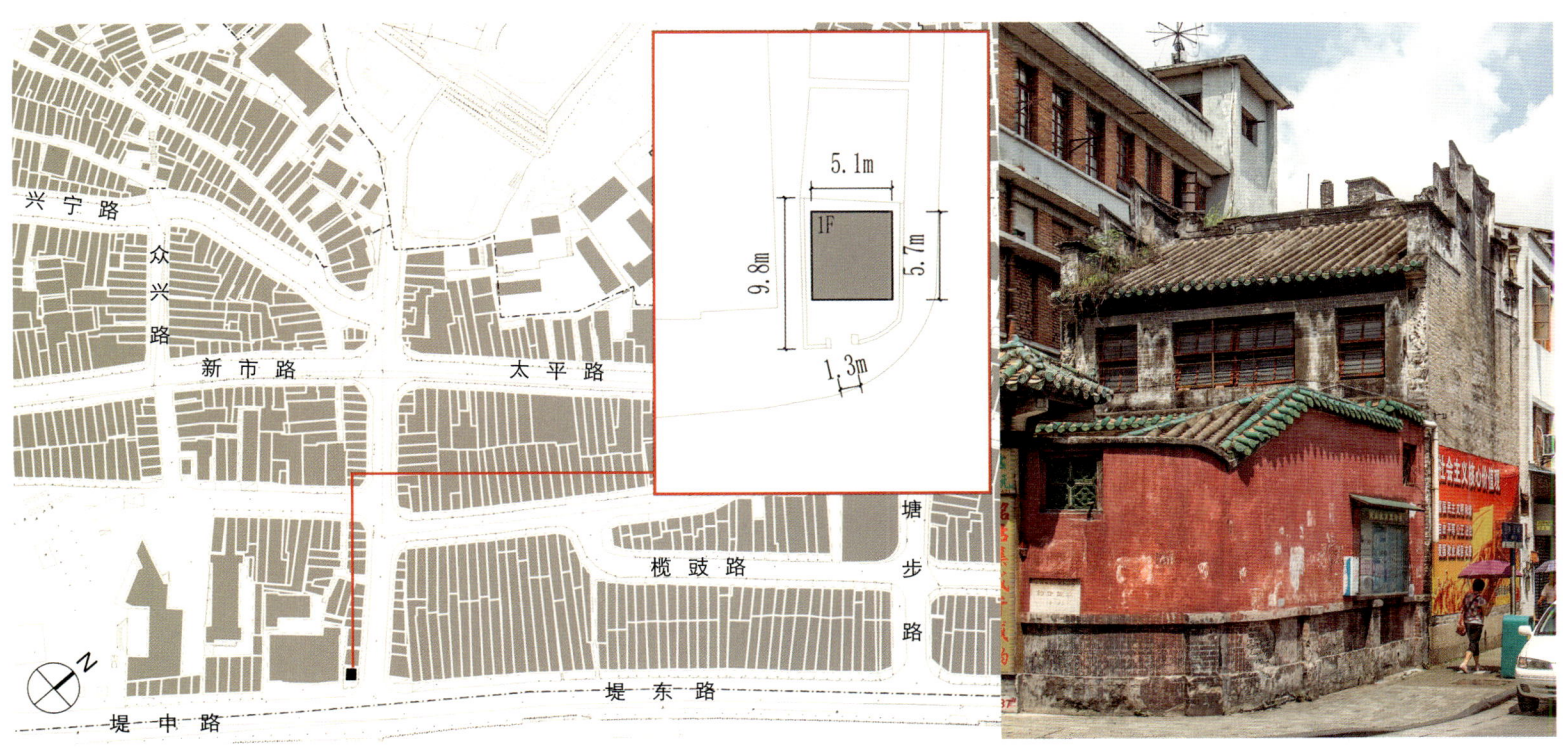

图2-2-22 区位图与平面轮廓图
PICTURE 2-2-22 LOCATION AND OUTLINE

图2-2-23 外观图
PICTURE 2-2-23 APPEARANCE

图2-2-24 正厅神龛细部
PICTURE 2-2-24 SHRINE

图2-2-25　正面放大局部
PICTURE 2-2-25　PORTION OF THE FACADE

图2-2-26　正厅梁架细部
PICTURE 2-2-26　STRUCTURE

图2-2-27 中山纪念堂正面
PICTURE 2-2-27 FACADE

### 2.2.5 中山纪念堂

中山纪念堂位于墟顶风貌区中部的中山公园内，是江门市为纪念辛亥革命和孙中山先生于1927年兴建的，1930年元旦落成，随后经过1950年、1965年、1980年三次修葺，现为江门市、县级文物保护单位。现建筑长40米，宽31.97米，占地面积950平方米，由放映室、戏台、化妆间及观众坐席等组成，顶部原为工字钢梁结构，1950年重修后改为钢筋水泥结构。

### 2.2.5 Sun Yat-sen Memorial Hall

Located in the Sun Yat-sen Park in the middle of the Xuding District, the Sun Yat-sen Memorial Hall was built in 1927 by Jiangmen City to commemorate Xinhai Revolution and Dr. Sun Yat-sen. It was completed in 1930 and went through three renovations in 1950, 1965 and 1980. It is now designated as a Cultural Preservation Site both at municipal and county levels. It covers a total area of 950m² with 40 meters in length and 31.97 meters in width. Composed of projection room, stage, dressing room and audience seats, the building adopted I-shaped steel girder, which was replaced by steel-cement structure in the renovation in 1950.

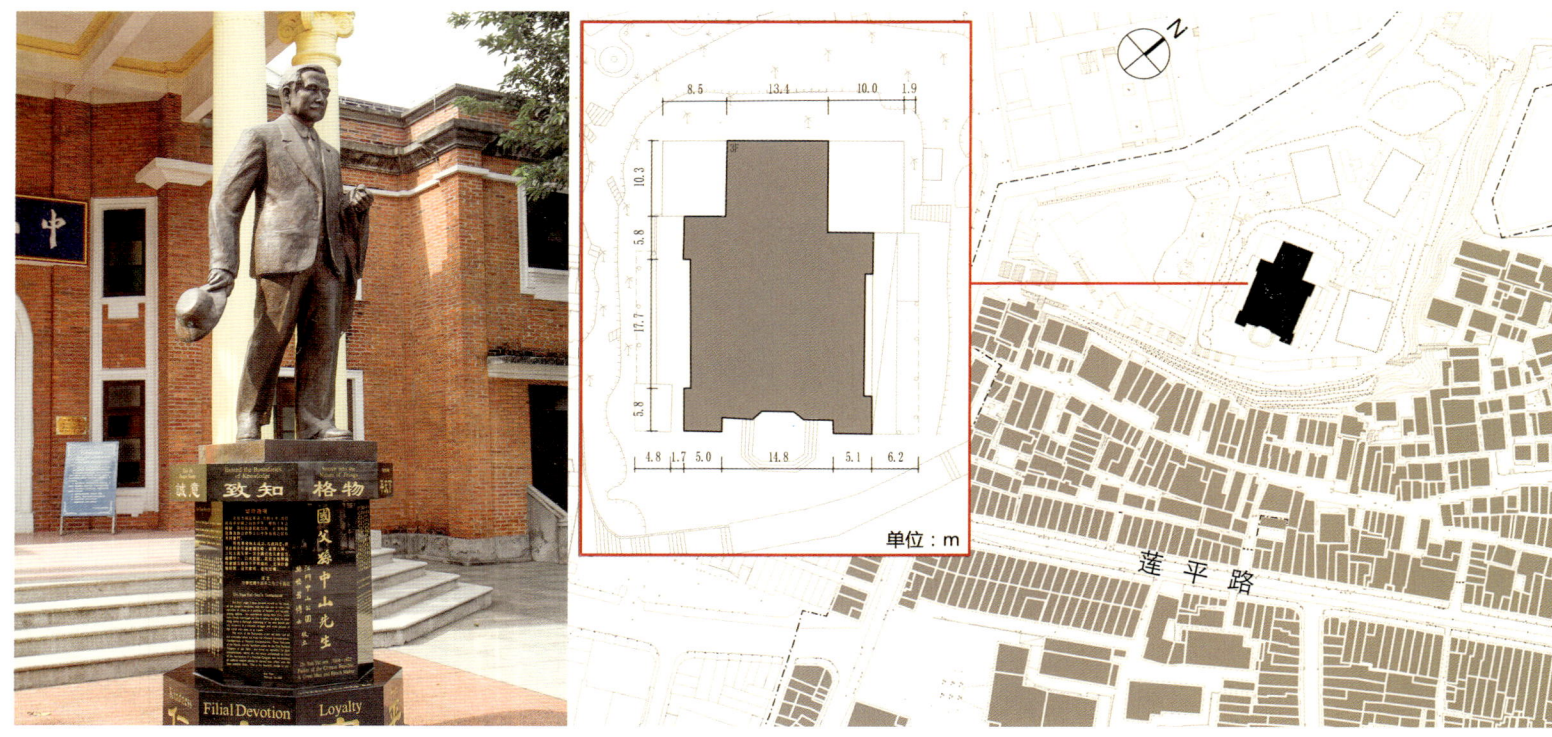

图2-2-28 孙中山雕像
PICTURE 2-2-28 STATUE OF SUN YAT-SEN

图2-2-29 区位图与平面轮廓图
PICTURE 2-2-29 LOCATION AND OUTLINE

图2-2-30 礼堂内景
PICTURE 2-2-30 INTERIOR

图2-2-31 前厅内景
PICTURE 2-2-31 LOBBY

图2-2-32 礼堂内景
PICTURE 2-2-32 INTERIOR

图2-2-33 当铺外观图
PICTURE 2-2-33 APPEARENCE

图2-2-34 远眺当铺
PICTURE 2-2-34 OVERLOOK

图2-2-35 当铺外观图
PICTURE 2-2-35 APPEARENCL

图2-2-36 正面局部
PICTURE 2-2-36 PORTION OF THE FACADE

## 2.2.6 莲塘南当铺

莲塘南当铺位于莲塘南街 20 号，建于民国时期。建筑长 9.40 米，宽 8.17 米，建筑占地面积为 76.8 平方米，建筑保存情况良好，进行过主面修复。旧时为当铺及储存当物的库房。建筑共五层，形似碉楼，一层外墙为红砂岩石，二层以上为青砖砌筑，锅耳山墙单檐布瓦硬山顶，上下五层均有防御性小窗眼，建筑结构牢固。

## 2.2.6 Liantangnan Pawnshop

Located at No.20 of Liantangnan Street, Liantangnan Pawnshop was built during the Republic of China. It covers a total area of 76.8m² with 9.4 meters in length and 8.17 meters in width. In good shape, the pawnshop has been renovated. It was a pawnshop as well as a warehouse to store the pawned goods. Five floors in total, the building looks like a watchtower. The external walls on the first floor were built with red sandstones and the second and above with plain bricks. It has panhandle-shaped pediments and concealed single eave gables with grey tiles. The whole building has defensive holes and is built with firm structures.

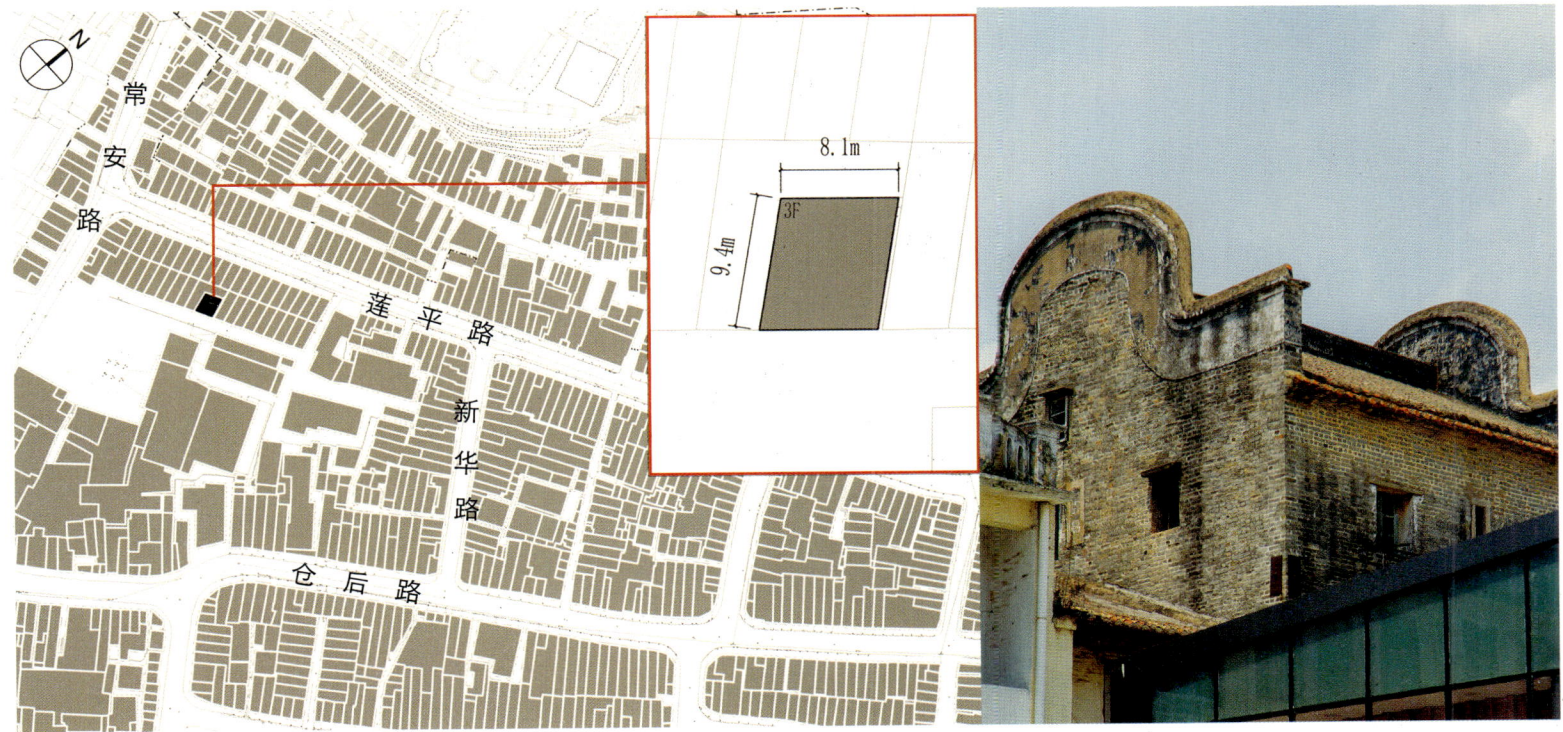

图2-2-37　区位图与平面轮廓图
PICTURE 2-2-37　LOCATION AND OUTLINE

图2-2-38　当铺外观图
PICTURE 2-2-38　APPEARENCE

图2-2-39 常安路街景
PICTURE 2-2-39 CHANG'AN ROAD

## 2.2.7 常安路

常安路步行街位于江门历史街区的西南部，南北走向，南接堤中路，北至范罗岗（中山公园附近），西接象溪路、紫茶路，东通莲平路、仓后路，全长860米。

常安路前身为常安涌，明朝后期，西江夹带的泥沙把常安路一带冲积成为陆地，在形成陆地过程中，来自范罗冈山丘的溪水又把淤泥冲开，形成一条河涌。康熙三年（1664年），朝廷下达迁海令，江门被划入迁海界内，居民悉数内迁。康熙八年（1669年），朝廷撤销迁海令，允许内迁居民回归复业。居民重返江门，寄"常安乐"之意，便把这条涌叫作"常安涌"。后来，涌两旁的居民多了起来，形成了长安街、长兴街，成为一个社区，便命名为"常安坊"。此后粤海关税口和千总衙署的开设，使得常安涌附近热闹非凡，曾有诗赞曰："酒榭歌台紫洞船，风光最好是营前。"

民国十八年（1929年），市政促进委员会成立，从民间集资20余万元白银，用以修筑长堤、钓台路，扩宽太平、塘步、新市、宝善、莲平、更兴等13条马路。常安涌也在这时被填平，铺上水泥路面成为马路，常安路便这样诞生了。之后几十年，常安路一直作为江门重要的商业街。21世纪初，江门市政府将常安路南段约220米改造成商业步行街，路面以花岗岩石板铺装，使老街重新焕发了生机。

## 2.2.7 Chang'an Road

Located in the southwest of the Historical Neighborhood, Chang'an Road Pedestrian Street points north-south direction. With a total length of 860 meters, it is connected with Dizhong Road in the south, Fanluogang Mountain (near the Sun Yat-sen Park) in the north, Xiangxi Road and Zicha Road in the west and Lianping Road and Canghou Road in the east.

Chang'an Road was a lake and has evolved into a piece of land by sediments and stones brought by the west river by the end of Ming Dynasty. In the process, the streams from the Fanluogang Mountain washed away the sludge and formed a river. In 1664 (the third year of Emperor Kangxi), the government issued a decree to remove citizens from the coastal areas, which included Jiangmen. Five years later in 1669, the government revoked the decree and those uprooted citizens were allowed to return to their hometown and resume their businesses. After the citizens went back, they named the river Chang'an which means eternal peace. More and more residents gathered along the river and then the Chang'an Street and Changxing Street came into being, and the area was named Chang'an neighborhood. The setup of Customs of West Canton and Qianzong Government in Jiangmen has brought vitality to Chang'an neighborhood and as the poem goes: "with wine, dances and songs on the Zidong boat, the best scenery ever is on the Chang'an river".

In 1929, the Municipal Administration Promotion Committee was established and built 13 roads including Changdi, Diaotai (Fishing Terrace), extended Taiping, Tangbu, Xinshi, Baoshan, Lianping and Gengxing with over 200,000 silver dollars funded from the public. The Chang'an River was filled and turned into a cement road at this time, then the Chang'an Road came into being. In the several decades after, Chang'an Road has always been an important commercial street. In the beginning of 21st century, Jiangmen government has renovated about 220 meters in the south of Chang'an Road with granite stones and turned the section of the road into a pedestrian street, bringing life back to the old street.

图2-2-40 区位图
PICTURE 2-2-40 LOCATION

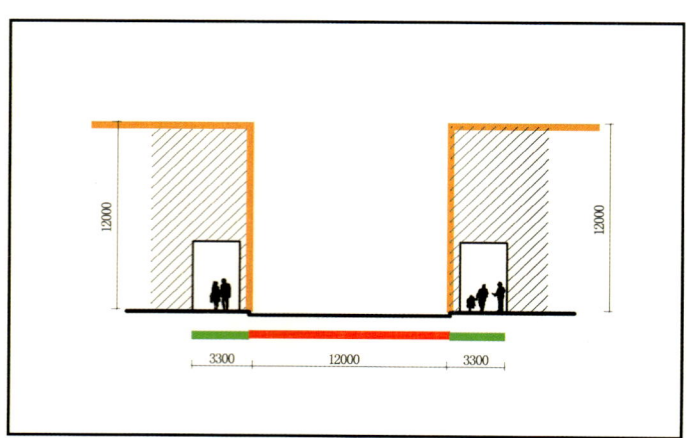

图2-2-41 街道剖面图
PICTURE 2-2-41 SECTION

图2-2-42 常安路街景
PICTURE 2-2-42 CHANG' AN ROAD

图2-2-43　常安路街景
PICTURE 2-2-43　CHANG'AN ROAD

图2-2-44　常安路街景
PICTURE 2-2-44　CHANG'AN ROAD

图2-2-45　堤中路街景
PICTURE 2-2-45　DIZHONG ROAD

图2-2-46 堤中路街景
PICTURE 2-2-46 DIZHONG ROAD

## 2.2.8 堤中路

堤中路位于蓬江北岸，骑楼风貌区南侧，街道呈东北、西南走向。东北接堤东路，西南连堤西路。堤中路长778米，车行道宽10米，两旁人行道各宽3米。此处原为河滩地，后成为住宅区。1930年拆屋筑堤建路，称"长堤"，此段居中，故称"堤中路"。商店、仓库及码头相继在此建起。建筑物为二、三层骑楼式旧楼房，仿古罗马式样。1950年后，逐步演变为城区主要商业区，沿河一边修筑防洪堤。1983年，拆防洪堤，建水磨通花栏杆。沿堤码头迁往北街，原码头改建为观河台。沿堤有画舫两家，为水上品茗好去处。华侨戏院、海员俱乐部、十五层商业大厦以及堤中百货商店等设于此。现在街道依旧保留路北侧的骑楼建筑风貌，建筑均经过改造。街道一派繁华的商业景象，为城市的主要交通干道。

## 2.2.8 Dizhong Road

Located in the north bank of Pengjiang River and in the south of Arcade Building District, Dizhong Road points the northeast and southwest direction. It is to the southwest of Didong Road and the northeast of Dixi Road. With a total length of 778 meters, Dizhong Road has a 10-meter wide roadway and two 3-meter wide sidewalks. Dizhong Road was a flood land and then turned into a residential area. In 1930, houses in the district were demolished and banks and roads were built, and the district was then called Changdi, which means long banks. Dizhong Road was named for its location in the middle of the Changdi district. Stores, warehouses and piers were built afterwards. Most architecture in the district is double or three-floored arcade-style old buildings. And the buildings imitate Romanesque styles. After 1950, Dizhong Road gradually evolved into a major commercial district and flood banks were built along the riverside which were replaced by water-grinded handrails in 1983 and the pier was renovated into a view deck. There were two beautifully decorated pleasure boats, an ideal destination for people to enjoy tea on the waters. Overseas Chinese Theater, Sailor's Club, Fifteen Floor Mansion and Dizhong Department Store were established here. Now the arcade buildings on the north side of the road were retained and renovated. Dizhong Road is now the arterial road in the city with prosperous commercial activities.

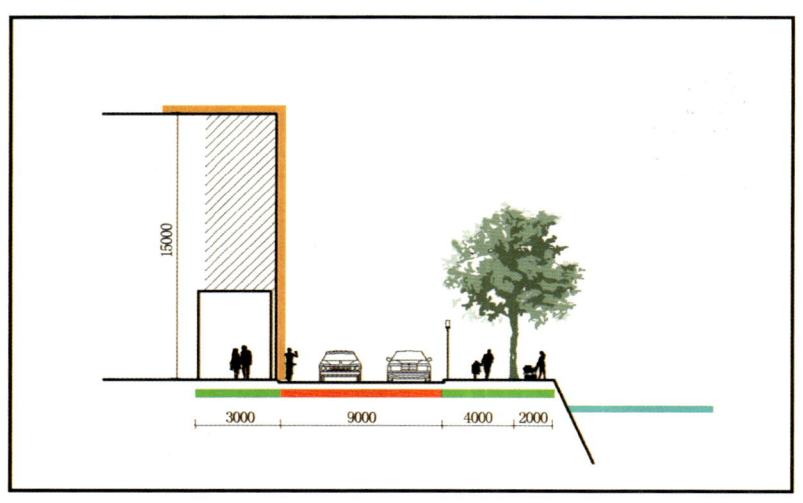

图2-2-47　街道剖面图
PICTURE 2-2-47　SECTION

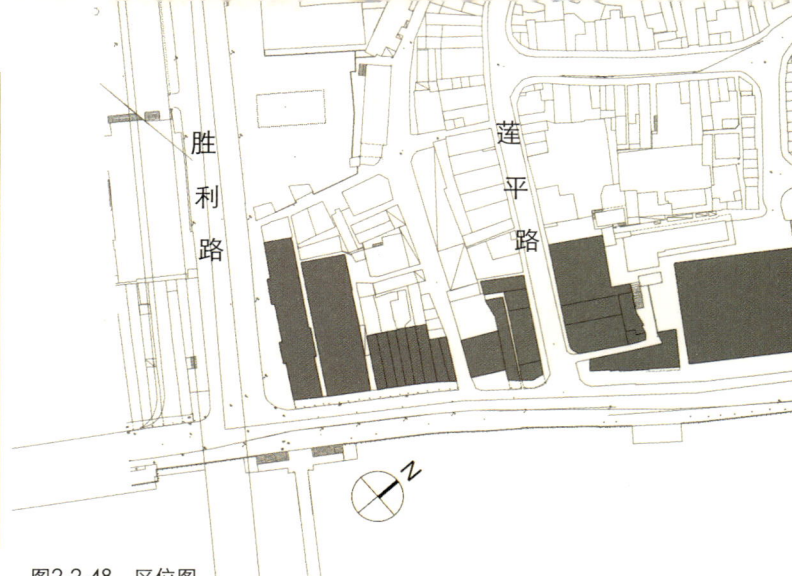

图2-2-48　区位图
PICTURE 2-2-48　LOCATION

图2-2-49　堤中路街景
PICTURE 2-2-49　DIZHONG ROAD

图2-2-50　堤中路街景
PICTURE 2-2-50　DIZHONG ROAD

图2-2-51　堤中路街景
PICTURE 2-2-51　DIZHONG ROAD

书院路　钓台路　榄豉路　塘步路

图2-2-52　堤中路街景
PICTURE 2-2-52　DIZHONG ROAD

图2-2-53 莲平路街景
PICTURE 2-2-53 LIANPING ROAD

## 2.2.9 莲平路

莲平路位于常安路步行街的北面，中山公园南面，为东西走向，与常安路北段呈T字形相交，东连兴宁路。该路由当时莲塘街与平安街合并而成，1930年筑马路时，各取一字称"莲平路"，长460米，宽8米，建筑物为二、三层骑楼式旧楼宇。莲平路1950年前多为金铺。1980年前一段时期，为居民住宅区。1981年后，商业网点逐步恢复，此地再现繁荣。莲平路现为商业区，有家具店、镜画店、服装店、小食店等。

现存骑楼多为砖木和砖混结构，风貌参差，其中不乏式样精美、浑厚大气的骑楼单体。骑楼底层为商铺，现以五金电子商店居多。

## 2.2.9 Lianping Road

Located in the north of Chang'an Road Pedestrian Street and to the south of Sun Yat-sen Park, Lianping Road, combining the then Liantang Street and Ping'an Street, points the east-west direction and is vertically crossed with the north section of Chang'an Road and is connected with Xingning Road in the east. Constructed in 1930, Lianping Road was 460 meters long and 8 meters wide with 1284 residents. Most architecture in the district is double or three-floored arcade-style old buildings. Before 1950, most of the stores were gold shops on the street and for some while before 1980, it was changed into a residential area and after 1981, the stores were brought back and the road was prosperous with business again. Lianping road is now a commercial district with stores selling furniture, paintings, clothes and food.

The arcade buildings retained now are mostly brick-wood or brick-concrete structures with different styles and features, among which some are exquisite and grand. The first floor of the arcade buildings are for commercial uses, and most are hardware stores nowadays.

图2-2-54 莲平路街景
PICTURE 2-2-54 LIANPING ROAD

图2-2-55 莲平路街景
PICTURE 2-2-55 LIANPING ROAD

图2-2-56 莲平路街景
PICTURE 2-2-56 LIANPING ROAD

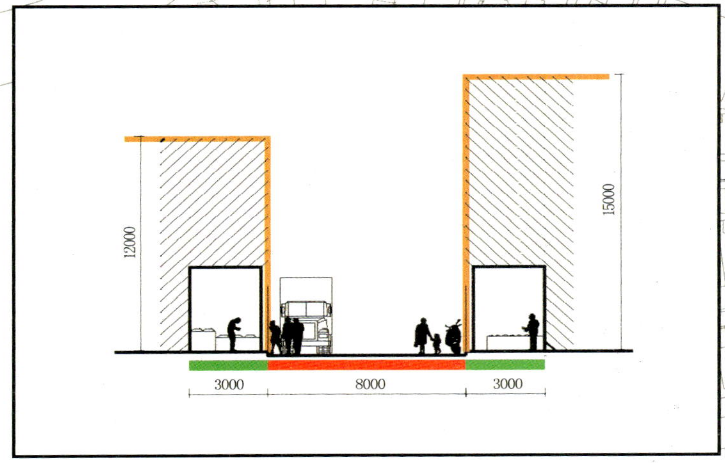

图2-2-57 街道剖面图
PICTURE 2-2-57　SECTION

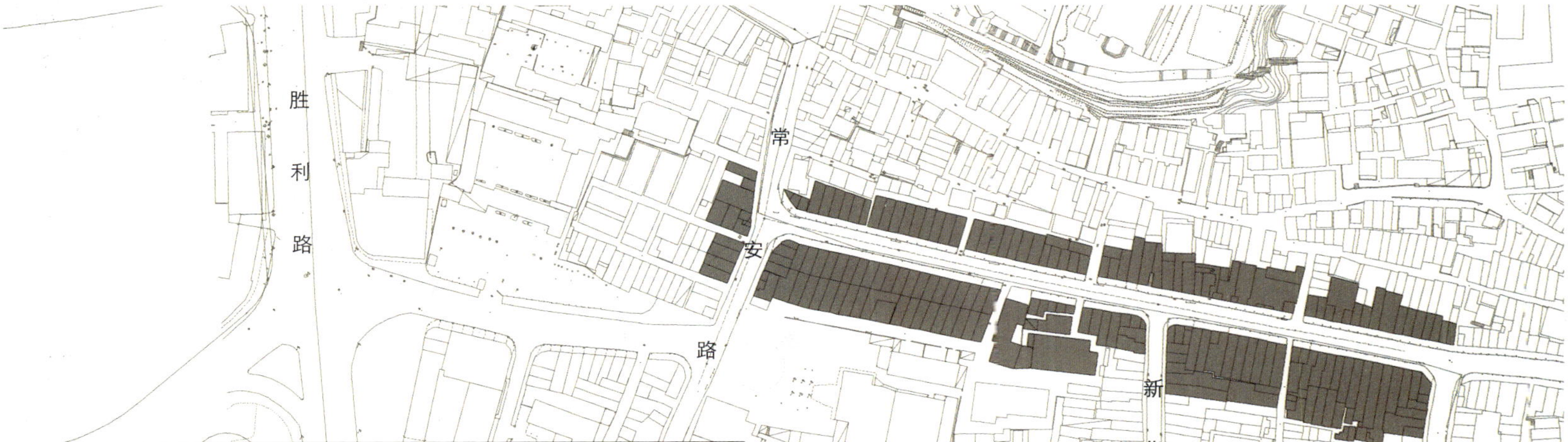

图2-2-58 区位图
PICTURE 2-2-58　LOCATION

图2-2-59 莲平路街景
PICTURE 2-2-59　LIANPING ROAD

图2-2-60 莲平路街景
PICTURE 2-2-60　LIANPING ROAD

图2-2-61 仓后路街景
PICTURE 2-2-61 CANGHOU ROAD

## 2.2.10 仓后路

仓后路位于骑楼风貌区中部，东西走向。西与常安路相交，东与新市路相接，长610米。车行道宽8米，两边的骑楼人行道各宽3米。该地为旧城区中心，居民近2000人。清道光年间（1821—1850年），本处地近河边，原设有盐埠，专供盐船装卸货物，盐埠后边有小巷习称"盐仓后街"。1927年江门筑马路，将此巷扩建为马路，故名"仓后路"。路两旁多为三、四层高的老式骑楼，建筑保存状况良好，现依旧沿用"上居下商"的使用模式。

## 2.2.10 Canghou Road

Located in the middle of the Arcade Building District, Canghou Road points the east-west direction. It is connected to Chang'an Road in the west and Xinshi Road in the east with a total length of 610 meters. It has an 8-meter wide roadway and two 3-meter wide sidewalks. At the center of the old downtown area, it had a population of nearly 2,000. From 1820 to 1850, Canghou Road was close to the riverside where it served as a salt port for salt commercial ships to unload goods. The lane behind the salt port was called Yancanghou Street. When the lane was expanded into a road in 1927, the road was called Canghou Road accordingly. Most of the buildings on this road are three to four-floored old arcade buildings. In good condition the buildings are still used for commercial purpose in the first floor and provide accommodation in higher floors.

图2-2-62 仓后路街景
PICTURE 2-2-62 CANGHOU ROAD

图2-2-63 仓后路街景
PICTURE 2-2-63 CANGHOU ROAD

图2-2-64 区位图
PICTURE 2-2-64 LOCATION

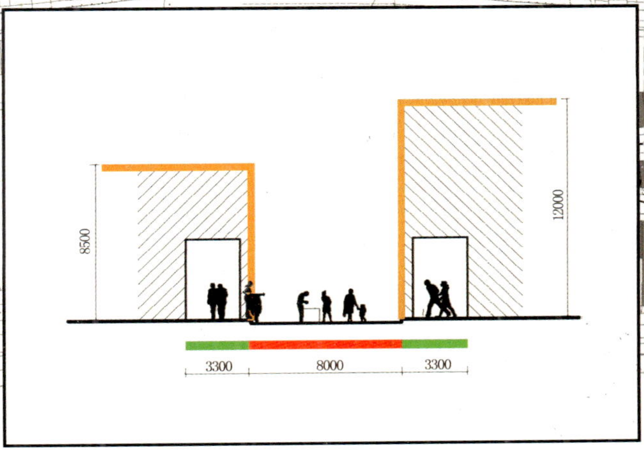

图2-2-65 街道剖面图
PICTURE 2-2-65 SECTION

图2-2-66 仓后路街景
PICTURE 2-2-66 CANGHOU ROAD

图2-2-67 仓后路街景
PICTURE 2-2-67 CANGHOU ROAD

图2-2-68 兴宁路街景
PICTURE 2-2-68 XINGNING ROAD

## 2.2.11 兴宁路

兴宁路位于骑楼风貌区的北部，东、西走向。西与莲平路、东与钓台路相通，长480米，车行道宽7.8米，两旁的骑楼人行道各宽约3米。清康熙三年（1664年）强令沿海居民内迁，五年后解禁，民归思安，取意吉祥，成街时初称"丰宁街"。街内多绸布店，时称绸布店为苏杭铺，故又称"苏杭街"。1929年筑马路时，易名为"兴宁路"，取兴盛安宁之意。建筑类型丰富，多为三、四层砖木结构骑楼式旧楼房。其时较著名的绸布店有卫海、昌兴、锦纶、美万、大成等。在路内沿石阶梯上京果街，其旁曾有闻名一时的"正三桁瓦"菜刀店铺。

## 2.2.11 Xingning Road

Located in the north of the Arcade Building District, Xingning Road points the east-west direction. It is connected to Lianping Road in the west and Diaotai Road in the east with a total length of 480 meters. It has a 7.8-meter wide roadway and two 3-meter wide sidewalks. In 1664 (the third year of Emperor Kangxi's reign), the Qing government issued a decree to force residents to move away from the coastal areas and when the decree was revoked 5 years later, those residents returned to their hometown and named the street Fengning to bring good luck. There were mostly silk stores on the street and was so called Suhang Street. Fengning Street was renamed as Xingning road meaning prosperity and peace in 1929 when a road was built. Most of the buildings on this road are three to four-floored old arcade buildings with brick-wood structures. In the old times, famous silk stores including Weihai, Changxing, Jinlun, Meiwan and Dacheng could be found here. Follow the stone steps in the road, the Nuts Street can be reached, and there was the famous kitchen knife store called Zhengsanhengwa nearby.

图2-2-69 兴宁路街景
PICTURE 2-2-69 XINGNING ROAD

图2-2-70 区位图
PICTURE 2-2-70 LOCATION

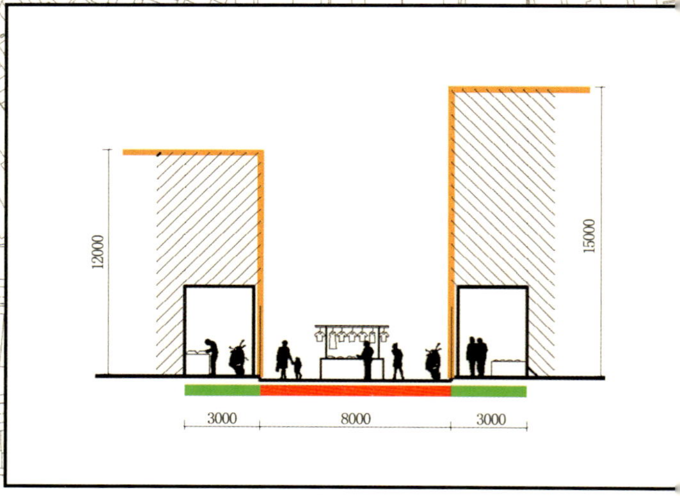

图2-2-71 街道剖面图
PICTURE 2-2-71 SECTION

图2-2-72 兴宁路街景
PICTURE 2-2-72 XINGNING ROAD

图2-2-73 兴宁路街景
PICTURE 2-2-73 XINGNING ROAD

图2-2-74 众兴路街景
PICTURE 2-2-74 ZHONGXING ROAD

## 2.2.12 众兴路

众兴路位于骑楼风貌区中部,南与新市路成十字形,北与莲平路成 Y 字形,南、北走向,长 180 米,宽 6~8 米。该路曾称"众兴街",1929 年筑马路时,改称"众兴路"。1949 年前设有零散商业服务点,后成为居民住宅区。1980 年后化肥设备配件厂综合贸易部及五金交电公司等商店相继设于此。建筑物多为二、三层旧式砖木楼房。现该道路两旁的建筑保存情况中等,大部分建筑依旧沿用"上居下商"的使用模式。

## 2.2.12 Zhongxing Road

Located in the middle of the Arcade Building District, Zhongxing Road points the south-north direction and forms a crisscross with Xinshi Road in the south and a Y shape with Lianping Road in the north. It has a length of 180 meters and a width of 6 to 8 meters. This road was named Zhongxing Street and renamed Zhongxing Road in 1929. Few commercial service stations were distributed in the road before 1949 which was then turned into a residential area. After 1980, the trade department of chemical fertilizer equipment factory and the hardware and electrical equipment companies were set up here. Most of the buildings on this road are two to three-floored old arcade buildings with brick-wood structures. In moderate condition, most of the buildings along the two sides of the road are still used for commercial purpose in the first floor and provide accommodation in higher floors.

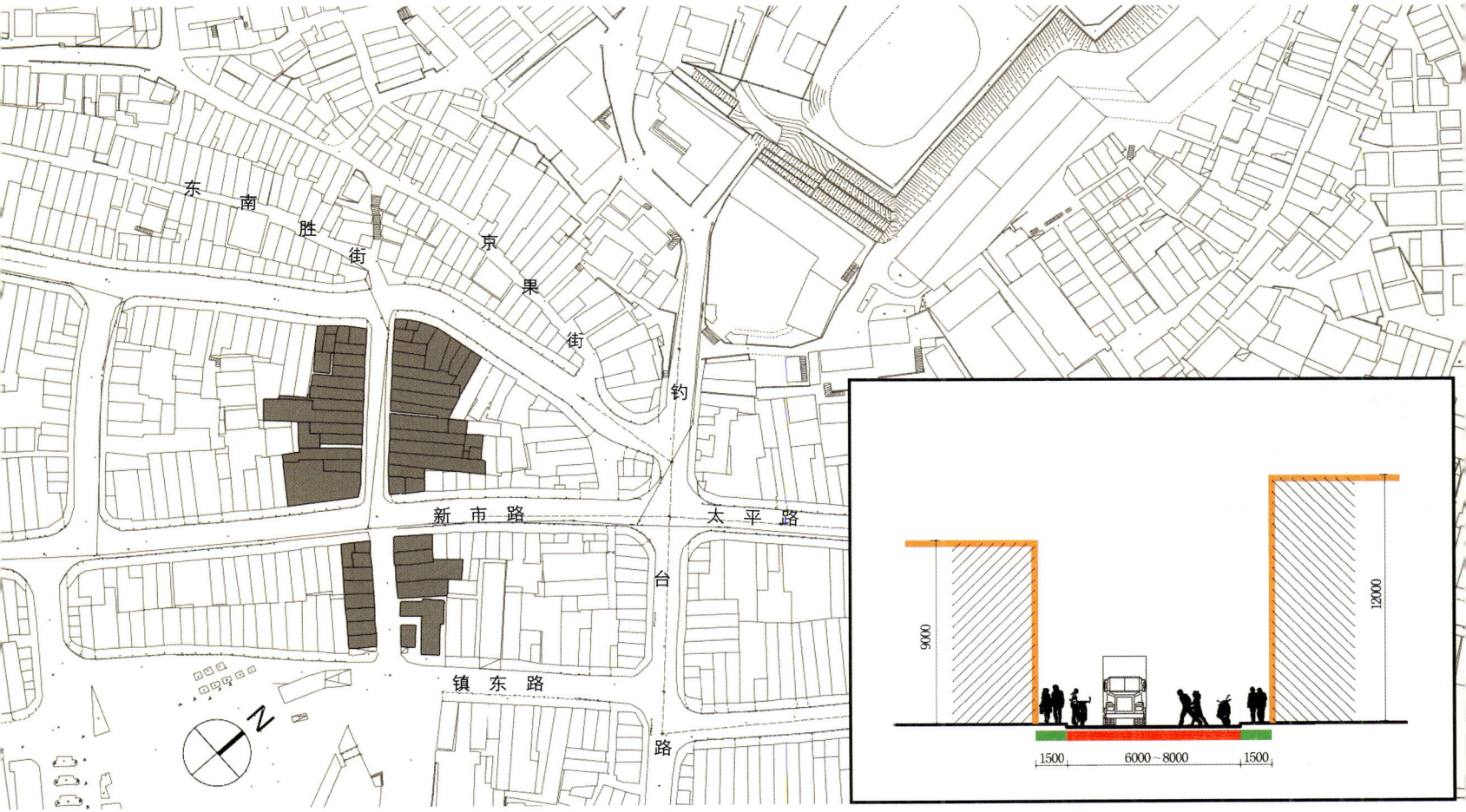

图 2-2-75 区位图
PICTURE 2-2-75 LOCATION

图 2-2-76 街道剖面图
PICTURE 2-2-76 SECTION

图2-2-77 新市路街景
PICTURE 2-2-77 XINSHI ROAD

## 2.2.13 新市路

新市路位于骑楼风貌街的中部，东、西走向，西接仓后路，东接钓台路，长300米，车行道宽8米，两旁骑楼人行道各宽约3米。街道两旁建筑物多为二、三层混合结构骑楼式旧楼房。这里原为蓬江一部分，几经淤积成沙滩。因地近江门旧墟场，市场逐渐扩展至此，至明末形成新市场，俗称"新市"。1933年前分属永兴、新市与竹地街。1933年筑马路，沿袭称"新市路"。骑楼街道风貌结构保存相对良好，部分建筑立面经过改造，大部分建筑首层依旧作商业用途。

## 2.2.13 Xinshi Road

Located in the middle of the Arcade Building District, Xinshi Road points the east-west direction and is connected to Canghou Road to the west and Diaotai Road to the east with a total length of 300 meters. It has an 8-meter wide roadway and two 3-meter wide sidewalks. Most of the buildings on this road are two to three-floored old arcade buildings with mixed structures. This road was part of Pengjiang River but was then turned into a flood plain. Being close to the old Jiangmen Market place, it became part of it when it expanded. By the end of Ming Dynasty, a new market was formed called Xinshi. It belonged to Yongxing, Xinshi and Zhudi Streets before 1933 and was renamed Xinshi Road in 1933. The styles and features of the arcade buildings are comparatively well preserved and part of the facade has been renovated. Most of the buildings are still used for commercial purpose on the first floor.

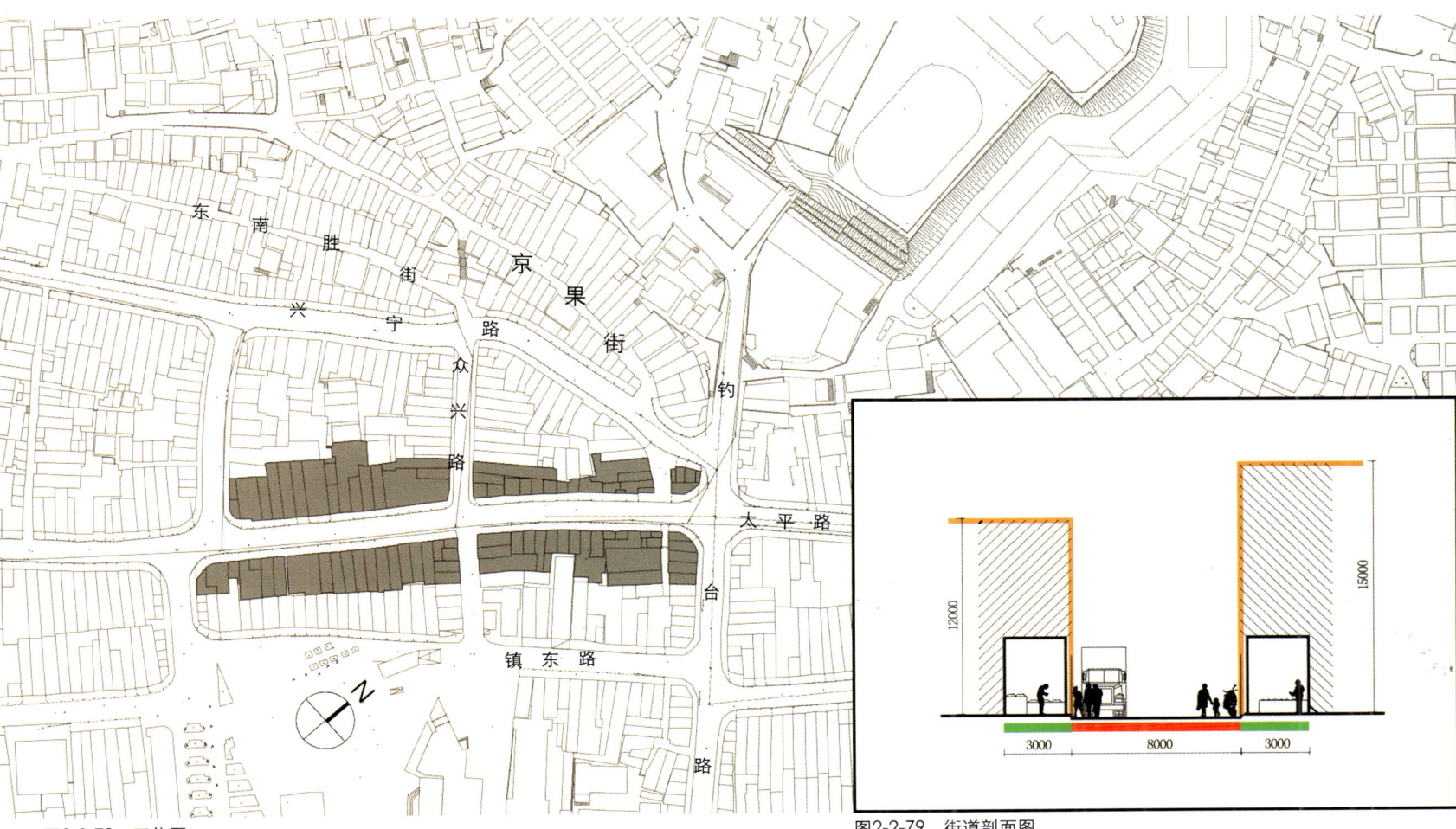

图2-2-78　区位图
PICTURE 2-2-78　LOCATION

图2-2-79　街道剖面图
PICTURE 2-2-79　SECTION

图2-2-80 太平路街景
PICTURE 2-2-80 TAIPING ROAD

## 2.2.14 太平路

太平路位于骑楼风貌区东部，东、西走向。西通钓台路，东与葵尾路、塘步路相交成Y字形，长100米，车行道宽8米，两旁骑楼人行道各宽3米。太平路昔日因专营海南土特产，故曾称"旧椰街"。清光绪十四年（1888年），设有慈善性质的"明善堂"。1929年筑马路，市民寄意太平盛世，改称"太平路"。1949年前此路段的商铺多经营绸布。民居均为二、三层砖木结构骑楼式旧楼房。江门市五邑发展公司长城分公司、太平小学及红十字会诊所等均设于此。

## 2.2.14 Taiping Road

Located in the east of the Arcade Building District, Taiping Road points the east-west direction. It is connected to Diaotai Road in the west and forms a Y shape with Kuiwei Road and Tangbu Road in the east with a total length of 100 meters. It has an 8-meter wide roadway and two 3-meter wide sidewalks. This road was named Jiuye Street for exclusively selling Hainan local specialties. In 1888, a charity institution Mingshan House was set up here. The road was renamed Taiping Road as citizens expressed good wishes for a peaceful and prosperous society. Before 1949, this road was mainly engaged in silk business. The residential buildings on this road are all two to three-floored old arcade buildings with brick-wood structures. Great Wall branch of Wuyi Development Company, Taiping Primary School and Red Cross Clinic are all located here.

图2-2-82 街道剖面图
PICTURE 2-2-82 SECTION

图2-2-81 区位图
PICTURE 2-2-81 LOCATION

图2-2-83 市场景象
PICTURE 2-2-83 INSIDE THE MARKET

## 2.2.15　水街农贸市场（榄豉路、新椰路）

水街位于骑楼风貌街的东侧，由榄豉路、新椰路组成，两段分别长177米和150米，宽8米，是江门市最后一个"马路市场"。市场兴起于20世纪中期，街道两旁为两、三层的旧式建筑，一楼多为小商铺，整条巷道被建筑挑出的铁皮雨篷所遮盖。雨篷下是用水泥砌成的台子，小商贩就将商品摆在台子上，供人选购。水泥台后面约3米处，就是临街的商铺，多是卖米、油和食品的，在街道的北端则集中卖服装。

水街农贸市场作为江门最后一个"马路市场"，是本土人民生活方式的见证，是街区生活中不可或缺的部分。蔬菜、水果、肉类、杂货，在这里都一应俱全。哪怕卖菜的人和买菜的人换了一代又一代，水街市场仍然几十年如一日，为老街的居民们提供最新鲜实惠的产品。在市场里，常常能遇到相熟的街坊，聊聊蔬菜价格、家长里短，充满了浓浓的生活气息。

白天，市场里人流如织，买卖声犹如一首无伴奏的歌曲，一派繁华景象，给人们带来虽时移世易但市声人情依旧的怀想。水街农贸市场，至今起码有五十年历史，是最有江门风情的大众市场。

## 2.2.15　Water Street Farmer's Market (Lanchi Road and Xinye Road)

Located in the east of the Arcade Building District, Water Street is composed of two sections-Lanchi Road and Xinye Road, with a respective length of 177 meters and 150 meters and a width of 8 meters. It is the last "roadway market" in Jiangmen. The market started in the 1950s and there were two or three-floored old buildings along the road. The first floors were mainly small stores and the whole lane was covered by iron-made rain sheds, under which there were cement platforms for small traders to display and sell their goods. About three meters behind the cement platforms were stores facing the streets, mainly engaging in businesses of rice, cooking oil and food. Stores in the north of the street mainly sold clothes.

As the last market on the street in Jiangmen, Water Street Farmers Market is the witness of the lives of the local resident, and an indispensable part of the neighborhood. Everything from vegetables, fruits, meat to grocery can be found here in the market. Although the buyers and vendors have changed in several generations, the market has remained as a venue that provides the locals with the most fresh and affordable products. In the market, people can always bump into familiar neighbors to chat about the price and family gossip which makes the market a place filled with life.

In the daytime, it is filled with the hustle and bustle as the locals gather here and the buyers and vendors call to each other like a chorus unaccompanied. This brings to people a sense of nostalgia where they feel their relationship lasts despite the change of times. Water Street Farmers Market is now a public market with at least fifty years of history.

图2-2-84　市场入口
PICTURE 2-2-84　THE ENTRANCE

图2-2-85　市场景象
PICTURE 2-2-85　INSIDE THE MARKET

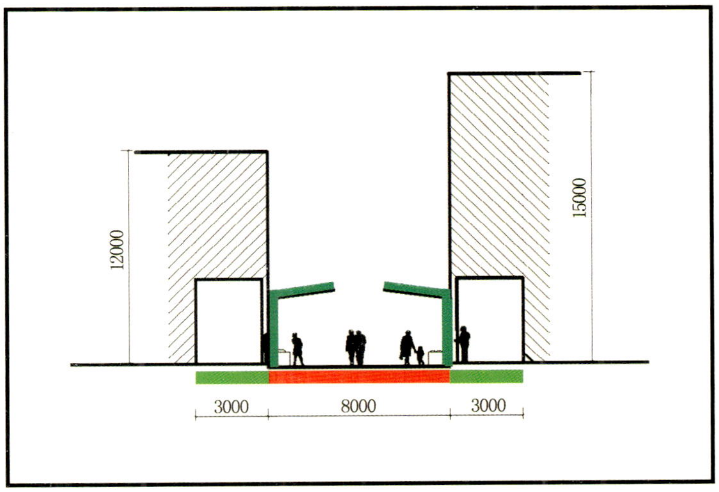

图2-2-86 街道剖面图
PICTURE 2-2-86 SECTION

图2-2-87 区位图
PICTURE 2-2-87 LOCATION

图2-2-88 市场景象
PICTURE 2-2-88 INSIDE THE MARKET

149

图2-2-89　市场景象
PICTURE 2-2-89　INSIDE THE MARKET

图2-2-90　市场景象
PICTURE 2-2-90　INSIDE THE MARKET

图2-2-91 市场周边街景
PICTURE 2-2-91 THE SURROUNDINGS

图2-3-1 石湾历史风貌区 鸟瞰
PICTURE 2-3-1 BIRD-VIEW

图2-3-2 石湾历史风貌区 鸟瞰
PICTURE 2-3-2 BIRD-VIEW

## 2.3 石湾历史风貌区
## 2.3 SHIWAN HISTORICAL DISTRICT

石湾历史风貌区位于江门历史街区的东部，西接大地塘连接太平路，东至跃进路，面积约8.4公顷。石湾历史风貌区的历史最早可追溯至明代，形成年代稍晚于墟顶，由于河道变迁，当时人们在蓬江边蓬莱山（现景贤中学）山下修筑民居，遂形成石湾村。在其后很长的一段历史时期中，石湾片区商贾云集、熙攘繁华，更有石湾庙、油糖会馆和雪峰寺三个有名的公共建筑，对江门蓬江区的发展产生了重要的影响。如今河道变迁、繁华散去，三大公共建筑也已变成古迹。今天，石湾历史风貌区仍保留了大量的砖木建筑和蜿蜒狭窄的石湾直街，历经沧桑，风貌犹存。穿行其间，转角不经意间邂逅青砖宅院，耳畔回荡民居里传来的粤曲声，一曲经年，回味悠长。

Located in the east of the Changdi Historical Neighborhood, Shiwan Historical District is connected with Daditang and Taiping Road to the west and Yuejin Road to the east with a total area of 8.4 hectares. Its history dates back to Ming Dynasty and was formed slightly later than Xuding District. Because of the changes in river course, local citizens built houses under the Penglai Mountain by the Penglai River and the Shiwan Village was formed. In a long period to come, Shiwan District witnessed hustle and bustle by gathering officials and businessmen. Three famous public buildings as Shiwan Temple, Oil and Sugar Guild, and Xuefeng Temple have exerted an important influence on the development of Pengjiang District. Now the river changed its course again and the hustle and bustle has gone. The three buildings have become historical sites, but a large number of brick-wood buildings and the zigzagging Shiwanzhi Street have been retained. After years of vicissitudes, their styles and features still exist. To walk through the streets, you may bump into an old plain brick house and enjoy the beautiful Cantonese tunes that can bring you lasting pleasure and inner peace.

图2-3-3　石湾历史街区街道
PICTURE 2-3-3　ALLEYS

图2-3-4　石湾历史街区历史建筑
PICTURE 2-3-4　HISTORICAL BUILDING

图2-3-5 启明里广场
PICTURE 2-3-5　THE QIMING LI SQUARE

图2-3-6 五角星幼儿园
PICTURE 2-3-6　FIVE-POINTED STAR KINDERGARDEN

图2-3-7 石湾历史街区街道
PICTURE 2-3-7　ALLEYS

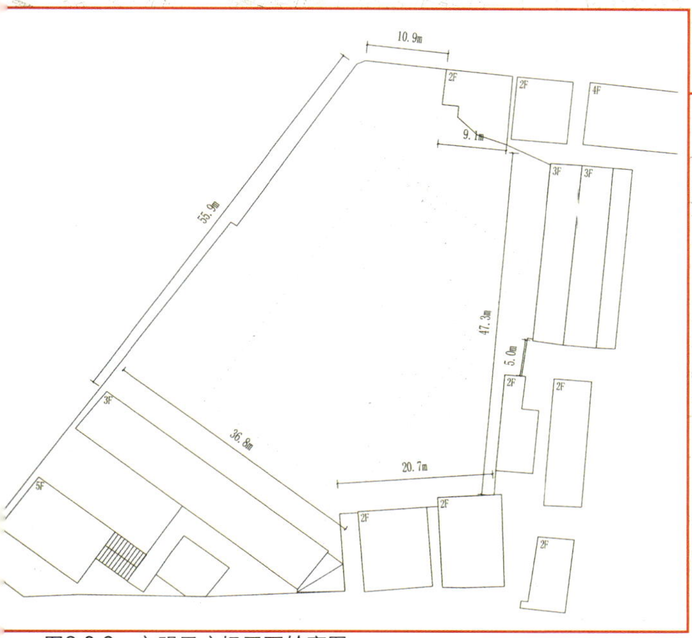

图2-3-8 启明里广场平面轮廓图
PICTURE 2-3-8 OUTLINE OF THE QIMING LI SQUARE

图2-3-9 区位图
PICTURE 2-3-9 LOCATION

图2-3-10 启明里广场
PICTURE 2-3-10 THE QIMINGLI SQUARE

图2-3-11 石湾历史街区街道
PICTURE 2-3-11 ALLEYS

## 2.3.1 新第里1、2、3号

新第里1、2、3号位于石湾历史风貌区中部，新第里南端，为一座三开间三层高的砖木结构民居，建于民国初期，整体长13.87米，宽11.57米，建筑占地面积为160.5平方米。建筑保存情况良好，内部有天井，一、二层门窗经过改造，三层阳台保留有石米制雕花栏杆以及科林斯柱式、雕花拱券，该建筑现作居住用途。

## 2.3.1 No.1 to No.3 of Xindi Lane

Located in the middle of Shiwan District and in the south of Xindi Lane, No.1 to No.3 of Xindi Lane are three brick-wood structures each with three floors. The buildings were built in the beginning of the Republic of China with a length of 13.87 meters and a width of 11.57 meters, covering a total area of 160.5m². In good condition, the buildings have a courtyard in the middle. The doors and windows on the first and second floors have been renovated and the third floor balcony has retained the beautifully carved chicken girt handrails and arches and the Corinthian Order pillars. The buildings still provide accommodation nowadays.

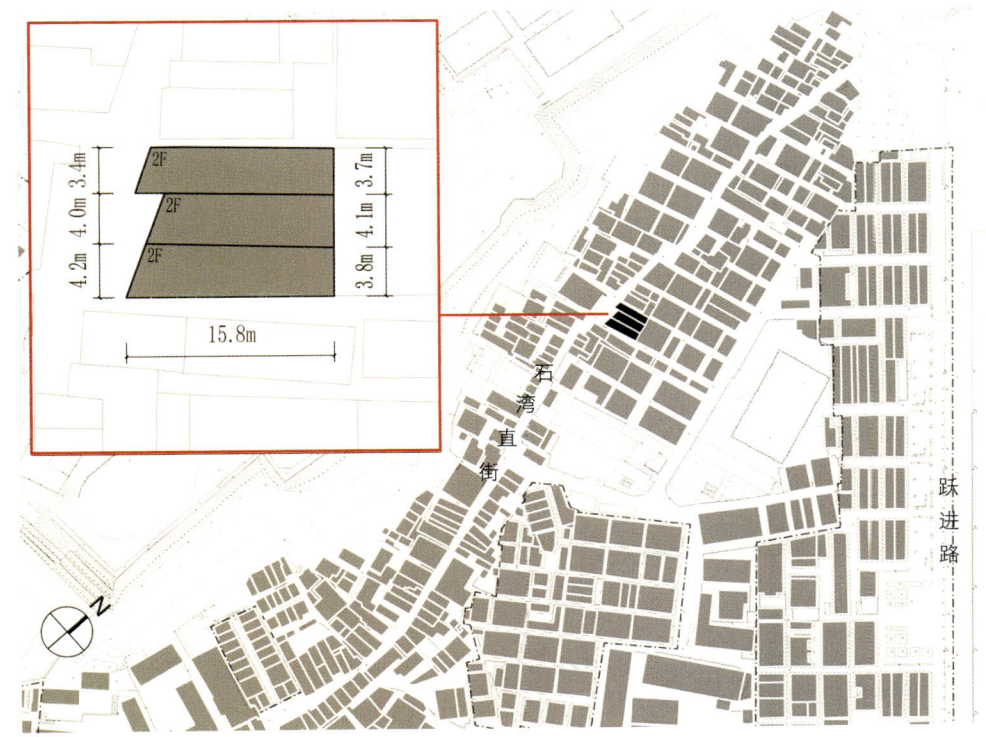

图2-3-12 区位图
PICTURE 2-3-12 LOCATION

图2-3-13 新第里1、2、3号外观图
PICTURE 2-3-13 APPEARENCE NO.1 TO NO.3 OF XINDI LANE

图2-3-14 新第里1、2、3号外观图
PICTURE 2-3-14  APPEARENCE

图2-3-15 内部局部
PICTURE 2-3-15  INTERIOR

图2-3-16 新第里1、2、3号外观图
PICTURE 2-3-16  APPEARENCE NO.1 TO NO.3 OF XINDI LANE

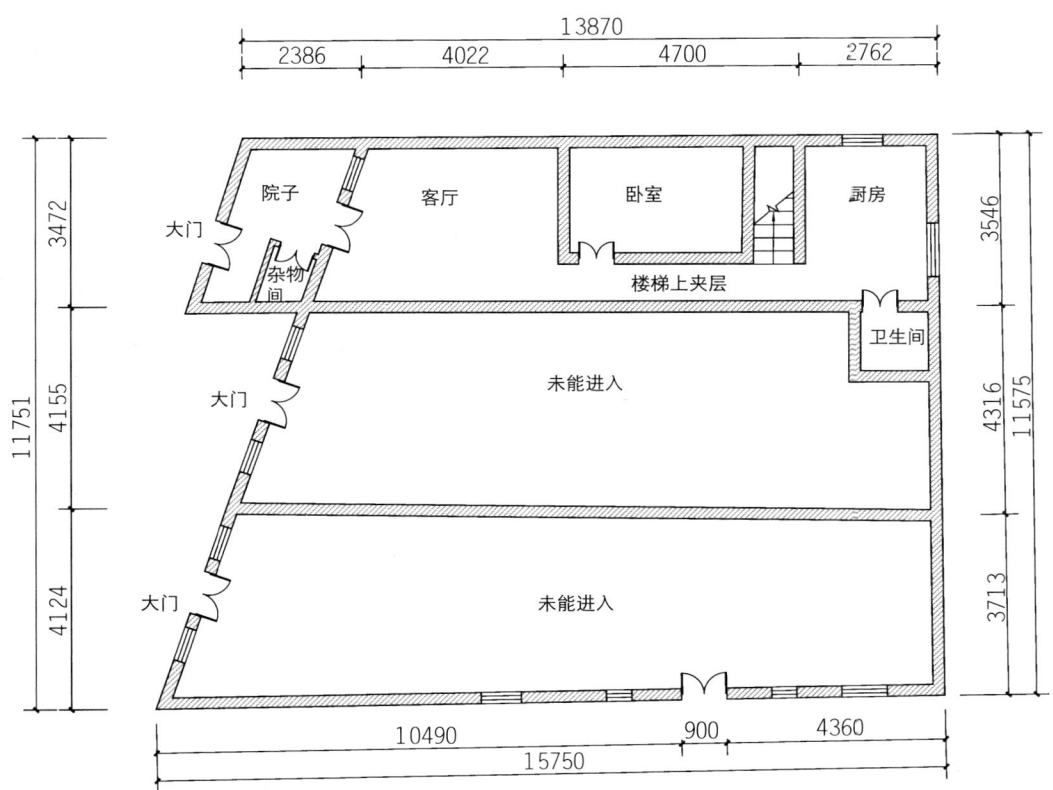

图2-3-17 首层平面图
PICTURE 2-3-17　FIRST FLOOR

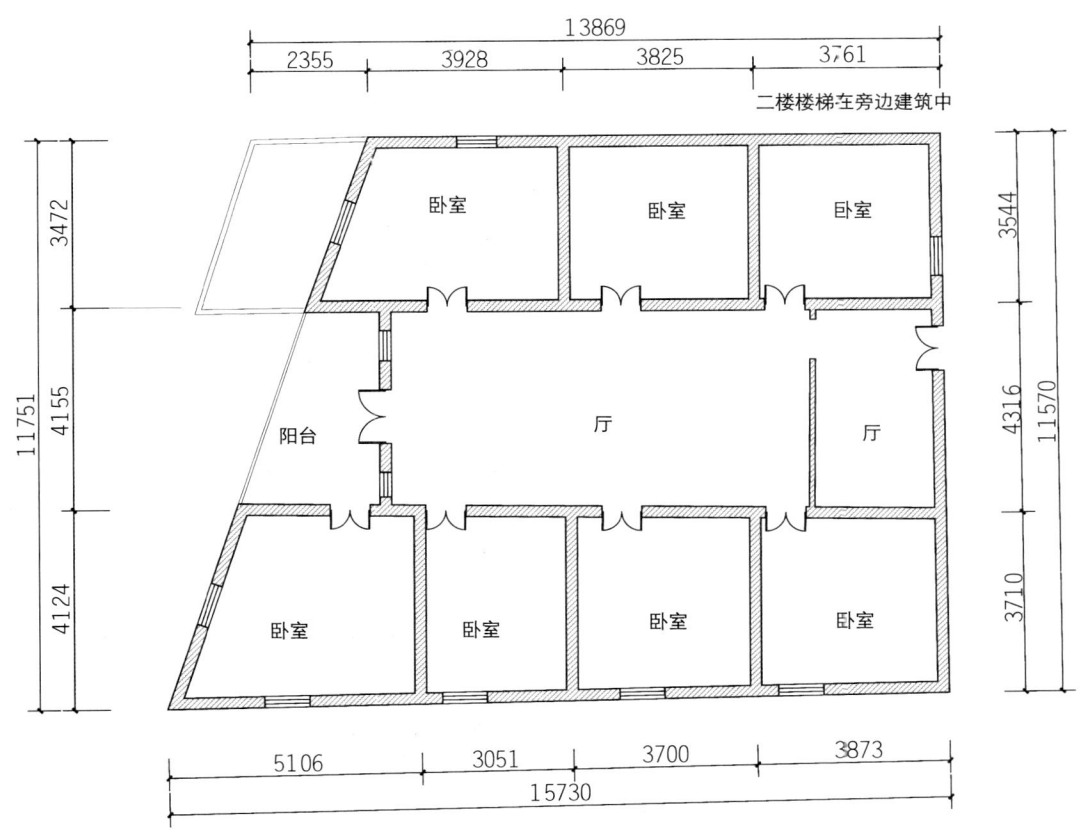

图2-3-18 二层平面图
PICTURE 2-3-18　SECOND FLOOR

图2-3-19 新第里15号外观图
PICTURE 2-3-19　APPEARENCE

图2-3-20 雕花细部
PICTURE 2-3-20　CARVING

## 2.3.2 新第里 15 号

新第里 15 号位于石湾历史风貌区北部，新第里西部，为一座一层高三开间的砖木结构祠堂，建于清末民初，整体长 9.7 米，宽 7.6 米，建筑占地面积为 73.7 平方米。建筑保存情况中等，为青砖砌筑，部分青砖遭到破坏。建筑屋顶为单檐布瓦。建筑结构样式基本保留，主入口有围墙围合成院，屋檐下的梅花灰塑保留完整。

## 2.3.2 No. 15 of Xindi Lane

Located in the north of Shiwan District and in the west of Xindi Lane, No.15 of Xindi Lane is a single floor brick-wood ancestral hall with three sections in width. The ancestral hall was built in the end of Qing Dynasty and the beginning of the Republic of China with a length of 9.7 meters and a width of 7.6 meters, covering a total area of 73.7m². In moderate condition, the hall was built with plain bricks, part of which has been destroyed. With single eave and grey tiles, the hall has maintained its basic style. There are walls surrounding the hall to form a courtyard and the plaster decorations of plums are well preserved.

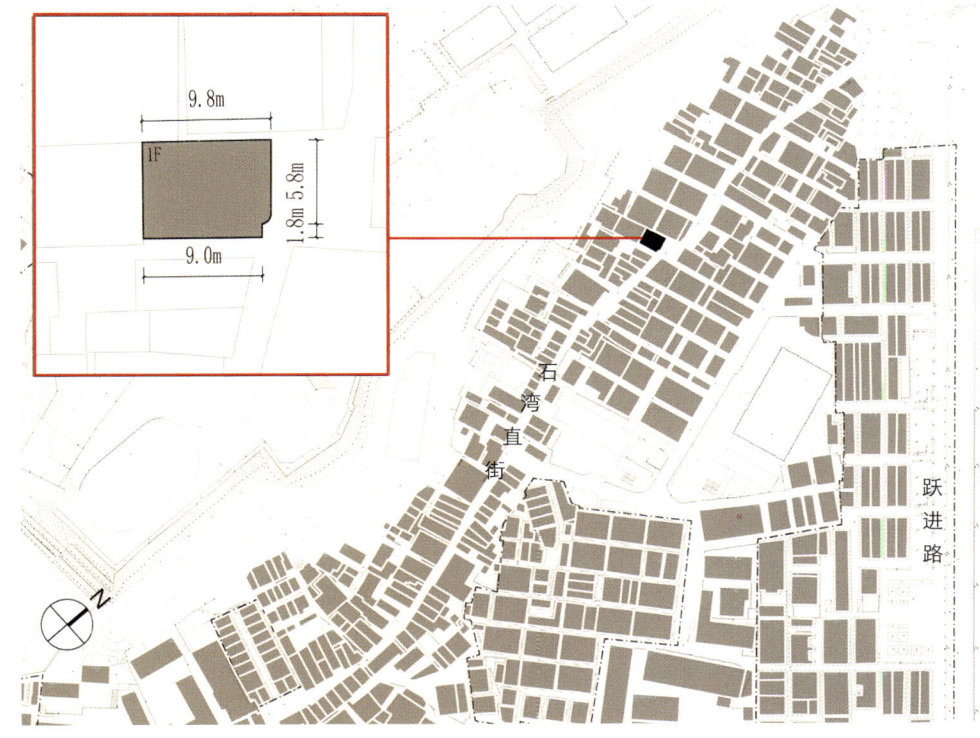

图2-3-21 区位图
PICTURE 2-3-21 LOCATION

图2-3-22 正立面放大局部
PICTURE 2-3-22 PORTION OF THE FACADE

图2-3-23 石湾真街、新第里街景
PICTURE 2-3-23 SHIWAN ZHI STREET & XINDI LANE

## 2.3.3 石湾直街、新第里

石湾直街与新第里南北相接，位于石湾历史风貌区西侧，东北、西南走向。西南接大地塘通太平路，东北与新第里相接出跃进路。两街道共长300米，宽2.5米。明代始建村落，因巷道弯曲，且多用条石（花岗岩）铺设，故称"石湾村"。后因市镇扩大，1935年经改造改称"石湾直街"。清代此街口建有石湾庙，为江门六庙之一。辛亥革命期间石湾庙曾用作商团公所。1926年石湾庙曾为当时市政府所在地。街道两旁大多数为民国时期的砖木结构建筑，样式为传统民居式，建筑保存状况良好，大多数建筑依旧有人居住。

## 2.3.3 Shiwanzhi Street and Xindi Lane

Located in the west of Shiwan District, Shiwanzhi Street and Xindi Lane are connected from south to north and point the northeast-southwest direction. With a total length of 300 meters and a width of 2.5 meters, the two streets are linked to Datangtong and Taiping Road in the southwest and Xindi Lane and Yuejin Road in the northeast. Shiwan Village was named so because there were a lot of curves in the lanes and roads when the village was built in Ming Dynasty and the roads were mostly paved by granite stones. Because of the expansion of the townships, the road was renamed Shiwanzhi Street in 1935 after renovations. There was the Shiwan Temple, one among the six temples in Jiangmen, at the entrance of the street in Qing Dynasty. It was used as a business guild during Xinhai Revolution and was the municipal government in 1926. Most of the buildings were brick-wood structures built in the Republic of China. In good shape, the buildings are traditional folk houses styles and most of them still provide accommodation.

图2-3-24 石湾直街、新第里街景
PICTURE 2-3-24 SHIWANZHI STREET & XINDI LANE

图2-3-25 石湾直街、新第里街景
PICTURE 2-3-25 SHIWANZHI STREET & XINDI LANE

图2-3-26 石湾直街、新第里街景
PICTURE 2-3-26 SHIWANZHI STREET & XINDI LANE

图2-3-27 石湾直街、新第里街景
PICTURE 2-3-27 SHIWANZHI STREET & XINDI LANE

图2-3-28 石湾直街、新第里街景
PICTURE 2-3-28 SHIWANZHI STREET & XINDI LANE

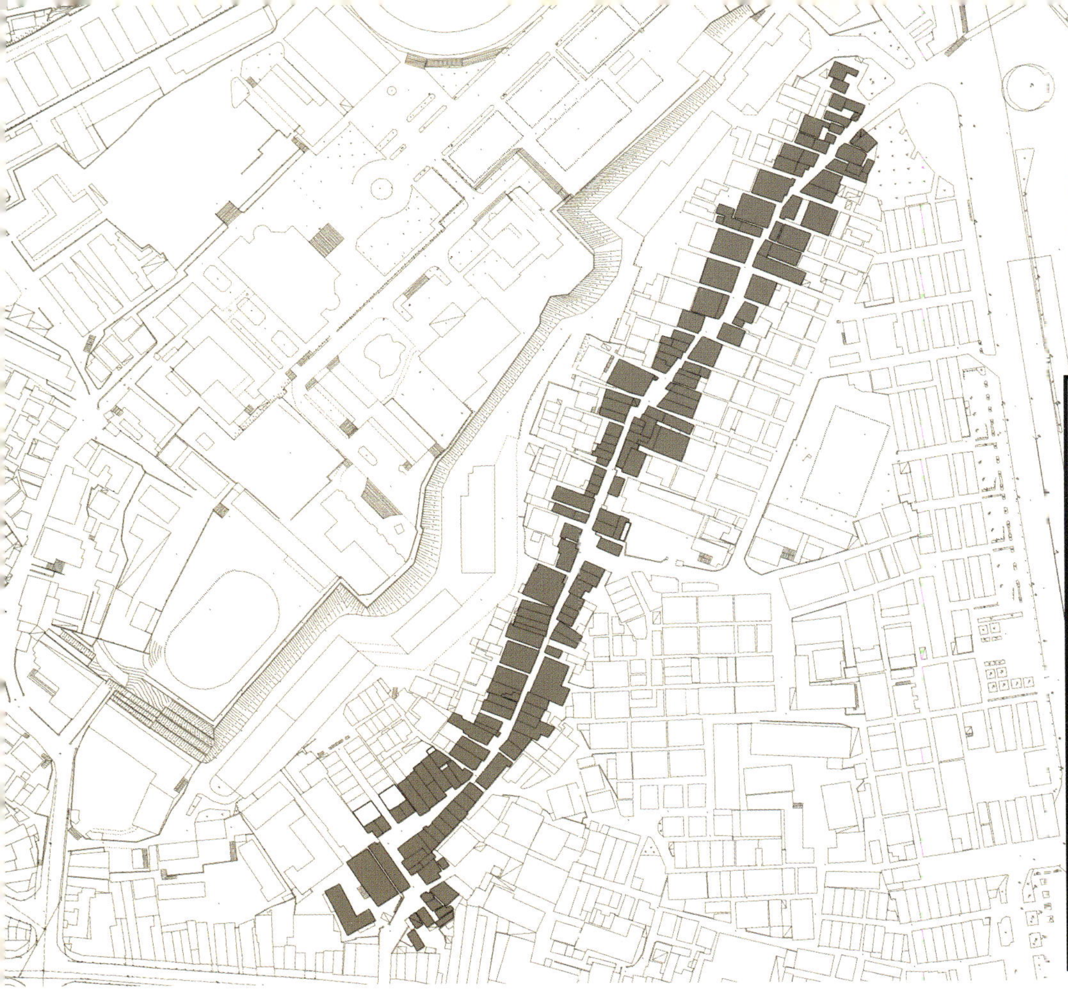

图2-3-29　区位图
PICTURE 2-3-29　LOCATION

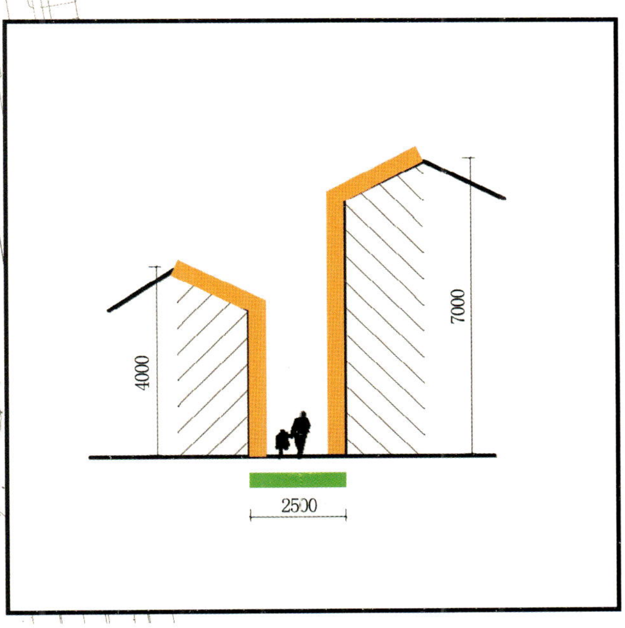

图2-3-30　街道剖面图
PICTURE 2-3-30　SECTION

图2-3-31　石湾直街、新第里街景
PICTURE 2-3-31　SHIWANZHI STREET & XINDI LANE

图2-3-32　石湾直街、新第里街景
PICTURE 2-3-32　SHIWANZHI STREET & XINDI LANE

图2-4-1 埠顶居住风貌区鸟瞰图
PICTURE 2-4-1 BIRD-VIEW

图2-4-2 埠顶居住风貌区鸟瞰图
PICTURE 2-4-2 BIRD-VIEW

# 2.4 墟顶居住风貌区
## 2.4 XUDING RESIDENTIAL DISTRICT

　　墟顶风貌区位于江门历史街区的中部，西接常安路，南抵莲平路，东至景贤中学，北至中山公园，包括墟顶、泰龙里、接龙里、京果街、卖鸡地等街坊，总面积约6.6公顷。墟顶居住风貌区的历史可追溯至明代，为江门历史街区中历史最为久远的风貌区，亦是江门城市的发源地。当时蓬江河道位于现中山公园山下，由于水运便捷，人们便在墟顶位置设置墟市，形成古代商贸和物流中心。后河道变迁，水退人进，墟顶大致保留了当时随地形布局的空间格局。现在墟顶居住风貌区内多为民国之后所建的居住建筑，街巷中点缀着些许商铺和药店，常见居民三五相约路边街头叙阔，有着浓浓的生活氛围。

Situated in the middle of the Changdi Historical Neighborhood, Xuding Residential District is connected to Chang'an Road in the west, Lianping Road in the south, Jingxian Middle School in the east and Sun Yat-sen Park in the north. It covers a total area of 6.6 hectares including Xuding Street, Tailong Lane, Jielong Lane, Nuts Street and Chicken Market. Dating back to Ming Dynasty, Xuding Residential District is one with the longest history within the Changdi Historical Neighborhood and is the cradle of Jiangmen's history. The river course of Pengjiang was then at the Mountain by the Sun Yat-sen Park. Because of the convenience of the water transportation, markets were set up in Xuding and ancient commercial and logistics center was formed. With the changes of the river course, Xuding has gathered more people and has maintained its layout based on its topography. Now the residential buildings in the district are mostly built after the Republic of China. Stores and pharmacies are distributed here and there in the streets and lanes and local people gather around by the roadside, a sketch of local life brimming with vitality.

图2-4-3 墟顶居住风貌区鸟瞰图
PICTURE 2-4-3 BIRD-VIEW

图2-4-4 墟顶居住风貌区街景
PICTURE 2-4-4 XUDING RESIDENTIAL DISTRICT

图2-4-5 区位图
PICTURE 2-4-5 LOCATION

图2-4-6 墟顶居住风貌区街景
PICTURE 2-4-6 XUDING RESIDENTIAL DISTRICT

图2-4-7 墟顶居住风貌区街景
PICTURE 2-4-7 XUDING RESIDENTIAL DISTRICT

图2-4-8 墟顶街街景
PICTURE 2-4-8  XUDING STREET

## 2.4.1 墟顶街

墟顶街位于墟顶居住风貌区中部，长约100米，地面为花岗岩条石铺地，街区风貌保存情况良好。该街区位于蓬莱山西侧，与蓬江南岸的烟墩山隔江而望，其地势犹如江门的门户。元末明初已有墟市在此设立，故称"江门墟"，又因地势较高，被称为"墟顶"。陈白沙先生（1428—1500年）曾作诗描述："十步一茅椽，非村非市廛。行人思店饭，过鸟避墟烟。日漾红云岛，鱼翻黄叶川。谁为问津者，莫上趁墟船。"可见当时的市集虽然简陋，只有几间茅屋，但每逢墟期，人们乘船由水路而来，经水埗头的石板台阶上岸交易各种日常所需的毛鸡、生猪、瓦缸等产品。江门墟形成之初，除每月初二、初五、初八约定俗成的墟期外，其余时间，各行各业的小贩也常聚在这里摆卖。

## 2.4.1 Xuding Street

Located in the middle of the Xuding Residential District, Xuding Street is about 100 meters long and in good condition with granite stone strips paving the ground. At the west of Penglai Mountain, Xuding Street faces Yandun Mountain on the south bank of the Pengjiang River, serving as a gateway to the Jiangmen River. Markets have been set up here in the end of Yuan Dynasty and the beginning of Ming Dynasty and were called Jiangmen Marketplace. Because of its high-lying position, it is called Xuding, meaning top of the market. Mr. Chen Baisha (1428-1500) once wrote a poem saying that although the marketplace was very simple and crude at the time with only a few thatched cottages, people would come by water when the market opens and get ashore via the stones steps to buy their daily necessities like chickens, hogs and pots. In the early days of the market, besides the second, fifth and eighth day on the lunar calendar as the conventional market days, Jiangmen Marketplace would be open to traders of all businesses to gather and sell their goods here.

图2-4-9 墟顶街街景
PICTURE 2-4-9　XUDING STREET

图2-4-10 墟顶街街景
PICTURE 2-4-10　XUDING STREET

图2-4-11 墟顶街街景
PICTURE 2-4-11　XUDING STREET

图2-4-12 墟顶街街景
PICTURE 2-4-12　XUDING STREET

图2-4-13 区位图
PICTURE 2-4-13 LOCATION

图2-4-14 街道剖面图
PICTURE 2-4-14 SECTION

图2-4-15 墟顶街街景
PICTURE 2-4-15 XUDING STREET

图2-4-16 墟顶街街景
PICTURE 2-4-16 XUDING STREET

173

图2-4-17 东南盛街街景
PICTURE 2-4-17 DONGNANSHENG STREET

## 2.4.2 东南盛街

东南盛街位于墟顶居住风貌区的东部,墟顶街南侧,东、西走向,东侧与新盛街相连,西侧直通兴宁路。街道长约176.8米,宽约3.4米。街道地面部分为花岗岩条石铺砌,街内里巷狭窄弯曲,道路不平。建筑物多为二、三层砖木结构旧民房。民房大多为青砖砌筑,建筑保存情况一般。大部分建筑现仍有居民居住。有的民房前有平台和台阶与街道相连,街道每隔20~30米有较大的空间,这些空间往往与民房前平台相连。街道主要通行行人和摩托车,局部宽阔的地方小型面包车也能开进来。街道两旁的民房界面多有塑料制雨篷飘出,街道以上空间也多有电线交叉穿越,连接两旁的民房。

## 2.4.2 Dongnansheng Street

Located in the east of Xuding Residential District and to the south of Xuding Street, Dongnansheng Street points east-west direction and is connected to Xinsheng Street in the east and Xingning Road in the west. The street, with a length of 176.8 meters and a width of 3.4 meters, was paved by granite stone strips. In the Street, the lanes are narrow and zigzagging with uneven pavement. Most of the buildings are two to three floored brick-wood structures. In moderate condition, most of the buildings are built with plain bricks and are still for residence. There are platforms or steps linking these buildings to the streets or to a relatively large space every 20 to 30 meters. Pedestrians and motorcycles can have access to these lanes and some broader place can allow small-sized minivan to pass. Most buildings have plastic rain shelters and electric wires up in the space intertwine and connect the houses on either side of the streets.

图2-4-18 东南盛街街景
PICTURE 2-4-18 DONGNANSHENG STREET

图2-4-19 东南盛街街景
PICTJRE 2-4-19 DONGNANSHENG STREET

图2-4-20　东南盛街街景
PICTURE 2-4-20　DONGNANSHENG STREET

图2-4-21　东南盛街街景
PICTURE 2-4-21　DONGNANSHENG STREET

图2-4-22　东南盛街街景
PICTURE 2-4-22　DONGNANSHENG STREET

图2-4-23 区位图
PICTURE 2-4-23 LOCATION

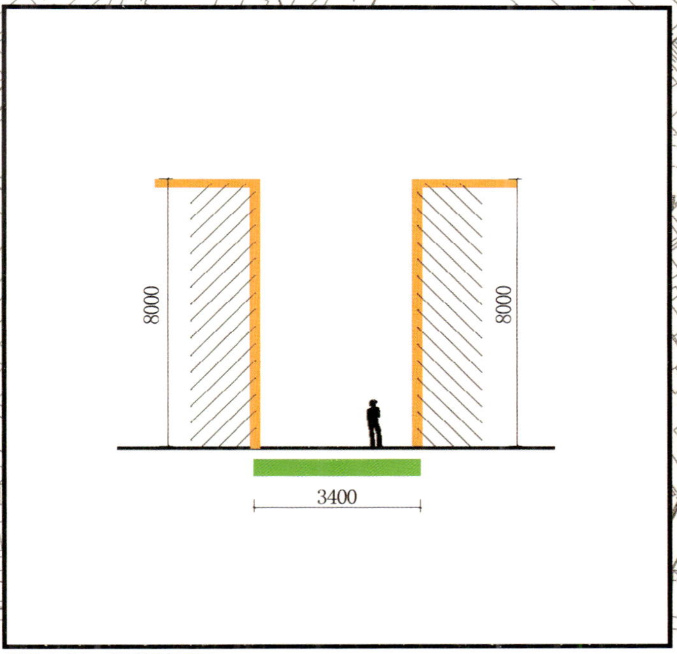

图2-4-24 街道剖面图
PICTURE 2-4-24 SECTION

图2-4-25 东南盛街街景
PICTURE 2-4-25 DONGNANSHENG STREET

图2-4-26 东南盛街街景
PICTURE 2-4-26 DONGNANSHENG STREET

图2-4-27 京果街街景
PICTURE 2-4-27 Nuts Street

### 2.4.3 京果街

京果街位于墟顶居住风貌区的东部，西接墟顶街，街道长约89米，宽3～4米，东西走向。旧江门墟时为干果（又称京果）摆卖地，故称"京果街"。后随江门城区扩展，渐变为居民住宅区。街道两旁建筑物多为二、三层砖木结构民房，建筑保存情况一般。由于地势坎坷，建筑入口很少使用趟栊门。现依旧有人居住及进行商业活动。当地著名小吃"绿豆饼"多在此销售。

### 2.4.3 Nuts Street

Located in the east of Xuding Residential District and to the west of Xuding Street, the Nuts Street points the east-west direction with a length of 89 meters and a width of three to four meters. There were often nuts sold on the streets during the market days and so the street was named after the trade. With the expansion of the downtown, the street was turned into a residential area. Most of the buildings along the street are two or three-floored brick-wood houses in moderate condition. Because of the rugged terrain, bar sliding doors were seldom used. Nowadays, the buildings are still used for residential and commercial purposes and the famous local specialty green bean paste pancake can be bought here.

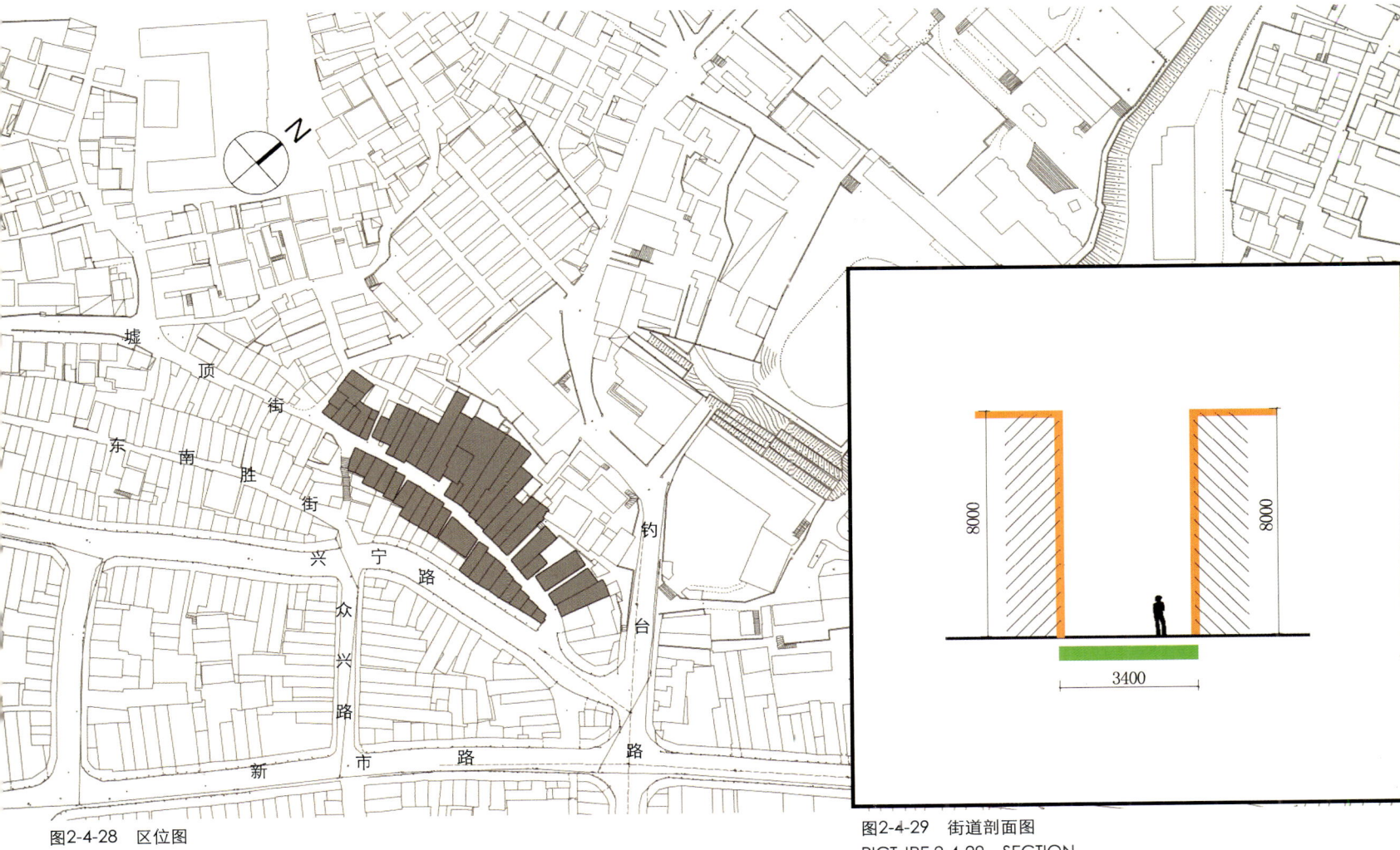

图2-4-28 区位图
PICTURE 2-4-28 LOCATION

图2-4-29 街道剖面图
PICTURE 2-4-29 SECTION

图2-4-30 新盛街街景
PICTURE 2-4-30 XINSHENG STREET

## 2.4.4 新盛街

新盛街位于墟顶居住风貌区的西部,东西走向,俗称"旧萝街"。街道长150米,宽2～4米。两旁建筑物多为民国时期所建二、三层砖木结构楼房,建筑保存情况一般。1935年经改造后,新盛街街内商业兴盛,专营"白事"之物。后取新兴繁盛之意,改名"新盛街"。旧时街内有正吉林斋堂、崇善堂、基督教堂等宗教活动场所,设棺材、故衣、家具、打铁、磨坊、制鞋等店铺,还有龙岗小学。1939年日寇入侵江门时曾在此设监狱一所,留下血泪斑斑。1950年后商业重心他移,此地逐渐变成居民住宅区。

## 2.4.4 Xinsheng Street

Located in the west of Xuding Residential District, Xinsheng Street points the east-west direction and was often called Jiuluo Street. With a total length of 150 meters, it is two to four meters wide. Most of the buildings are two to three floored brick-wood structures in moderate condition. This road mainly engaged in funeral affairs related businesses after renovations in 1935. It was named Xinsheng Street for being burgeoning and prosperous. There were religious buildings including Zhengjilin Buddhist Hall, Chongshan Buddhist Hall and a Christian church, and stores engaging in businesses like coffins, grave clothes, furniture, blacksmith, mill, shoemaking, etc., and there was also the Longgang Primary School. It further added a miserable stroke to the history when the Japanese army set up a prison here upon their aggression into Jiangmen in 1939. After 1950, its commercial activities have transferred to other places and the street is mainly for residence now.

图2-4-31 区位图
PICTURE 2-4-31 LOCATION

图2-4-32 街道剖面图
PICTURE 2-4-32 SECTION

图2-4-33　永安按当铺周边街景
PICTURE 2-4-33　THE SURROUNDINGS

## 2.4.5 永安按当铺

永安按当铺，又称"永安按"，建筑坐西向东，位于墟顶居住风貌区南边，建于民国时期，为江门市级文物保护单位。建筑东西长8.9米，南北宽8.1米，建筑占地面积为72平方米。建筑分为四层，高约15米。用青砖、花岗岩和红砂岩砌筑，底层墙体有半米之厚，单檐布瓦顶，上下四层均有防御性射击孔5个，屋内还有一口直径为0.58米的水井。永安按当铺旧址为旧时当铺及储藏当物的库房，旧时称为"石屎楼"，兼具实用和防御功能，十分坚固，对于研究江门商业和经济发展等具有重要价值。

## 2.4.5 Yong'an Pawnshop

Located in the south of Xuding Residential District, Yong'an Pawnshop sits against the west and faces the east. Built in the Republic of China, it is now designated as a Municipal Cultural Preservation Site with a length of 8.9 meters and a width of 8.1 meters, covering a total area of 72 m². It has four floors with a total height of 15 meters. The building was built with plain bricks, granite stones and red sandstones with the walls thick as half meters in the lower floors. It has single eave and grey tiles and 5 defensive shooting holes in each floor. There is a well with a diameter of 0.58 meters in the house. The former site of Yong'an Pawnshop was used as warehouse to store the pawns, which was called Shishi Tower. With combined functions of pawnshop and defensive use, the building stands firm and is of great value for the study of the commercial and economic development in Jiangmen.

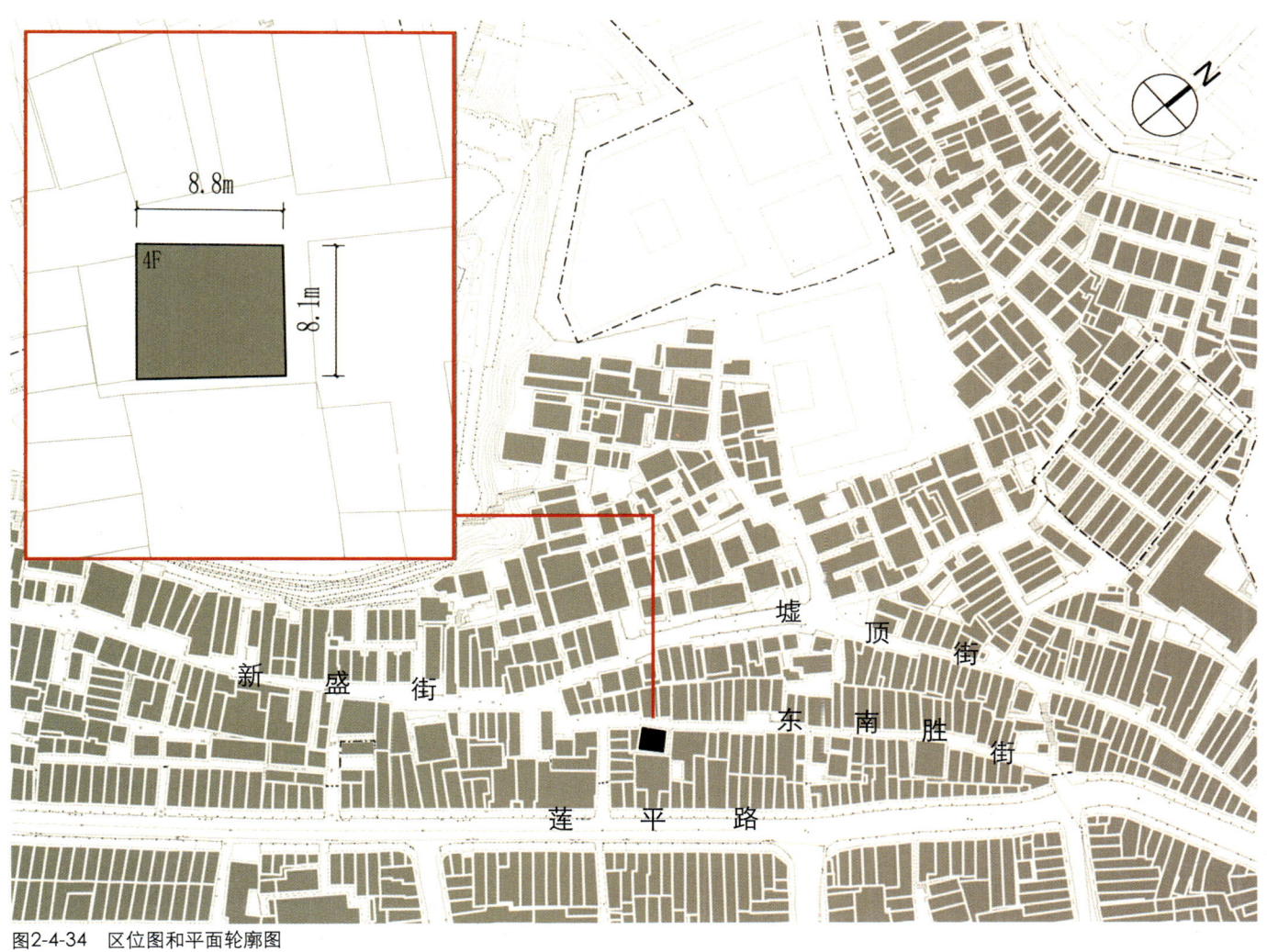

图2-4-34 区位图和平面轮廓图
PICTURE 2-4-34 LOCATION AND OUTLINE

图2-4-35 三十三级台阶
PICTURE 2-4-35 THIRTY-THREE Stone Steps

## 2.4.6 三十三级台阶

三十三级台阶位于墟顶街往兴宁路走的方向上，又称"水埠头"，为从前墟顶街对外交流的重要码头，趁墟者和货物就是由此上落。水埠头脚下原有石碑一方，高约1米，上面刻有"江门"二字，作为地方标志，现该石已不知去向。从前趁墟的人都是划艇或是搭乘墟船由水路而来，通过这里上岸做买卖。石级附近曾经产生过一个对江门有很大影响力的刀具品牌"三桁瓦"。现台阶结构保存完整，两边为沿地势抬高的民居，建筑保存情况一般。

## 2.4.6 Thirty-three Stone Steps

Thirty-three Stone Steps, also called Shuiputou, is located on the road from Xuding Street to Xingning Road. It was an important pier for Xuding Street to conduct external exchanges. Traders and goods will get ashore here. There was a stone tablet which is about one meter tall at the pier carved with Jiangmen as a local mark. At that time, all the traders came by water and had to climb the steps to get ashore and do business. There was a very famous kitchen knife brand called Sanhengwa, which exerted great influence on Jiangmen. The steps are well preserved and the elevated houses on both sides are in moderate condition.

图2-4-36 区位图
PICTURE 2-4-36 LOCATION

图2-4-37 台阶局部
PICTURE 2-4-37 THE STEPS

# 3 保护与复兴
Protection and Regeneration

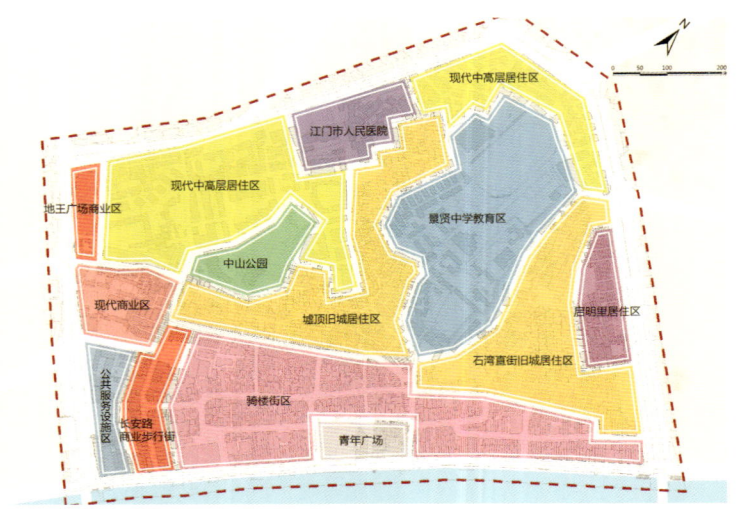

图3-1-1 现状功能分区
PICTURE 3-1-1 EXISTING FUNCTION DISTRIBUTION

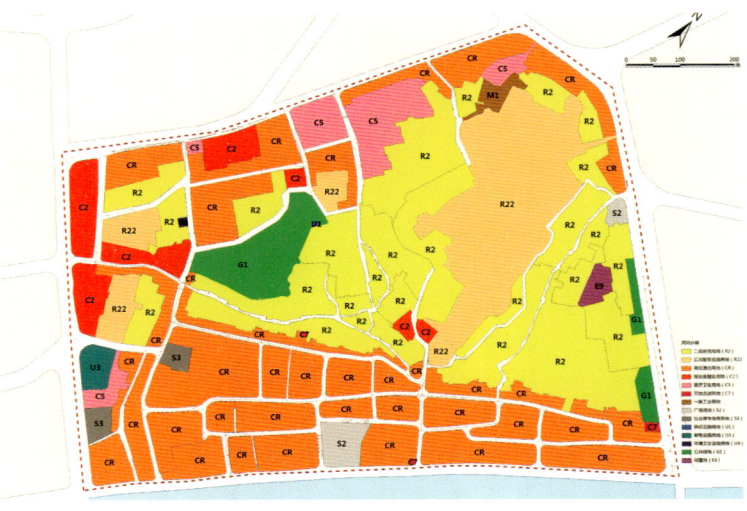

图3-1-2 现状土地性质
PICTURE 3-1-2 EXISTING LAND USE

图3-1-3 街区设计示意图
PICTURE 3-1-3 RENDERING OF BLOCK DESIGN

# 3.1 保护与复兴实施策略
## 3.1 STRATEGY FOR PRESERVATION AND RESTORATION

作为江门城市发展的起源地，历史街区的历史价值不仅在于广泛分布的文物建筑和历史建筑，更重要的是历史街区内的整体格局经历了长时间的历史变迁，显现出历史发展脉络的独特性和显著性，其所承载的社区生活和民俗文化也同样具有深厚的历史文化内涵。如今，历史街区的发展面临着内部与外部的双重挑战，长堤历史街区的保护和复兴工作任重而道远。

### 3.1.1 保护与复兴目标定位

江门长堤历史街区作为江门市重要的生态人文区域和历史文化遗产，通过对以历史街区为核心的历史文化遗产及其环境进行有效保护与永续利用，有利于推动江门市的文化建设和社会综合发展。

目标定位：

将历史街区打造成为江门发源地历史文化展示区、五邑特色文化旅游街区、五邑传统与特色商业街区、浓郁侨乡风情的传统居住区、富有活力的滨水休闲街区。

江门发源地历史文化展示区：强调街区在江门发展历史中的标志性和唯一性，深度挖掘并重点保护街区内历史文化资源，将街区塑造成江门历史文化展示区。

五邑特色文化旅游街区：以五邑传统墟市和特色商贸、侨乡特色文化为亮点，积极推动和发展文化旅游经济，开展华侨寻根游和特色文化游，以旅游的繁荣带动历史街区的发展和兴旺，使其成为五邑地区乃至全省的特色文化旅游街区。

五邑传统与特色商业街区：调整商业结构，升级和优化现有商业形态，扩大服务和辐射范围，打造为以服务江门市为主的骑楼特色商业中心；引进代表地方传统与特色的商业，通过同类集聚形成专业特色街；提升为社区服务的配套商业，满足市民日渐增长的生活需要。

浓郁侨乡风情的传统居住区：保留特色华侨居住建筑，对建筑进行修缮，重现原始风貌；改善居民生

As the birthplace of the Jiangmen City, the value of historical neighborhood does not only lie in the listed and historical buildings. The overall layout has gone through the change of time and represents the uniqueness of historical development. The community life and folklores are of historical significance. Currently the development of the historical neighborhood is facing challenges, both internally and externally. There is a daunting task for the preservation and restoration of Changdi Historical Neighborhood.

### 3.1.1 Preservation and Restoration Positioning

The Changdi Historical Neighborhood of Jiangmen City is an important area for eco-environment, cultural development and the preservation of cultural and historical heritage. The effective protection and sustainable use of the historical and cultural heritage (the core area is the Changdi Historical Neighborhood) will benefit the overall cultural and social development of Jiangmen.

Positioning:

The Historical Neighborhood will become a display area for history and culture showing the origin of Jiangmen. It will also boast Wuyi Special Tourism Zone, Wuyi Traditional and Commercial Zone, Residential Area with Overseas Chinese Characteristics and a vibrant waterfront recreation zone.

The display area showing the birthplace of Jiangmen will highlight the iconic and unique position of the neighborhood. The rich historical and cultural resources will be further tapped so that it can be a cultural presentation.

Wuyi Special Tourism Zone: It will feature Wuyi traditional market, special businesses and culture that is unique to the hometown of Overseas Chinese. Cultural tourism will be boosted with tourism programs of Overseas Chinese tracing their roots. The whole neighborhood will be boosted by tourism and become a special cultural tourism zone in Wuyi or even the entire province.

Wuyi Traditional and Commercial Zone: The business structure and forms will be upgraded and optimized. The service will be expanded and the Qilou commercial center will be built. Businesses representing local traditions and character will be brought in to create a special commercial street. The supporting businesses for the community will be updated to meet the people's growing needs.

Residential District with Overseas Chinese Characteristics: The special residential buildings for Overseas Chinese

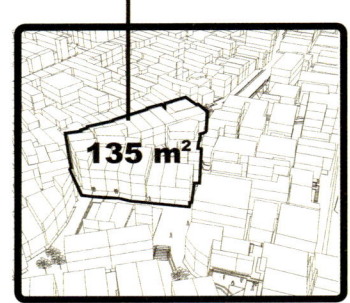
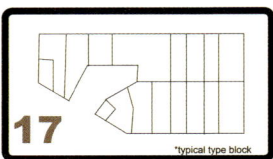

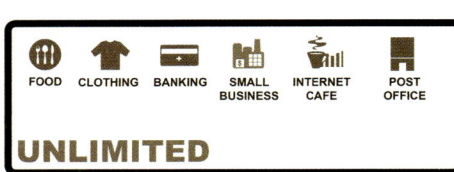

**AVERAGE SIZE BLOCK**
街区尺度接近平均值

**PARCELS OF LAND**
产权数量

**BUILDINGS**
房屋数量

**POTENTIAL GROUND-FLOOR SERVICES**
首层空间潜在服务功能

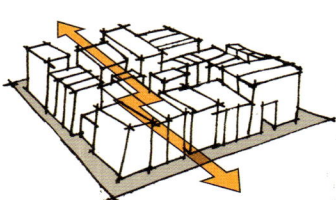
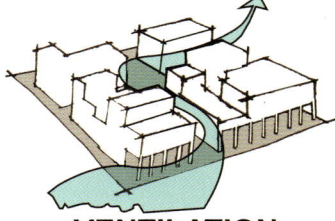
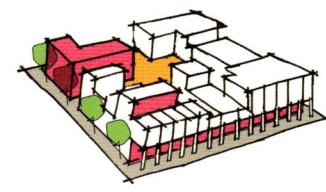

**FIRE SAFETY**
消防疏散

access dangerous areas
快速疏散路径

**VENTILATION**
群体通风

channel winds to improve health and sanitation
通过风道提升卫生与健康程度

**ACTIVATE**
活力

infill and repurposing vacant & underutilized spaces
恢复闲置空间原有功能或赋予新功能

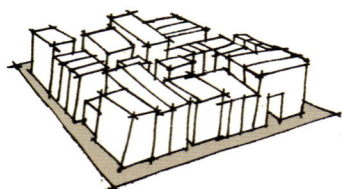
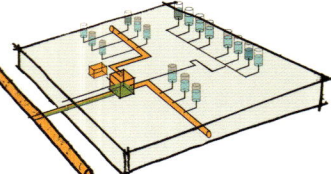
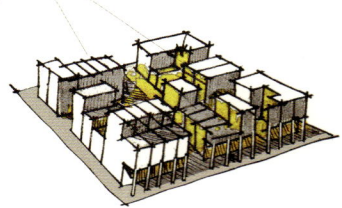
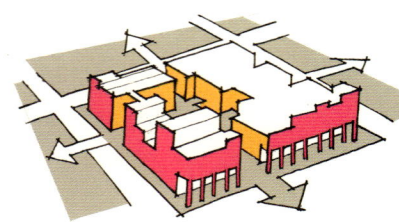

**EXISTING**
现状

**INFRASTRUCTURE**
基础设施

sewer & storm water 排污与排水设施
electric transformers 电力转换设施
technology services 技术维修服务

**SHADE & LIGHT**
采光与遮阳

shelter from summer heat
夏日遮阳设施

public lighting (natural/electric)

**CONNECT**
联系

connect locally inside
提供对内服务
serve regionally outside
对外提供服务

图3-1-4 街区修复研究
PICTURE 3-1-4 RENOVATION OF THE BLOCKS

活环境，提高居民生活质量，重现居民传统生活气息和生活习俗，打造为市级侨乡传统居住区的示范点。

富有活力的滨水休闲街区：以堤中路和青年广场为中心，发展滨水主题的休闲商业，改善滨水的休闲环境，引入多样化的休闲和节庆活动，打造江门市最富活力的滨水休闲区。

### 3.1.2 整体保护、渐进式的街区修复策略

在江门历史街区的保护中，必须坚持整体保护和渐进式更新相结合，进行全面系统的规划，这是实施历史街区保护与更新的着力点。

江门历史街区的整体性保护不仅涉及历史风貌建筑物质空间环境的问题，还涉及非物质文化遗产的保护与传承、旧城区生活环境的改善与提升以及社会网络结构的维持和培育等问题。在江门历史街区的保护中，一切执行手段必须符合联合国教科文组织和中华人民共和国的相关法令、标准、宣言和国际公约，这是保护工作开展的前提条件。整体性保护，其实也是保护应遵循的重要原则之一。坚持整体保护，维护了江门历史街区文化景观的多样性，如地理环境特征、地域特征、文化特征、功能属性等，使得历史街区承载的丰富文化得以完善地传承发展。

历史街区内居住人口多，权属复杂，大规模的改造无法做到公正公平，同时大规模改造方式也必然会破坏城市原有的肌理，因此可采取渐进式更新的改造策略。每一阶段的建设周期短，易于筹措资金，易于见效，容易被居民接受，也有利于从改造中总结经验教训并适时调整。江门历史街区应遵循"小规模、渐进式、多样化、微循环"的保护整治方式。通过对历史街区内基础设施和风貌的改造提升，避免大规模改造与搬迁，让街区重现往日的生机与活力。

### 3.1.3 街区与地域文化复兴

每个地域都有各自的历史，它存留在建筑与城市当中，融汇于每个人的心理体验和生活感受中。然而，在现代化大生产的冲击下，人们渴望打破地域的界限，加入到更大范围的经济交往中去。于是，大批廉价、灰色、简单的低廉建筑拔地而起，改变了传统街区附近的城市景观。地域文化也逐渐地被现代快餐文化所取代。然而，在现代文明带来巨大物质和精神财富的同时，人类却迷失在单调平庸的钢筋混凝土森林里。历史街区作为凝聚了历史记忆的、展现了历史风貌的城市独特场所，应作为城市发展

will be kept and restored to display its original shape. The living conditions and quality need to be improved and the original lifestyle will be brought back. Efforts shall be made to build a demonstration zone.

Vibrant Waterfront Recreation Zone: The center of the zone will be Dizhong Road and Youth Square. The waterfront leisure business will be developed along with the improvement of the environment. A variety of recreational activities and festivals will be introduced to create the most dynamic waterfront recreation area in Jiangmen.

### 3.1.2 Renovation for Phased Renewal and Overall Protection

The preservation projects need to be carried out in a phased manner and stick to the overall protection plan. A comprehensive planning is needed for the preservation and renewal of the historical neighborhood.

The overall protection plan is not only related to physical environment like the historical building, but also the protection and inheritance of intangible cultural heritage, the improvement of the living environment of the old town and the maintenance and cultivation of social network. In the implementation, every action must comply with UNESCO and the People's Republic of China's laws, standards, declarations and international conventions, which is a prerequisite for protection. The integrity protection is also essential to keep the cultural landscape diversity, such as geographical characteristics, local features, cultural characteristics and functions. In this way the folk culture will be able to continue.

The historical neighborhood has big population and complex ownership. Large-scale transformations cannot be fair and equitable and will destroy the original structure. Therefore small steps need to be taken in the transformation. Each project should have short cycle, be easy to raise funding and effective. The residents are more likely to accept small projects. In addition, lessons can be learned from small projects and adjustments can be made. So the adjustments should be small-scale, gradually carried out and diverse. Large-scale renovation and relocation needs to be avoided. The transformation and upgrading of the infrastructure in the historical neighborhood will bring back the vitality of the past.

### 3.1.3 Blocks and Local Culture Renaissance

Each region has its own history embedded in the buildings, the city and in each person's psychological and life experience. However, under the impact of modern mass production, people are eager to break the geographical boundaries and get involved in a wider range of economic exchanges. Thus, a large number of cheap, grey, simple new buildings came up and changed the traditional neighborhoods. And the regional culture is gradually replaced by the modern fast-food culture. However,

**block types**
街区类型

**CONCEPTUAL STRATEGIES:** 概念策略

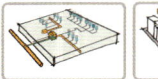 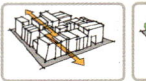 

INFRASTRUCTURE 基础设施 | FIRE SAFETY 消防疏散 | ACTIVATE 活力 | CONNECT 联系

**TYPICAL STREET** 典型街区

**COMB BRUSH PATTERN** 梳型道路规划

**BLOCK TYPE A**

**CONCEPTUAL STRATEGIES:** 概念策略

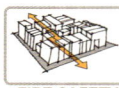 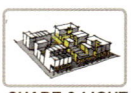  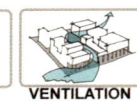

FIRE SAFETY 消防疏散 | SHADE & LIGHT 采光与遮阳 | ACTIVATE 活力 | VENTILATION 群体通风

**TYPICAL STREET** 典型街区

**LINEAR PATTERN** 直线形路径

**BLOCK TYPE B**

**CONCEPTUAL STRATEGIES:** 概念策略

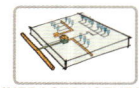  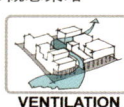

INFRASTRUCTURE 基础设施 | FIRE SAFETY 消防疏散 | VENTILATION 群体通风

**TYPICAL STREET** 典型街区

**SQUARE PATTERN** 广场型路径

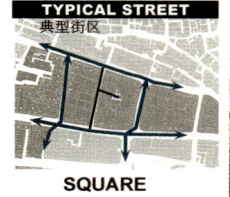   

**BLOCK TYPE C**

**CONCEPTUAL STRATEGIES:** 概念策略

 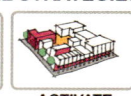 

FIRE SAFETY 消防疏散 | ACTIVATE 活力 | CONNECT 联系

**TYPICAL STREET** 典型街区

**IRREGULAR PATTERN** 非正常路径

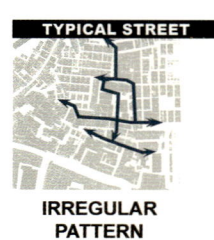    

**BLOCK TYPE D**

图3-1-5 街区修复研究
PICTURE 3-1-5 RENOVATION OF THE BLOCKS

图3-1-6：水街市场
PICTURE 3-1-6　SHUIJIE FARMERS MARKET

图3-1-7：水街市场
PICTURE 3-1-7　SHUIJIE FARMERS MARKET

图3-1-8　钓台故居
PICTURE 3-1-8　DIAOTAI FORMAL RESIDENCE

图3-1-9 基督教江门堂
PICTURE 3-1-9  CHRITIAN CHURCH OF JIANGMEN

图3-1-10 钓台故居
PICTURE 3-1-10  DIAOTAI FORMAL RESIDENCE

图3-1-11 莲塘南当铺
PICTURE 3-1-11  LIANTANGNAN PAWNSHOP

进程中受到保护的对象。经历了数百年的社会变迁，江门仍然保持着悠久而独特的历史文化传统，历史街区内有着集纳江门人智慧精华的重要历史积淀。地域文化是彰显历史街区独特性特征的载体。因此，地域文化复兴是历史街区保护与更新的核心。

#### 3.1.3.1 文化场所网络与可达性

江门历史悠久，人才辈出，历史名人有明末著名理学家陈白沙、民主革命先驱陈少白、近代中国第一个飞行家冯如、著名侨领司徒美堂、近代史上的风云人物梁启超等。著名的思想家、教育家、科学家，对古代和近代中国的发展有着深远的意义。江门是一个侨乡，明楼、华侨园林、骑楼商业街、近代西洋建筑和青砖华侨大屋，展示出浓郁的传统建筑地域特色。将江门沿江传统街区的复兴，与江门名人故居、华侨文化等其它文化区统筹考虑，加强文化区域间文化场所的可达性，通过水路、绿道、公共汽车交通、轻轨，加强市中心区与滨水区的连接，完善步行网络，使文化场所连接起来，促进城市旅游发展。

#### 3.1.3.2 丰富多样的混合功能

强调该街区在江门发展历史中的标志性和独一性，深度挖掘并重点打造街区内历史文化资源，将街区塑造成江门历史文化展示区。而创造有活力的城市历史文化区，多样性的功能和活动在空间和时间上的集中混合至关重要。简·雅各布强调将绝大多数的城市功能适当合理地包容在城市的街区内，以保证在街区的空间中产生能获得极富活力的建成环境质量的"丰富的多样性"。混合功能开发，不仅为城市市民提供消费的便利，产生丰富的城市生活，还可以更有效地利用空间与其它各种资源，是实现城市街区可持续发展的重要途径。

混合功能开发，应强调布局小规模和多样化的文化商业，如主题墟市、民俗工艺、创意集市、土特产街、古玩字画、传统手工作坊、特色餐饮、休闲商业、家庭旅馆等，规划布局华侨会馆、历史博览等文化地标类功能，为市民提供多元化的公共活动空间。同时以文化带动当地居住生活的复兴，在保持原有居住功能的基础上，改善其居住环境，恢复原有居住功能。

#### 3.1.3.3 文化设施、文化产业、文化活动

通过建设"文化旗舰项目"改善旧城形象，提高知名度，是城市复兴的重要方法之一。建议在石湾直街入口，结合主题集市广场，将其改造成石湾直

when people enjoy the enormous material and spiritual wealth brought by modern civilization, they are lost in the monotonous and mediocre concrete forests. The historical neighborhoods are a combination of historical memory and the city's unique historic character and should be protected during urban development. After several centuries of social change, Jiangmen still retains its long and unique historical and cultural traditions. The historical neighborhood keeps the wisdom of local people as well as important historical heritage. Thus the regional cultural renaissance is the core of the protection and renewal of the region.

#### 3.1.3.1 Cultural Places and Accessibility

Jiangmen has a long history with numerous talented people. The historical figures include famous Confucian scholar Chen Baisha in Ming Dynasty, democratic revolutionary pioneer Chen Shao-Bai, the first aviator Feng Ru in modern China, the famous overseas Chinese Situ Meitang and Liang Qichao, a renowned man in China's modern history. Those famous thinkers, educators and scientists have far-reaching impact on ancient and modern China. Jiangmen is city for the Overseas Chinese, the Ming House, Overseas Chinese Garden, Qilou Commercial Street, modern Western architecture and brick houses, all demonstrating strong local traditional architecture and geographical characteristics. The revival of the historical neighborhood needs to consider the old houses of celebrities and the overseas Chinese culture. The connectivity among the cultural places needs to be enhanced with waterways, greenways, bus transportation and light rail. The city center needs to be connected to the waterfront area and the pedestrian network needs to be improved. The connectivity for cultural sites will promote urban tourism development.

#### 3.1.3.2 Multiple Functions

The historical neighborhood is highly symbolic and unique in the history of Jiangmen. The historical resources need to be tapped and the neighborhood needs to become a history and culture display area. The mix of multiple functions is quite important for creating a vibrant historical neighborhood. Jane Jacobs once stressed that streets should encompass most of the city functions so that the space could be vibrant, diverse and good in quality. The development of multiple functions do not only make life easier for the residents and produce dynamic city life, but also make full use of other resources such as space. This is quite important for the sustainable development of streets.

The layout in the neighborhood emphasizes small-scale and diverse cultural businesses such as bazaars, folk crafts, creative market, special product street, antiques and paintings, traditional hand workshops, catering, leisure, hotels and guest houses. Cultural landmarks such as Overseas Chinese Hall and History Museum should be included to provide diverse public space. The cultural programs can also revitalize the life of local people, improve their living conditions and keep the residential functions.

图3-1-12 南芬里
PICTURE 3-1-12 NANFEN LANE

图3-1-13 水街农贸市场
PICTURE 3-1-13 SHUIJIE FARMAERS MARKET

图3-1-14 水街农贸市场
PICTURE 3-1-14 SHUIJIE FARMAERS MARKET

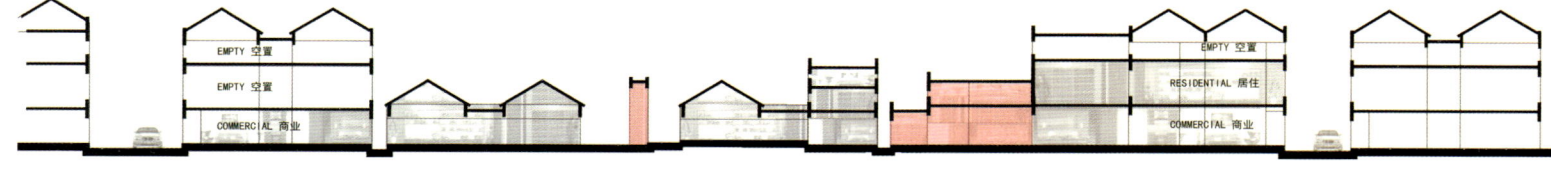

**SECTION OF ORIGINAL BLOCK**
改造前街区剖面

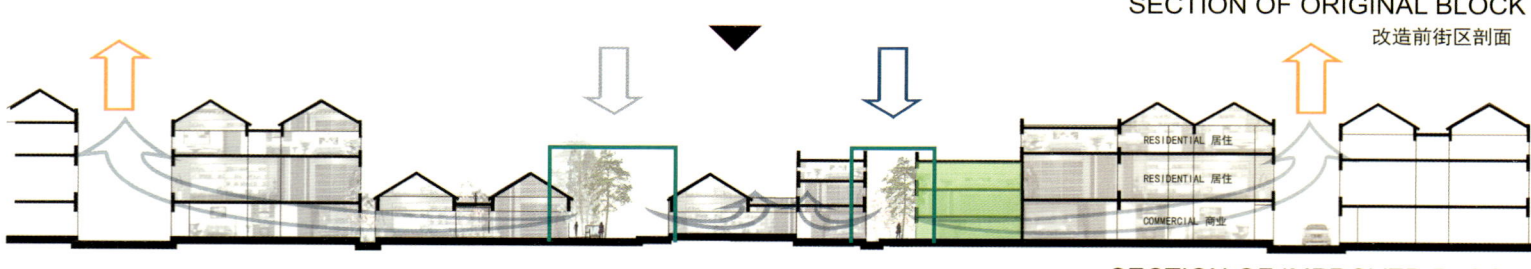

**SECTION OF IMPROVED BLOCK**
改造后街区剖面

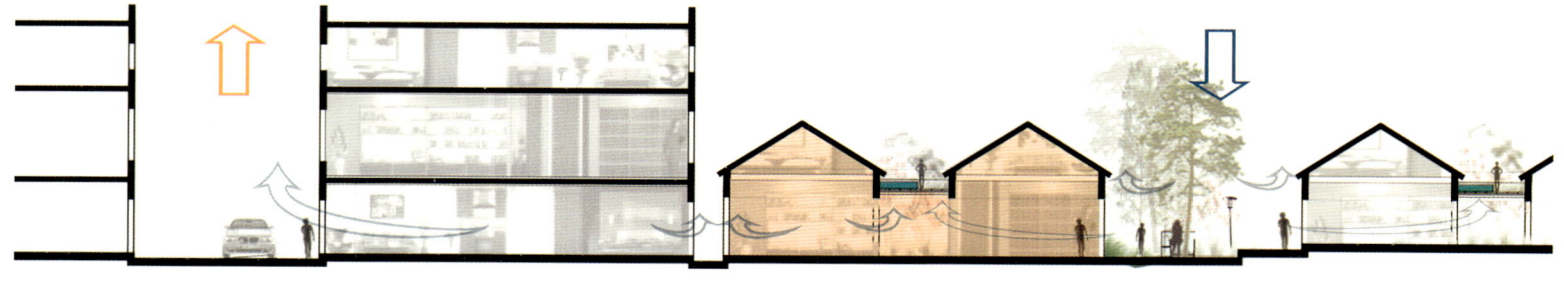

**SECTION OF COURYARD**
庭院及公共空间剖面

图3-1-15 街区剖面设计示意图
PICTURE3-1-15 BLOCK DESIGN

街历史和民俗博物馆区，作为展示江门起源的基地，通过多样的方式展现华侨文化。通过华侨会馆的入驻，加强与海外华侨的联系，开展多种旅游、夏令营、商贸、投资等交流活动；通过举办文化活动，提升文化资源对城市的影响；通过市场引导，积极吸引社会资金，使文化产业与创意产业成为振兴城市经济的支柱产业。将文化产业作为复苏经济与社会的一种手段引入到城市更新地区，这对旧区重新振兴、城市特色保护与发扬以及历史文脉延续都有重要意义。

充分利用当地民俗资源，结合民俗节庆、文化活动的开展，将日常活动、定期的活动与大型活动相结合，激发居民的自豪感和自信心，使当地居民受惠，使江门得益。

### 3.1.4 生态技术的应用

历史街区的保护与复兴，不仅要注重对街区的历史环境、社会生活环境的研究，还要注重街区生态环境的研究。

滨水地区开展可持续规划设计方法和生态技术的探讨，以最大化地展示和提供河岸空间的最佳享受为目标，在对历史和现状水系进行考察分析的基础上，着重研究河岸两边的滨水空间的城市设计策略，以实现"改善水质量、提高沿岸水岸线视觉通达性及实际可达性、开展保护环境教育"等滨水城市生态发展目标。

街区内部的保护更新，注重江门地方气候特点，见缝插绿，修复街巷等公共开放空间，用被动式生态技术策略改善居住环境。

### 3.1.5 保护与复兴的多方探索

历史街区的保护和复兴需要全社会的关注，需要以多种方式和途径全面探索保护与更新的策略与方法。以城市设计工作坊的方式搭建长堤历史街区保护与更新规划设计的交流平台，国际知名的城市设计及景观设计学者、美国加州大学伯克利校区的Peter Bosselmann教授携其指导的研究生团队赴华南理工大学建筑学院开展江门历史街区国际联合城市设计工作坊活动，与华工师生一起，现场考察调研，与居民及地方管理部门访谈，就历史街区的保护更新问题开展相关的学术交流活动。分为6组不同专业背景的中外混合团队，在借鉴国际历史街区复兴经验的基础上，结合江门市和历史街区的实际条件，

#### 3.1.3.3 Cultural Facilities, Industries and Activities

The cultural flagship projects are important ways to improve the old town's image and gain reputation in urban revitalization. The Shiwanzhi Street History and Folklore Museum can be built at the entrance of the street along with the market square. As the birthplace of Jiangmen, the neighborhood should showcase the overseas Chinese culture through a variety of ways, such as travel, summer camps, trade and investment and other exchanges. The cultural events will enhance the impact of cultural resources and the guidance will attract social funds so that the cultural industries and creative industries will become pillar industries in the revitalization of the urban economy. The cultural industries are important for economic and social recovery and urban renewal, the protection of local characteristics and the continuity of historical context.

The local folklore resources need to be tapped. The folk festivals, cultural activities, daily and regular events need to be hosted to boost the residents' sense of pride and confidence and the city will benefit from such programs.

### 3.1.4 Application of Eco-technology

The protection and revitalization of historical neighborhood requires not only the study into its history and social life but also research into its eco-environment.

A study of sustainable planning and design method and eco-technology in the water-front area is conducted with the aim to maximize the demonstration and enjoyment of the riverbank space. On the basis of an investigation into the historical and current water systems, the study focuses on the urban design strategy of the riverbank space along the both banks of the river. It helps to attain the eco-development goal of improving the water quality, enhance the visual effect and accessibility of the waterfront area and carrying out education on environmental protection.

The protection and regeneration inside the neighborhood emphasize on the climate conditions of Jiangmen, create green space wherever possible and restore alleys, streets and other public open space. The living environment is enhanced through a passive strategy of eco-technology.

### 3.1.5 Efforts from Multiple Stakeholders

The protection and rehabilitation of historical neighborhoods need the attention of the whole society and a variety of ways to fully explore strategies and methods of conservation and renewal. An Urban Design Workshop was established for the preservation and renewal. The team was led by internationally renowned urban design and landscape design scholar, Professor Peter Bosselmann from the University of California, Berkeley and his research team. The workshop also had students from School of Architecture, South China University of Technology. They conducted site visits and investigations, interviewed the residents and local authorities and had academic exchanges on the protection and renewal of the historical neighborhood. The team was divided into

## TRADITIONAL WAY 传统雨水，黑水和灰水系统

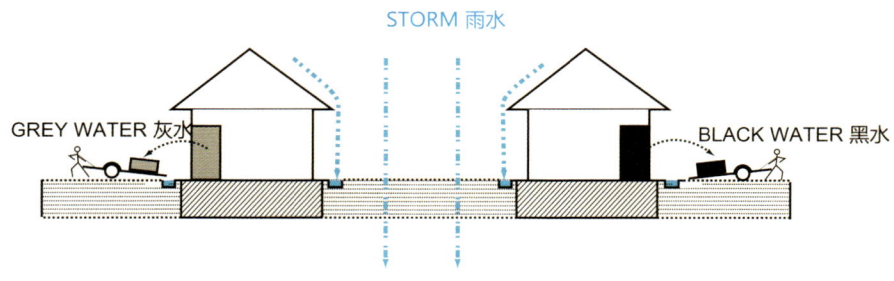

In traditional way, the storm drainage system function depend on the gradient of the street surface and it can content the need of the old street if each part contact well.
传统的途径：排水系统的运作是依赖于街道表面的坡度。如果每个区域联系紧密，这种方式可以满足历史街区的排水需要。

In traditional way, light rain could infiltrate directly into soil underground, rainstorm could be drained by open channels and underdrain. The grey water from the kitchen and the black water will be collected by manual tools In this way, people created a mode to collect blue water, grey water and black water separately and this way is 'low-technic'and environmentally friendly.
对于传统的黑水和灰水系统，小雨可以直接渗流进入土层，大雨可以通过明渠和暗沟排走，厨房和洗浴的灰水和厕所的黑水将采用人工收集处理。通过这种途径，当时的人们成功地将雨水、灰水和黑水分类收集处理，并且低技术、环保。

## MODERN WAY 当前的雨水，黑水和灰水收集系统

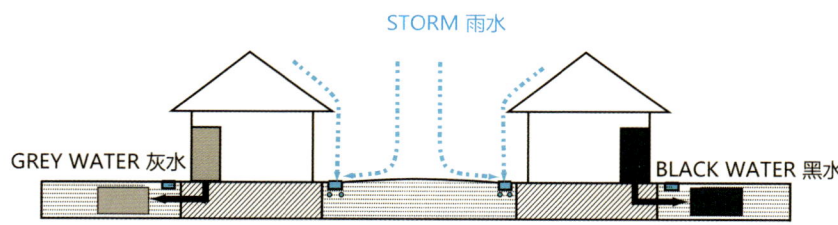

In modern way, the storm drainage system function depend on the gradient of the storm pipe and if the newly-built one ignore the elevation of old area, not only the rainfall can not be drained but also will flow backward.

In modern way, most part of the surface is covered by concrete and many open channels and underdrain are replaced by modern storm sewers, so rainfall can only be drained by modern storm sewers which are not enough for the entire area. The gray water from the kitchen and the black water is collected by cesspools and then drained to the city sewage treatment plant.
当前的现状是：大多数的地表都被混凝土所覆盖，绝大多数的原有水渠和暗沟都不复存在，取而代之的是现代的排水管。而新设置的排水管不能满足整个历史街区的排水要求。来自厨房的灰水和厕所排出的黑水都先排入化粪池，再集中排入城市的污水处理厂。

当前的排水系统的运作变成依赖于排水管道的坡度。如果周边的新建项目不充分考虑历史街区内的街道标高，不仅历史街区内的雨水难以排除，还可能导致雨水的倒灌。

图3-1-16 排水系统研究
PICTURE 3-1-16 RESEARCH OF THE DRAINAGE SYSTEM

对江门长堤历史街区的空间发展定位和城市设计对策进行了探索,以丰富的设计创意演绎出历史与现代交融、充满地域特色的城市设计成果,受到了参加活动的专家学者以及政府领导的好评。来自国内外不同高校的教师与学生、专家学者、当地居民、地方政府部门相关人士,以城市设计工作坊为契机,共同探讨历史街区的保护与复兴方案,集思广益,为江门市长堤历史街区的保护与复兴献计献策。历史街区的保护与复兴,需要广泛的全社会的公众参与,需要多方位的全面探索。

江门长堤历史街区的保护与复兴,首先应做好全面的系统规划,重点从以下几个方面对历史街区进行规划设计:

土地利用规划:继续保持街区的混合用地特点,历史街区土地利用以商住混合用地和居住用地为主,其次还有商务设施用地、公园用地、中小学用地等。骑楼区主要以商住混合用地为主。

道路交通规划:维护和加强原有肌理致密的传统街巷特色,加强街区内支路网密度,通过道路设计和交通管制策略减少整个街区的通过性交通。重新划定街区内的道路等级,设置车行道、人-摩托车混行道和步行道三种。要限制车速,保证行人安全和保持街区宁静的氛围。整体上提倡混行及慢行的概念,打通尽端式巷子,创造良好的步行环境和步行线路,减少机动车的使用。通过部分道路的疏导,可减少历史街区内滨水部分的车流量,为滨水地区的慢行化提供良好基础。北部和西部根据规划设计,整合现有街巷、通道和未被利用的道路,与南部旧区交通结合,形成有机系统。根据现状和设计,在各个片区及滨江地区附近建立地下和地面停车场。

公共空间开放体系规划:通过针灸式的空间梳理,增加公共空间数量,建立连续而层次丰富的步行网络。在西部、中南部、东部三个公共中心形成核心广场空间,与骑楼步行街区相互连接。强化东西向的空间发展轴,增加居住区街头绿地空间。适当开发街区内部空间的商业公共功能。梳理出一条连续完整的重点步行路径,即常安路步行街—骑楼院落组团—青年广场—骑楼街道—石湾直街商业街—启明里沿街带状绿地—滨江休闲步行带。

景观系统规划:根据景观风格的不同可以归纳为七种景观分区,这七种独具特色的景观分区有机地构成一个整体,并形成具有地域特征的长堤历史街区的景观系统,各景观分区内又分布着景观节点。它们通过一条滨江景观轴以及一条历史文化景观轴

six sub-groups with Chinese and foreign members. They learned the international practices of protecting historical neighborhood, investigated Changdi and Jiangmen, explored the urban design and spatial positional of Changdi Historical Neighborhood and worked out a design that blended modern and history elements in addition to local features. The plan got favorable reviews from the government officials and experts. The teachers and students from different universities, scholars, experts, local residents and government officials took this opportunity to study the renewal and preservation of the Changdi Historical Neighborhood and brainstormed together, trying to work out feasible plans The preservation and renewal need full public participation and analysis from all perspectives.

Jiangmen Changdi Historical neighborhood needs comprehensive planning and the focus should be put in the following areas:

Land use: The mixed-use neighborhoods will be kept, namely mixed-use (commercial and residential) land and residential land, followed by business facilities, parks and school sites. The Qilou streets are mainly dominated by commercial and acommodation buildings.

Road traffic planning. The traditional dense alleys will be kept and strengthened. The road network needs to have higher density. The road design and traffic control will reduce pass-through traffic. The road grading will be modified. There will be three categories: the road for vehicles, mixed-use road (for people and motorcycle) and pedestrian road. A limit of the vehicle speed will be set to ensure neighborhood tranquility and the safety of pedestrians. The concept of mixed traffic and slow traffic will be encouraged. The decapitated alleys will be modified to be more walkable and the use of motor vehicles will be reduced. The diversion of some of the roads will reduce traffic in the waterfront area and provide a good foundation for slow traffic. According to the plan, the existing streets, roads and unused channels in the northern and western part will be modified and connected to the southern part to establish a comprehensive system. The overground and underground parking lots will be built in all sections and the waterfront area.

Public space system planning: The detailed analysis needs to be conducted and the public space needs to be increased to build a multi-level pedestrian network. The public centers in the west, mid-south and east will form the core area connected by the Qilou pedestrian streets. The west-east development axis needs more green space in the residential area. The commercial resources can be further tapped. A major walking path needs to be in place, namely Chang'an Road Pedestrian Street, the Qilou buildings, Youth Square, Shiwanzhi Commercial Street, Greenland at Qiming Lane and Waterfront Recreational Zone.

Landscape planning: There can be seven different landscape zones. The seven unique landscape zones form the Changdi Historical Neighborhood with local geographical features. Each zone has different landscape sites and views. The different zones are connected by the waterfront axis and historical and cultural axis.

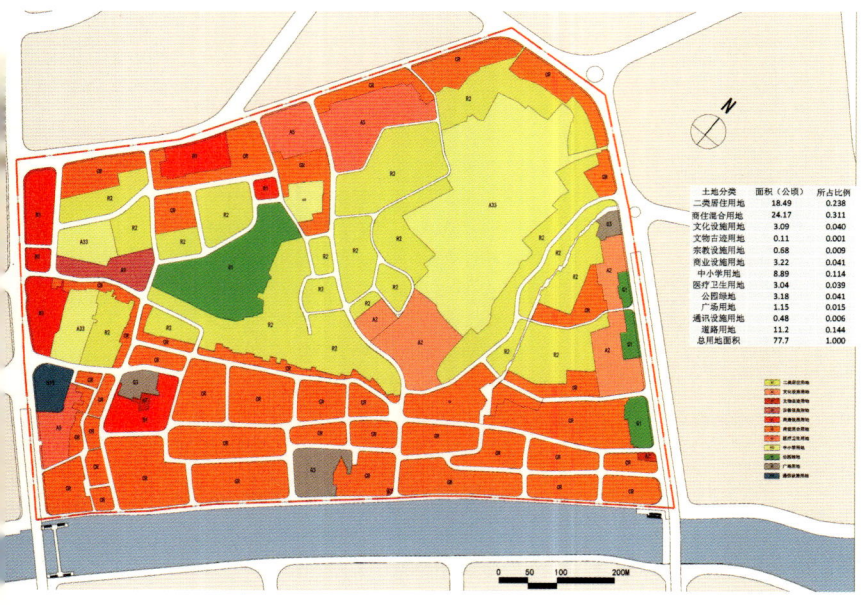

图3-1-17 土地利用规划示意图
PICTURE 3-1-17 LAND USE PLANNING

图3-1-18 道路交通规划示意图
PICTURE 3-1-18 TRAFFIC PLANNING

图3-1-19 公共空间开放体系规划示意图
PICTURE 3-1-19 PUBLIC SPACE SYSTEM

图3-1-20 景观系统规划示意图
PICTURE 3-1-20 LANDSCAPE SYSTEM PLANNING

图3-1-21 视线走廊规划示意图
PICTURE 3-1-21  VIEW CORRIDOR PLANNING

图3-1-22 分期建设规划示意图
PICTURE 3-1-22  PHASED CONSTRUCTION PLANNING

图3-1-23 人口广场设计示意图
PiCTURE 3-1-23  ENTRANCE SQUARE DESIGN

201

图3-1-24 开放空间设计示意图
PICTURE 3-1-24 OPEN SPACE DESIGN

串联成一个整体,同时,形成多个景观特色类型分区。

公共服务设施规划:街区现今拥有总人口约16300人,总人口数约2100户,根据规划研究,远期将达到18000人。规划使用公共设施二级分布,即居住区级—居住小区级分布。按历史文化保护的需要,定位居住区级用地,需配置居住区级的公共服务设施。

保护与更新时序设想:规划应分近期和远期两个阶段,近期应主要对部分保护建筑进行修缮,对各街块划定的更新地块(包括青年广场和启明里)进行更新开发,对景观标识系统的建设进行完善,以及对部分市政设施进行更新和环境景观进行改造。远期则完成街区大部分历史建筑的修缮与更新、完成旅游展示系统的建设,对骑楼街商业业态进行调整,对街区环境进行改造更新,将街区打造成为具有浓郁历史氛围和人文气息的传统街区。

开发强度控制:应平衡区域内的开发强度,控制好整体容积率。开发建设以保护街区风貌为特色,适当降低墟顶居住区的居住密度并限制其开发强度,保证居住环境质量。历史街区的保护更新应结合江门整体的城市发展,实现资源的优化配置。

建设高度控制:规划应对江门历史街区内所有区块内的新建和改建建筑按区块分别设置高度控制指标。应通过详细的城市设计制定石湾直街周围的历史风貌区控制高度以及骑楼风貌区等特色区的建设控制高度。

## 3.1.6 旧城开发资金筹措

资金问题一直是旧城更新中的一个核心要素,而这也是目前国内历史街区保护面临的一个严峻问题。国内历史街区尽管遭受了一定程度的破坏,但通常具有一定规模,整体传统风貌特色尚存,同时这些街区亟需进行保护与更新。旧城开发资金筹措面临挑战,一方面,保护与更新的成本很高,所需的金额数量庞大,而目前国内主要还是靠政府财政手段;另一方面,国家财政投入的历史文化遗产保护的资金十分有限,而且就这部分资金也大部分投入于文物古迹等其他保护项目中,这两方面矛盾冲突非常剧烈,甚至构成了决策方案成败的关键因素之一。再好的方案,没有资金投入依然是纸上谈兵。

旧城改造带来了巨大的资金压力,从而影响了改造的进程。资金方面的问题主要表现在:一方面,开发商对于基础设施的改善和公共空间、建筑的更

Public facilities planning: Currently the neighborhood has a total population of 16300 people with 2100 households. According to our research, the population is expected to reach 18000 in the long term. There are two types of public facilities, namely public facilities for large residential areas and normal residential areas, which means Residential facilities should be built in the areas according to its scale and also in line with the needs of historical and cultural protection

The timing for preservation and renewal: The planning should be divided into two stages, the short-term planning focuses on the restoration of buildings, the re-development of different blocks (including the Youth Square and Qiming Lane), the improvement of the signposts on the street, the municipal facilities and environmental landscape. In the long term, most historical buildings will be renovated and updated, the tourism display system will be finished, the Qilou commercial street will be renovated and the environment will be improved. Ultimately the neighborhood will feature rich historical and cultural atmosphere.

The degree of development: The development should be balanced within the region to control the overall plot ratio. The development should protect the original features and lower the residential density. The quality of living environment must be ensured. The protection projects need to adapt to Jiangmen's overall master plan and optimize the resources.

Limit on the height of buildings: The height limit will be set to all new buildings and renovated buildings. A detailed urban design shall set the height limit to buildings in the historical neighborhood around Shiwanzhi Street and the Qilou District.

### 3.1.6 Fundraising for the Urban Renewal Project

Fundraising has always been an issue in the re-development of the old towns. It is also a serious problem that most historical neighborhoods face in the preservation. Despite the fact that many historical neighborhoods suffer serious damage, large areas are still kept out there. There is an urgent need for protection and renewal. Fund-raising for the urban renewal project is now a great challenge. On one hand, there is high cost in protection and renewal and a huge amount of money is needed. Currently they mainly rely on government finance. On the other hand, the financial investment in the protection of historical and cultural heritage is very limited and most go to the cultural relics protection projects. There is a huge conflict out there and it is one of the key factors for success. No matter how good a plan is, it means nothing without capital investment.

The renewal projects face tremendous financial pressure and the transformation process is affected. The major issues are as follows: the developers are reluctant to invest in infrastructure improvement and public space. On the other hand, because there is no direct benefit in the management and maintenance of public space, the developers don't want to be responsible for that. If all the expenses are borne by the government, it will be overburdened.

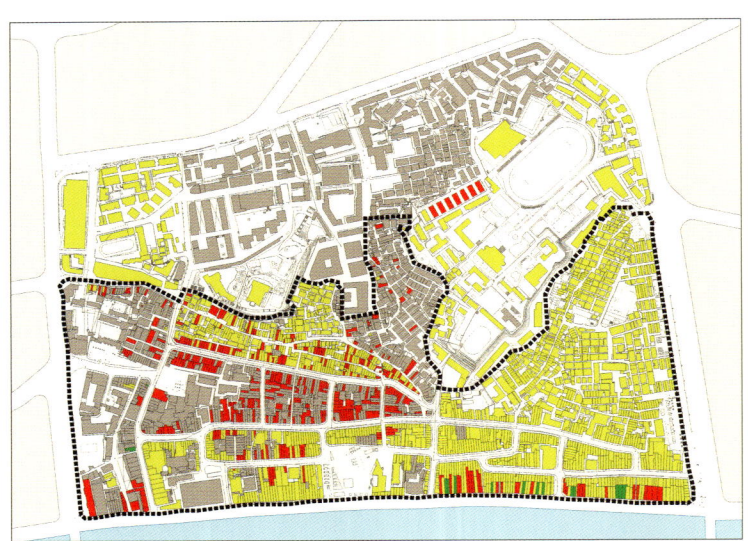

**OWNERSHIP MAP**
产权性质分布图

STATE OWNED 公共产权
PRIVATELY OWNED 私有产权
BOTH 混合产权
UNKNOWN 产权不明

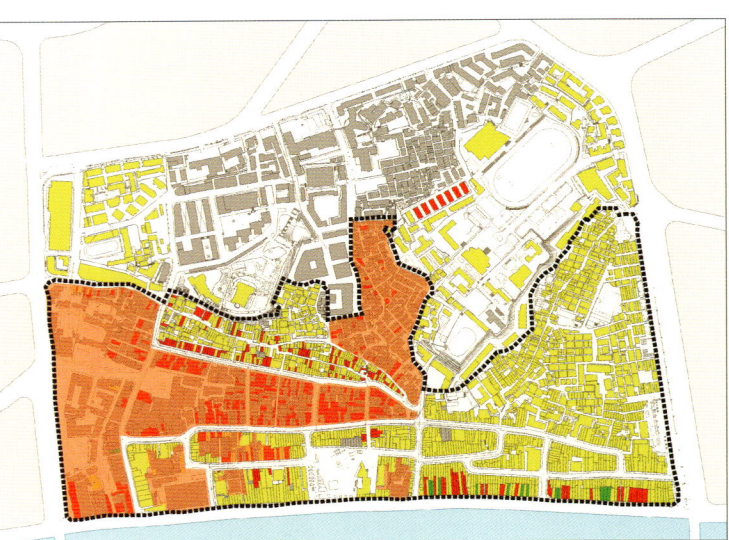

**STATE OWNERSHIP CONCENTRATION**
公共产权集中区域

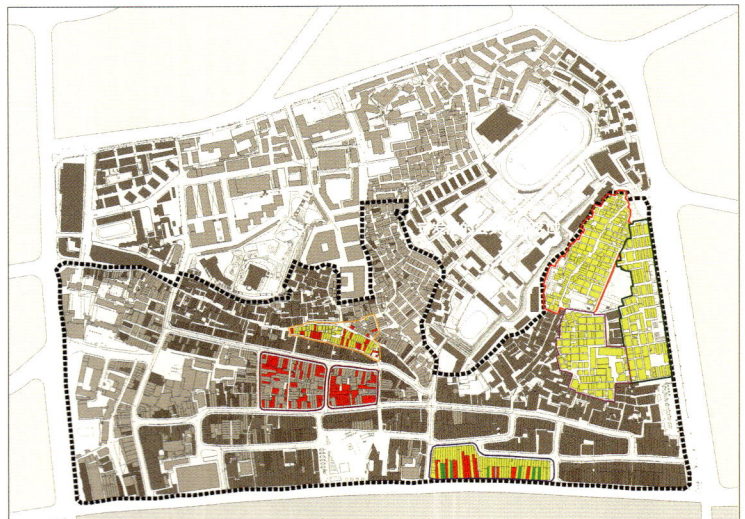

**OPPORTUNITY SITES**
可实施区域

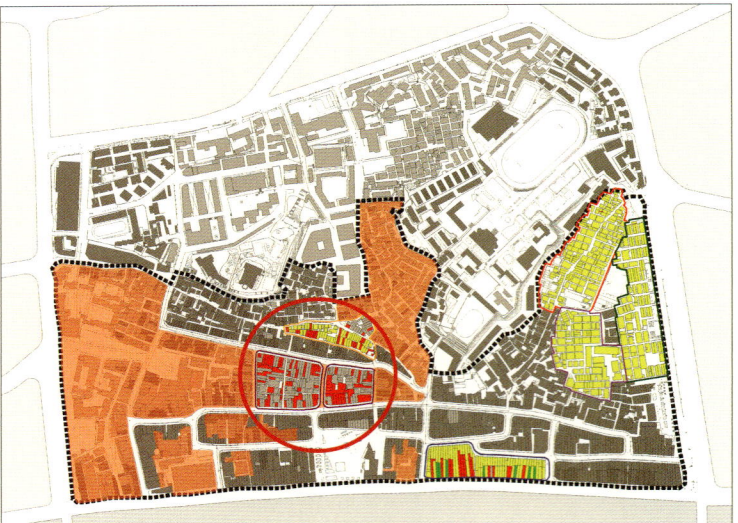

**OPPORTUNITY SITES IN STATE OWNED AREAS**
可实施的公共产权区域

图3-1-25 产权研究
PICTURE 3-1-25  PROPERTY DESIGN

图3-1-26 钓台故居
PICTURE 3-1-26 DIAOTAI FORMAL RESIDENCE

新不愿投资；另一方面，对于建成后的公共空间的管理与维护由于无直接效益而不愿负责。如果全部由政府负担，则致使政府负担过重。

在江门历史街区保护与更新中，应当综合各种资金筹措方式，如政府拨款、金融市场融资、居民自筹融资、市场融资和政策扶植融资，实现城建投资主体由依靠政府向依靠社会，由来源于财政向来源于市场的转变，建议探索一条由政府投入、社会参与、引进外资等多渠道、多元化的新路子。

In the protection and renewal of the historical neighborhood, multiple ways of financing should be adopted including government funding, financing from the market, self-financing of residents and support policies. The source of funding should be moved from the government to the general public and the market. An effective way of financing needs to be in place with the combination of government investment, social participation and outside investment.

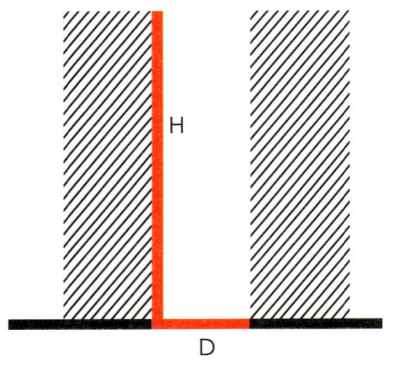
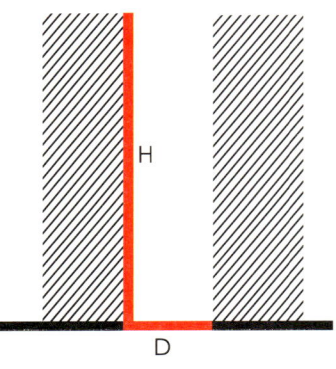

龙聚里街区路
（宽4~6米，D/H为1/1~1/2）

启明里巷道
（宽1.5~2米，D/H为1/4~1/6）

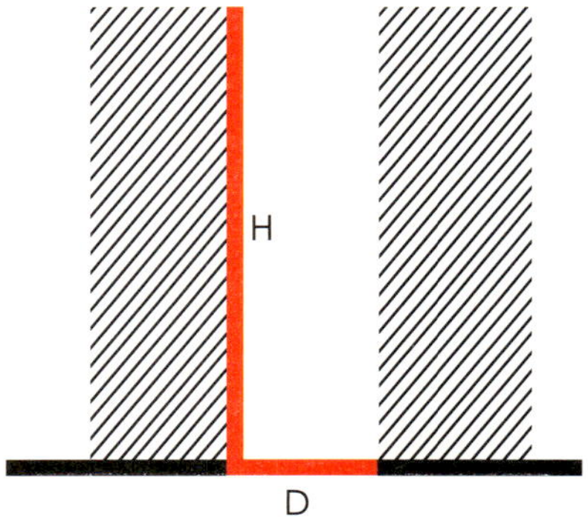

龙聚里街区路
（宽1~1.5米，D/H为1/5~1/6）

图3-2-1 典型街巷剖面示意图
PICTURE 3-2-1 TYPICAL ALLEYS SECTION

图3-2-2 南芬里街区广场
PICTURE 3-2-2 NANFEN LANE SQUARE

## 3.2 历史街区的保护与更新
## 3.2 PROTECTION AND REGENERATION

### 3.2.1 街巷体系和公共空间的发展

历史街区内部各具特色的街巷体系是构成历史街区空间形态的重要骨架，也是内外部交通联系的基本网络。更新改造需要合理地平衡传统街区尺度、道路形式与现代交通、安全等生活及生产要求之间的关系，有效保护城市空间结构和形象的历史风貌，同时也要保证城市发展的功能合理和便利舒适。街巷空间的规划设计应结合历史街区的特色，区内以步行和非机动车交通为主，以对具有丰富历史价值的街巷进行有效的维护和优化；同时也通过完善和修补原来的街巷结构，保证机动车在局部范围和时间上的合理使用；重新恢复山水景观与街巷体系有机渗透和结合的景观及步行体系。

街区内传统建筑开间小而进深大，传统街巷尺度宜人，街区形成致密的肌理。尊重当地石湾直街与小巷的肌理，保护与完善传统街道的空间，注重街道潜在价值的挖掘与提升，体现传统街区的场所感，强化具地域特色的城市空间意象，增强居民的归属感与社会的凝聚力。传统街区中的新建建筑不应破坏历史街区的总体风貌、巷道肌理，而要延续老街区的空间形态并与老街区相协调。

### 3.2.2 弘扬特色与场所再造

重点抓住历史街区的侨乡、墟市、商贸文化，通过对历史建筑的保护和历史信息点的重新塑造，重点打造街区内历史文化资源，将街区塑造成江门最具特色的传统街区，使其成为江门乃至五邑地区的特色文化名片。通过对公共空间的梳理与改善和特色活动的策划，使历史街区汇聚街道巷道民俗生活体验，重新建立正在衰败的江门传统生活场所和建筑空间，并将其打造为传统与现代相融合的历史街区魅力场所。

#### 3.2.2.1 骑楼风貌区

骑楼风貌区位于街区的南部，跨越街区东西两端，包括堤中路、常安路、书院路、仓后路、新市路、莲平路、兴宁路、太平路、葵尾路、上步路等，面积为24.68公顷。应维持该片区的街道格局及街区肌理，重点保护骑楼街的面貌及商业氛围。新增道

### 3.2.1 The Development of Street System and Public Space

The street system in the neighborhood is the important framework for the space and internal and external transport links. The renewal needs reasonable balance on the scale of traditional neighborhoods, the form of the roads, modern transportation, security and other relations between life and production. The urban spatial structure and image needs to be protected and the functions of urban development need be reasonable and convenient. The planning and design of street space should consider local characteristics. Walking and non-motorized transport take up most part. Streets with rich history need to be effectively maintained and optimised. The original streets will be repaired and improved and motor vehicles can be used in a limited scale and time. The landscape view will be brought back and a walking system that fits the system will be established.

The traditional buildings in the neighborhoods have small width and big depth. The width of streets is reasonable and the neighborhoods are well structured. The structure of Shiwanzhi Streets and small lanes need to be respected. During the protection and restoration of the traditional neighborhoods, the potential value of the streets can be explored to create the setting atmosphere. The city spatial image with local features will be enhanced and residents will have a stronger sense of belonging and gathering. The new buildings in the old town should not destroy the overall landscape and structure of the historical neighborhood. The spatial form will be kept and match the existing streets.

### 3.2.2 Highlighting the Unique Style and Remaking of the Place

The planning needs to focus on the culture of bazaars, commerce and Overseas Chinese. The re-branding of the history information, the protection of historical buildings, the use of cultural resources will make the neighbourhood most special in entire Jiangmen and a cultural representation of Jiangmen or even Wuyi. The analysis of public space and planning of special events will bring folklore experience and rebuild the declining traditional life settings and architecture space that fits the modern society.

#### 3.2.2.1 Qilou District

Qilou District is in the southern part of the historical neighborhood and spans through the east and west end. It includes Dizhong Road, Chang'an Road, Shuyuan Road, Canghou Road, Xinshi Road, Lianping Road, Xingning

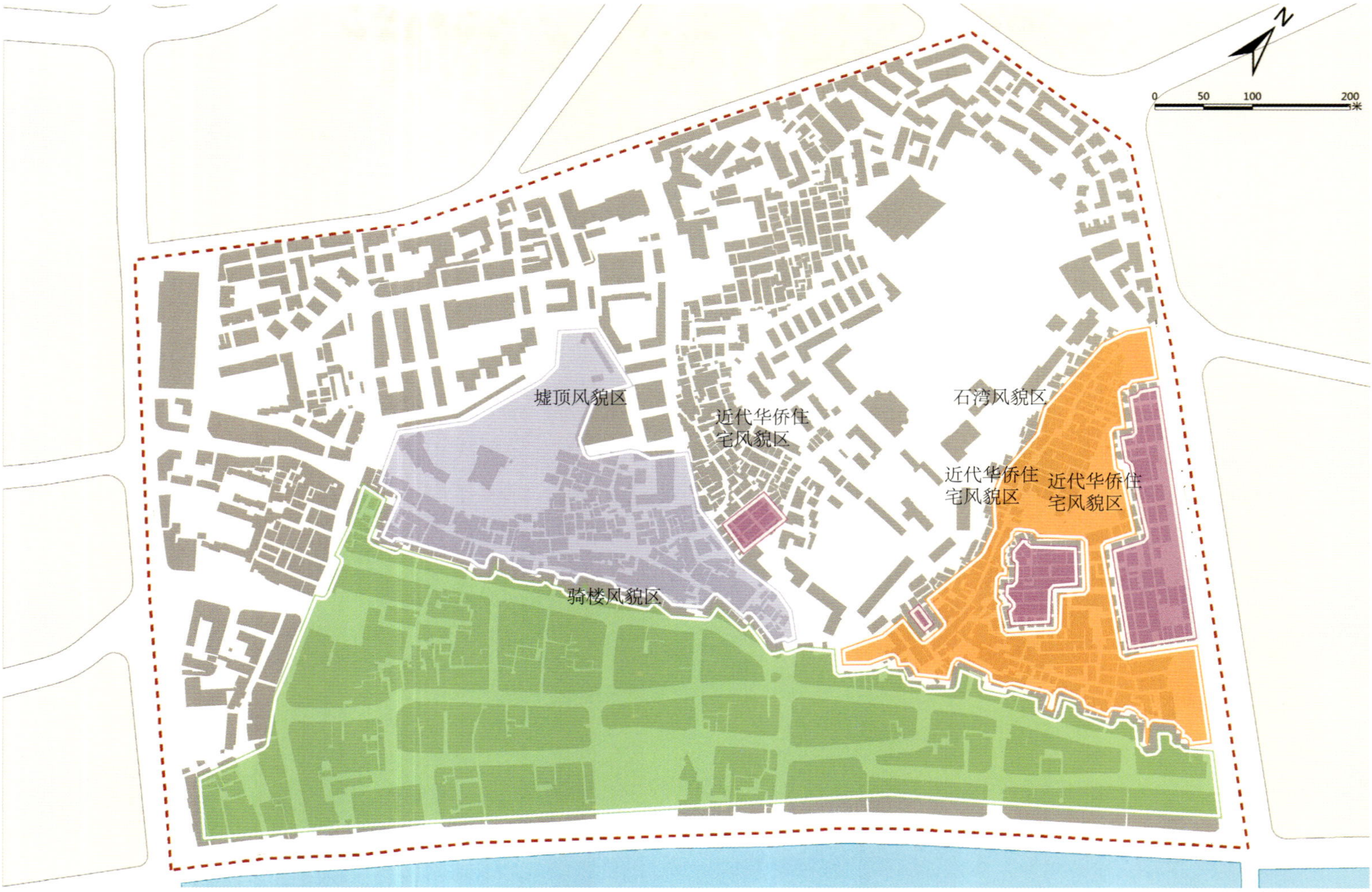

图3-2-3　历史街区风貌分区图
PICTURE 3-2-3　STYLE ZONING MAP OF HISTORIC DISTRICT

图3-2-4　新市路
PICTURE 3-2-4　XINSHI ROAD

路不应超过现有道路的尺度。维持骑楼街界面的连续性，禁止大面积拆除骑楼建筑，新建沿街建筑应维持原界面连续性，并建议鼓励采用传统骑楼形式。巷口宜采用牌坊等立面构筑物保持连续性。保持骑楼廊下空间的畅通。改善街区内建筑的通风、采光、市政设施和消防问题。新建建筑按照建筑控制导则，鼓励居民、租户自主地改造更新。

地块内部有价值的历史建筑年久失修，无人利用。建议修缮有价值的历史建筑，用作社区活动中心，丰富居民生活的同时可令历史建筑价值最大化。在开放空间方面，各区块采取多入口设计，增强区块与周边街道的联系，减少阻隔感。以现有街巷为基础做适当拓宽，必要时拆除少量质量差的建筑。在交通节点种植景观性的树木，丰富社区景观。

#### 3.2.2.2 石湾历史风貌区

石湾历史风貌区位于街区的东部，由景贤中学、太平路、葵尾路和跃进路围合而成，包括新第里、石湾直街、长庆里、启明里、南芬里和龙聚里等，面积9公顷。规划维持该片区的街道格局及街区肌理，重点保护启明里、南芬里和龙聚里的建筑群风貌。新增道路不应超过现有道路的尺度。延续石湾直街的传统风貌，并逐步对沿街建筑进行维修改造更新。将原有小学和幼儿园空地作为商业和居住开发用地，建筑应按照建筑导则设计和建造。改善街区内建筑的通风、采光、市政设施和消防问题。新建建筑按照建筑控制导则，鼓励政府主导下、有开发商介入的维修与建设。

#### 3.2.2.3 墟顶居住风貌区

墟顶居住风貌区位于街区的中部，由墟顶街、京果街、莲平路和兴宁路围合而成，包括墟顶、余庆里等，面积 2.34 公顷。规划维持该片区的街道格局及街区肌理，重点保护余庆里建筑群风貌。新增道路应与现有道路的尺度相协调。延续墟顶街、京果街等传统街巷的传统风貌与空间尺度，并逐步对沿街建筑进行维修改造更新。改善街区内建筑的通风、采光、市政设施和消防问题。制定新建建筑控制导则，鼓励居民、租户自主地改造更新。

#### 3.2.2.4 石湾直街改造设计

石湾直街东邻城市主干道跃进路，西接景贤中学，北接江华一路，南临太平路骑楼街和水街菜市场。石湾社区总面积 10.18 公顷，包括启明里、南芬里、

Road, Taiping Road, Kuiwei Road and Shangbu Road and covers an area of 24.68 hectares. To keep its existing structure and layout, it is important to keep the original shape and commercial atmosphere. The new roads should not be wider than existing roads. The continuity of the Qilou needs to be kept and large-scale demolition of Qilou will be prohibited. The new buildings need to keep the original shape and are suggested to be Qilou. Facade architectures like memorial archways can be built at the entrance of the alley. The space below the arcade needs to be smooth. Ventilation, lighting, fire and municipal facilities need improvement. The new buildings need to be controlled and residents and tenants are encouraged to do their own renovation work.

For the unoccupied buildings with historical values, we suggest to use them as community center after repairing, so as to enrich citizens' life while maximizing their historical values As for open spaces, to improve connectivity with surrounding areas and reduce barriers, multi entries should be designed in the project. Lanes and streets will be expanded and certain buildings in poor conditions will be dismantled. Plants can be planted at key traffic junctions, so as to enrich the overall landscape of the community.

#### 3.2.2.2 Shiwan Historical District

The Shiwan Historical District is located in the eastern part of the neighborhood, encircled by Jingxian Middle School, Taiping Road, Kuiwei Road and Yuejin Road. It includes Xindi Lane, Shiwanzhi Street, Changqing Lane, Qiming Lane, Nanfen Lane and Longju Lane. It covers an area of nine hectares. The existing layout and landscape needs to be the kept with the focus on the buildings in Qiming Lane, Nanfen Lane and Longju Lane. The traditional features of Shiwanzhi Street need to be kept and the buildings will be renovated. Following the architectural guidelines, the open space of the primary school and kindergarten will be developed into commercial and residential land. Ventilation, lighting, fire and municipal facilities in the district need improvement. The new buildings need to be controlled and developers are encouraged to get involved under the guidance of the government.

#### 3.2.2.3 Xuding Residential District

The Xuding Residential District is located in the middle of the neighborhood, encircled by Xuding Street, Jingguo Street, Lianping Road and Xingning Road. It includes Xuding and Yuqing Lane and covers 2.34 hectares. The planning keeps its existing layout and structure and emphasizes on protecting the landscape of Yuqing Lane. New roads should be coordinated with the old ones. The traditional features of Xuding Street and Jingguo Street need to be kept and the buildings will be renovated. Ventilation, lighting, fire and municipal facilities in the district need improvement. The new buildings need to be controlled and residents and tenants are encouraged to do their own renovation work.

## Future development stategy:（建筑形态设想）

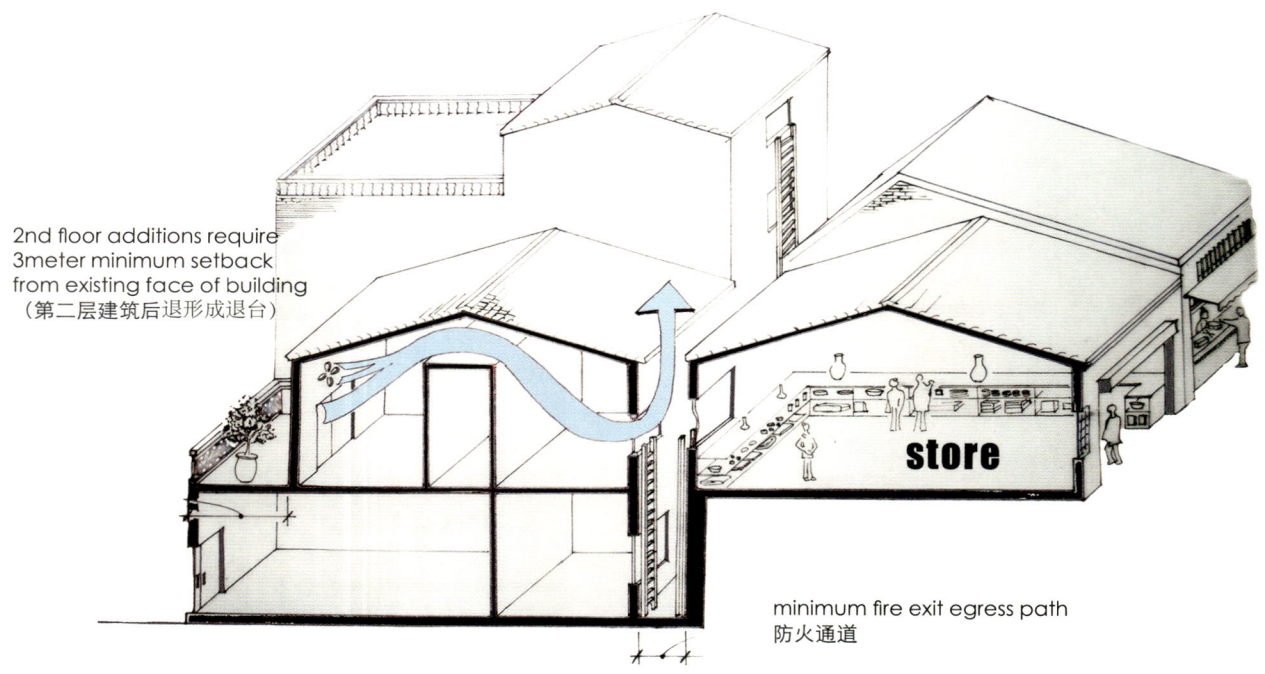

图3-2-5 建筑形态研究
PICTURE 3-2-5 RENOVATION OF THE BUILDING

图3-2-6 启明里建筑群
PICTURE 3-2-6 QIMING LI ARCHITECTURE

龙聚里、石湾直街、新第里、长庆里等多个里坊，现主导功能为居住功能。

石湾社区保留了大量不同时期的建筑。石湾社区历史久远，历史建筑保存丰富，文化积淀深厚。它是江门历史的见证。石湾直街和墟顶、常安路、长堤风貌街是一个整体，是宝贵的侨乡历史文化遗产，是江门历史发展的见证，是江门的"根"。它是江门商业发展的见证。历史上，石湾直街一带商店林立，商业繁茂。它是江门建筑的荟萃。石湾直街保留了大量传统民居和侨房，保留了趟栊门、锅耳山墙等传统建筑元素，是江门不可多得的财富。

保护设计主要包括通过对保留历史风貌建筑的修缮，吸引特色作坊、传统手工艺、特色餐饮、古玩字画等传统特色商业业态，打造石湾直街文化休闲品牌。通过对历史风貌建筑的修缮、维修、改造，使历史风貌建筑满足现代使用的需求，可吸引华侨相关人士到此投资置业、商务办公或居住会友。

**3.2.2.5 余庆里改造设计**

余庆里位于历史街区的中心位置，狗山的山脚，也有通向滨江的廊道连接，有着独特的山水格局。地块位于三个不同的历史片区（石湾直街、墟顶、骑楼街）和重要街道之间。地块紧邻两条内干道，有很强的公共性，也有很高的可达性。

江门历史街区许多建筑都沿狗山山脚布局，因此设计方案希望能够恢复山势，展现老江门的山水特色。

由于历史上江门历史街区的兴旺和侨乡的回归，余庆里就位于两条重要街道（墟顶街和石湾直街）之间，内部有很多有历史价值的建筑和街道空间。因此，应很好地保留这些建筑和梳理街道空间，联系两片传统居住区，宣传江门历史文化。

江门历史街区是源于自发形成的墟市，由于江门滨江的便利和其墟市的兴盛，更由于海关的入驻，江门历史街区渐渐演变成一个历史上的重要地区。余庆里适宜传承集市展销文化，同时这种文化功能也与江门如今日益发展的手工业相匹配，定能带动街区发展，成为街区特色。

**3.2.3. 历史风貌建筑保护更新和新建筑发展**

**3.2.3.1 保护历史风貌建筑**

江门沿江传统街区的传统建筑成组成群，整体

**3.2.2.4 Design of the Shiwanzhi Street**

Shiwanzhi Street borders the major road Yuejin Road in the east, Jingxian Middle School in the west, Qilou Street of Taiping Road and Shui Street market in the south. The Shiwan community covers 10.18 hectares, including Nanfeng Lane, Qiming Lane, Longju Lane, Shiwanzhi Street, Xindi Lane and Changqing Lane. It is a residential area.

Shiwan community keeps many buildings of different eras. It has a long history and is rich in cultural and historical resources, a witness of the history of Jiangmen. Shiwanzhi Street, Xuding, Chang'an Road and Changdi Historical Neighbourhood are a complete community and precious historical and cultural heritage of the Overseas Chinese. Historically, many shops lined up at Shiwanzhi Street and the business flourished. It is the melting pot for different buildings in Jiangmen. Shiwanzhi Street also keeps many residents' buildings that have traditional elements such as dragon doors and walls. These are all Jiangmen's treasures.

The design plan will renovate the listed buildings and attract workshops, traditional arts and crafts, food and drink, antiques and paintings and other traditional characteristics of commercial activities to build a leisure and culture brand. New buildings with traditional features will be built in the middle area close to Longju Lane and Qiming Lane and they will fit into the traditional buildings and become pleasant residential areas. The renovation and repair of historical buildings will let them adapt to the needs of modern society. It is hoped that the Overseas Chinese can choose here to invest, open business or live and meet friends.

**3.2.2.5 Design of the Yuqing Lane**

Yuqing Lane is at the central area of the historical neighbourhood and the foot of the Dog Mountain. There are links to the waterfront area so the landscape is quite unique. Yuqing Lane is located in three different historical districts (Shiwanzhi Street, Xuding and Qilou Street) and important traffic pass-ways. The area neighbours two major roads. It is essentially public and highly connected.

Many historical districts are scattered along the Dog Mountain. So the plan hopes to revitalize such features and show the characteristics of old Jiangmen.

As the historical neighborhoods prospered and the Overseas Chinese came back, Yuqing Lane was formed between two important roads, Xuding Street and Shiwanzhi Street with many valuable historical buildings and streets. The area, if well preserved, can maintain the historical buildings, clean up the street spaces and connect the two traditional residential areas, all with an aim to promote the history and culture of Jiangmen.

Jiangmen historical neighborhoods originated from self-formed markets and evolved into an important region with the easy access brought by the river, the prosperity of the market and the presence of the Customs office. According to the plan, this area is suitable for the promotion of market exhibition and sales culture, which is in line with the increasingly developed handicraft industry in Jiangmen.

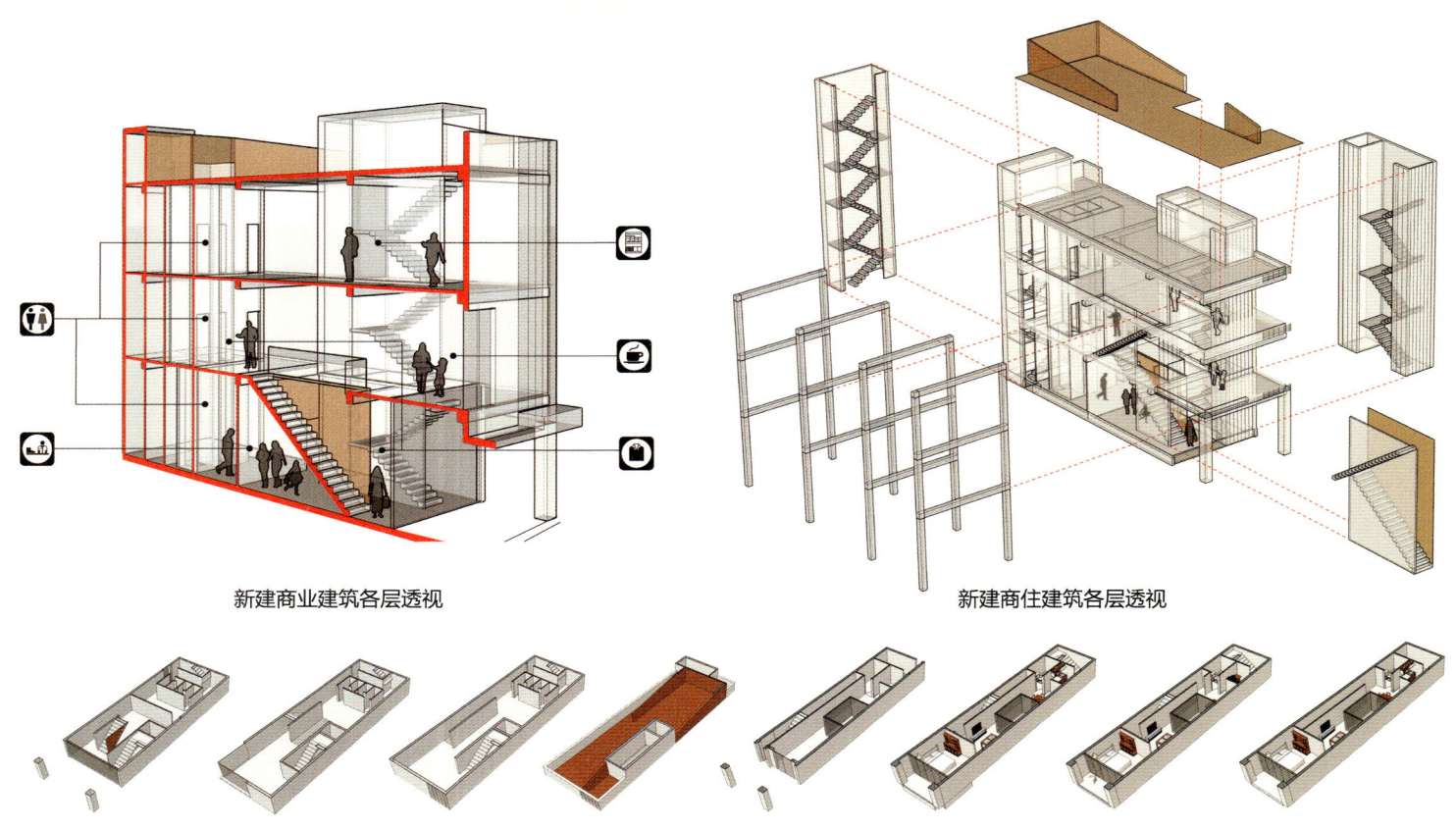

新建商业建筑各层透视　　　　　　　　　　　新建商住建筑各层透视

图3-2-7　骑楼建筑改造策略
PiCTURE 3-2-7　STRATEGY OF ARCADE BUILDING TRANSFORMATION

图3-2-8　骑楼街塘步路
PICTURE 3-2-8　TANGBU ROAD IN THE ARCADE STREET

风貌特色明显。街区有市级文保建筑数座,应严格按照文物保护法规和历史名城保护法规进行保护。区内尚存富有特色的青砖大屋、骑楼建筑群在江门的其它小区已不多见,应保护好这些具有文化内涵的侨乡建筑。对传统建筑的更新改造,不应破坏传统街区的风貌和格局。在保持原有空间格局的前提下,可适当进行功能置换和调整,满足现代商业和居住要求,保护历史风貌建筑的同时使其能够重焕生机。

以尊重历史街区整体风貌和推动历史街区更新发展为出发点,针对不同的旧建筑选择不同的更新方式:拆除乱搭建等不适宜建筑;对具有历史价值但建筑质量不能满足现代功能需求的建筑进行局部改造;对具有历史价值且建筑质量完好的区域进行以保护为主的局部修缮。新建筑设计在区位、体量、高度、立面和材料选择上均充分考虑对周边历史街区的影响并与历史街区的传统风貌和建筑风格相协调。

#### 3.2.3.2 骑楼街保护与更新

应维持骑楼建筑传统风貌,禁止对传统骑楼建筑任意拆除、改建。对风貌较好的骑楼建筑进行加固和修复,对风貌一般和较差的骑楼建筑进行整饰和改造。

整饰和改造应尽可能展示历史原真性,积极运用传统元素和材质。对风貌和质量较差的沿街建筑以及开发地块,可采用置换的方式,新建骑楼建筑的高度不超过20米,体量与尺度应与周围建筑协调。新建骑楼建筑的外立面应保持街道界面的连续性,外立面的控制线宜与邻近建筑协调。

骑楼改造示范地块居于整体设计区域中较内部的位置,南临书院路滨江路骑楼重点展示区域,西接常安路商业步行街,东侧是石湾直街和启明里民居集中区。若将整体区块理解为一个整体,滨江路书院路一带的骑楼和石湾直街及墟顶一带的民居可进行全面的修复和整饰,尽可能地保留其艺术、建筑和文化价值。而作为被这些重点地块环绕的地块,一方面拥有临街骑楼中西合璧的特色立面,一方面却因为长期的乱搭乱建和自行改造失去了骑楼典型的内部空间,削减了此地块的价值。

#### 3.2.3.3 传统天井式建筑的保护与更新

维护传统天井式建筑的传统风貌,禁止对传统建筑任意拆除、改建。对风貌较好的传统天井式建筑进行加固和修复,对风貌一般和较差的传统天井

This will be a local feature and will certainly boost the development of the whole neighborhood.

### 3.2.3 Protection & Renewal of Historical Buildings and Development of New Buildings

#### 3.2.3.1 Protection of Historical Buildings

Traditional buildings in the neighborhoods cluster as communities and groups, so that historical features in the traditional neighborhoods along the river are well presented. Buildings designated as Municipal Cultural Preservation Sites are well protected according to laws and regulations on protection of cultural relics and historical cities. The fact that brick houses and Qilou are already very rare in other neighborhoods alerts us to upgrade protection efforts in the hometown of overseas Chinese. While we should keep in mind that certain adjustments to the function of the buildings are allowed to meet the requirement for commercial and residential uses, unique features and layout of traditional buildings should be well maintained.

Our protection work is based on promoting the renewal of historical neighborhoods while respecting its overall style and features. Renewal plans should be tailored to different types of buildings: dismantling illegal buildings that do not fit in; renovate certain parts of the historical buildings that cannot meet the requirements of modern use; protect and renovate those with important historical value and in good shape. Newly planned buildings should fit in with the traditional features and architecture styles in the neighborhood and take into consideration such factors as location, size, height, material uses and external wall decoration, etc.

#### 3.2.3.2 Protection and Regeneration of Qilou (Arcade Building)

Traditional features in the Qilou should be kept and any arbitrary removal or rebuilding is forbidden. Qilou with intact features will be repaired and preserved, while those in moderate and poor conditions will be regenerated and rebuilt.

Traditional elements and materials are preferred to keep the authenticity of the buildings in regeneration and renovation. Poorly built and presented buildings and land blocks along the street can be replaced by arcade buildings lower than 20 meters. The new buildings should fit in with their surroundings in scale and size and the style of external walls should be kept consistent with the whole street and building line should also match architectures nearby.

The central part of the neighborhoods is selected as the demonstration project for arcade protection and renewal, with the key demonstration area of Qilou on Shuyuan Road and Binjiang Road to the south, Chang'an Pedestrian Street to the west and Shiwanzhi Street and Qimin Lane residential area to the east. If we take the neighborhoods as an integrity, Qilou on Shuyuan Road and Binjiang Road, and residential buildings on Shiwanzhi Street and Xuding Street should be repaired and renewed so as to keep their

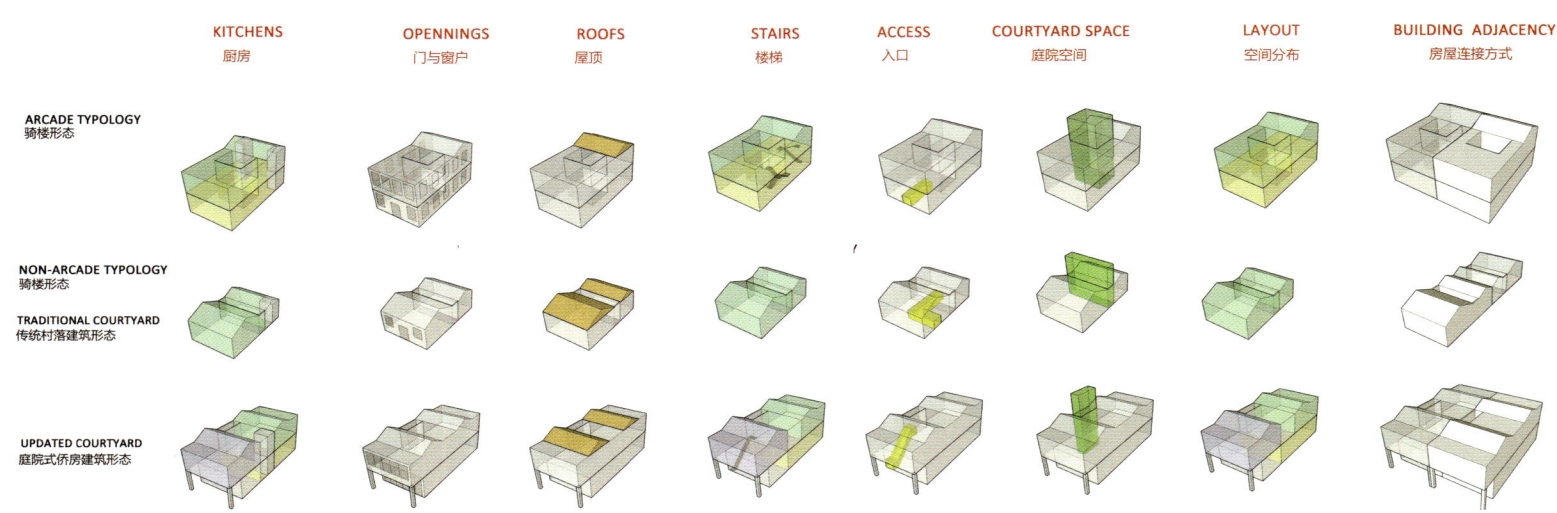

图 3-2-9 建筑类型学研究
PICTURE 3-2-9 RESEARCH OF BUILDING TYPOLOGY

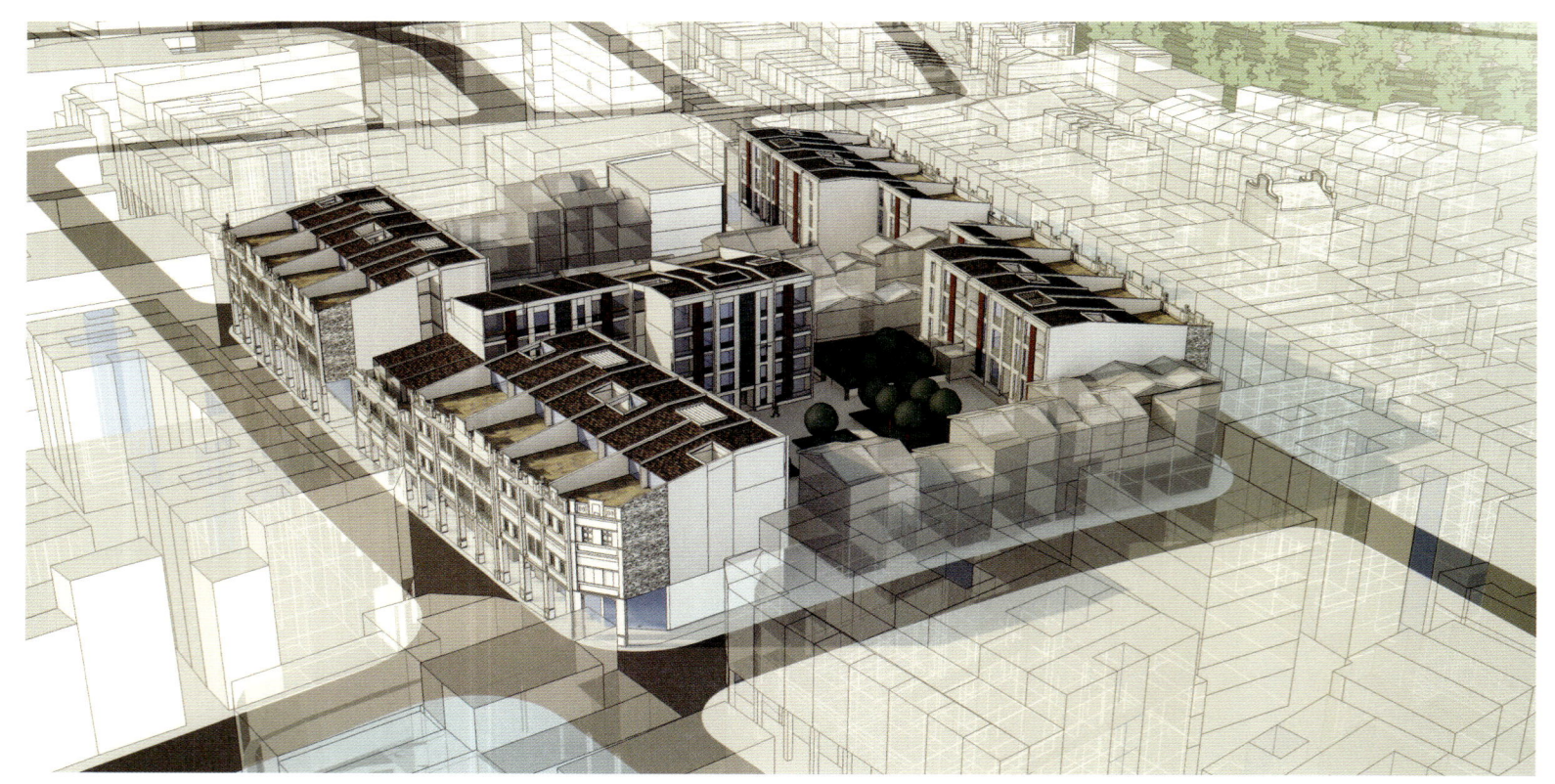

图 3-2-10 骑楼示范点改造设计效果图
PICTURE 3-2-10 REFORM OF ARCADE STREET

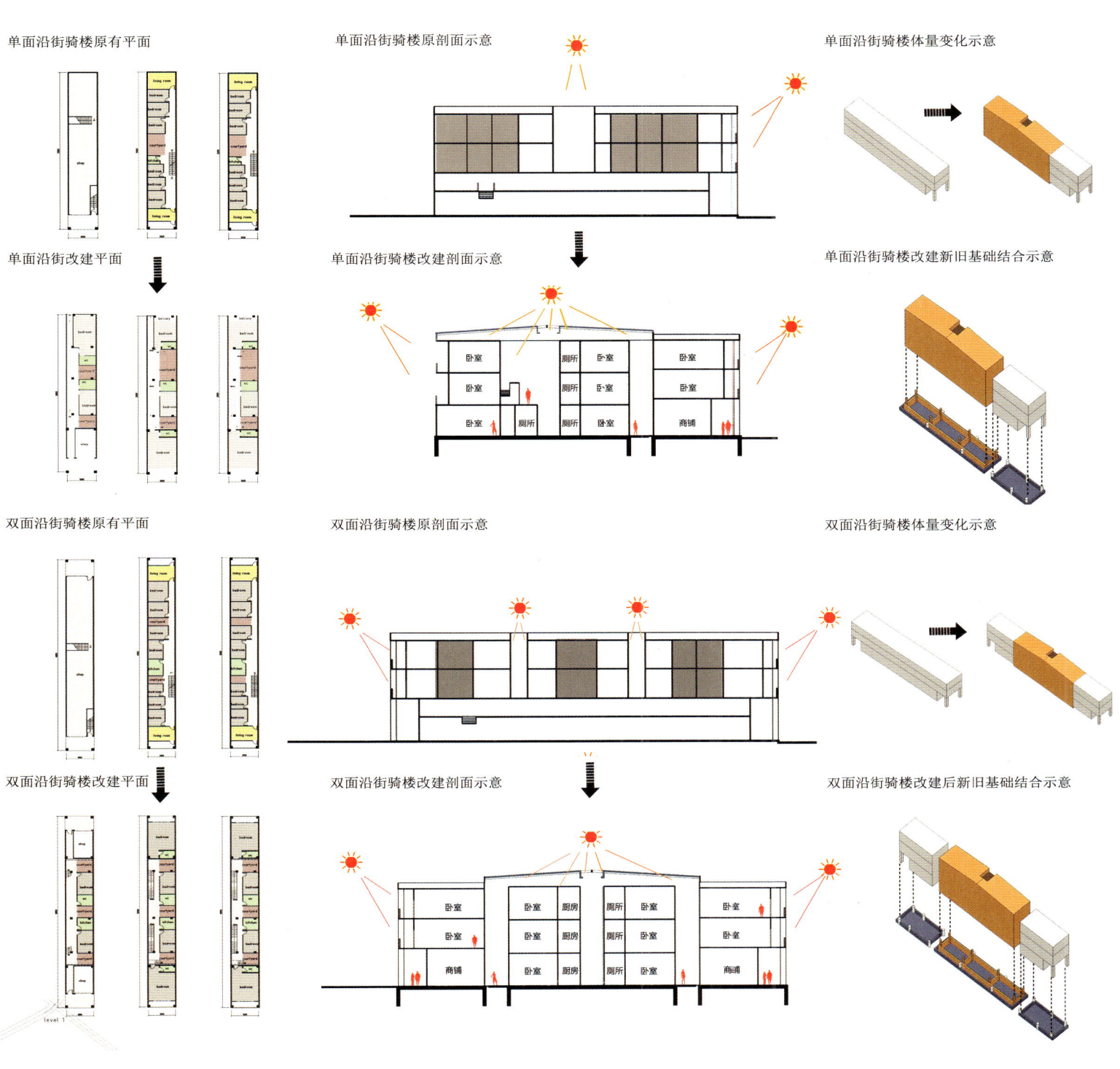

图3-2-11 骑楼改造示意图
PICTURE 3-2-11 TRANSFORMATION OF ARCADE STREET

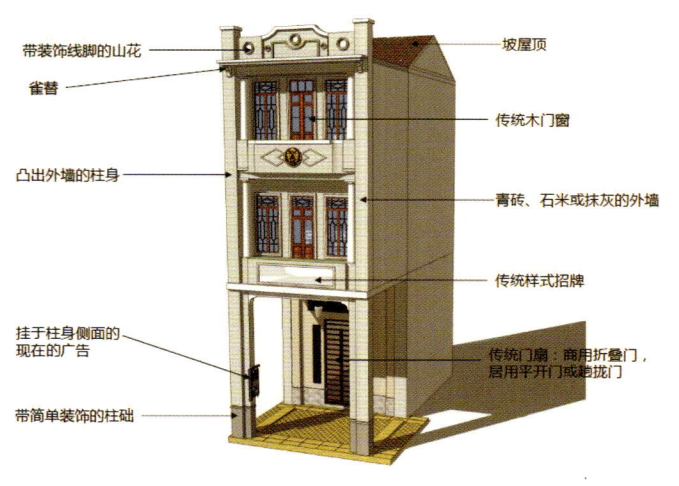

图3-2-12 骑楼修缮示意图
PICTURE 3-2-12　RENOVATION OF ARCADE STREET

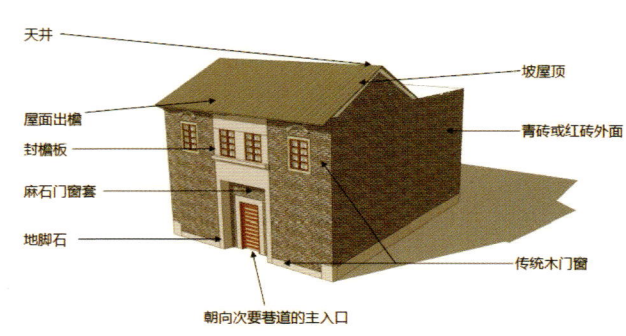

图3-2-13 传统天井式建筑修缮示意图
PICTURE 3-2-13　RENOVATION OF TRADITION PATIO BUILDING

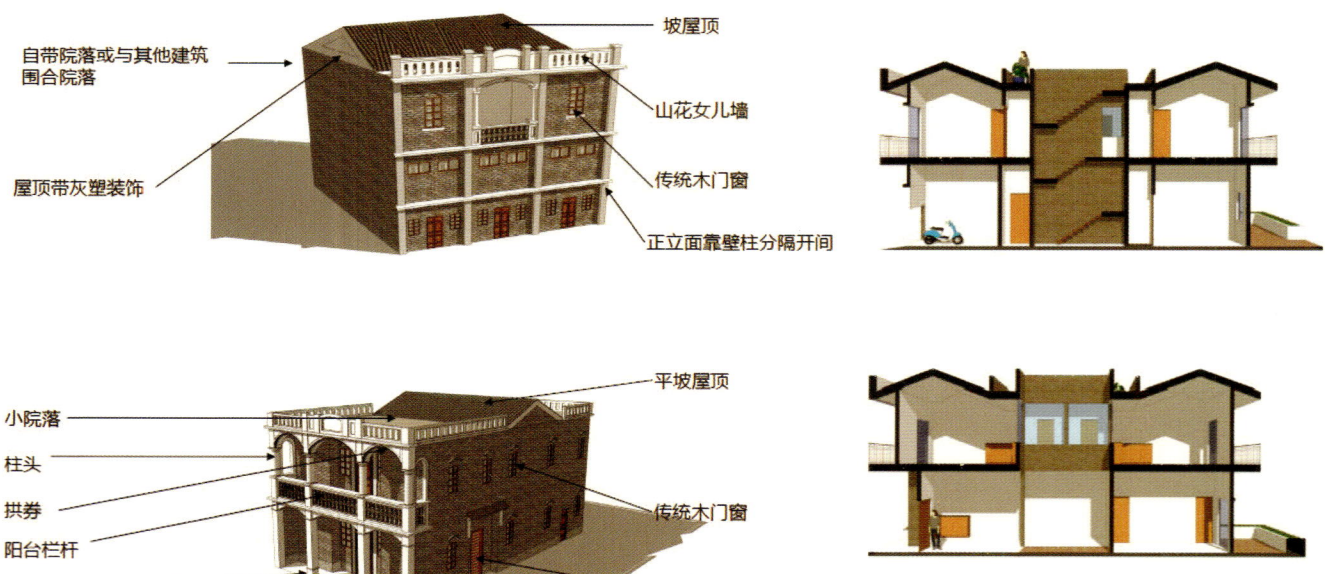

图3-2-14 传统院落式建筑修缮示意图
PICTURE 3-2-14　RENOVATION OF TRADITIONAL PATIO BUILDING

式建筑进行整饰和改造。加固和修复应考虑历史原真性及维修的可读性与可逆性。整饰和改造应在历史原真性的基础上，积极运用传统元素和材质。

对风貌和质量较差的建筑以及开发地块，可拆除风貌不协调的新建建筑，新建建筑的高度不超过15米，正立面宽度不超过20米，宜采用竖向线条划分开间和虚实，建筑的体量与尺度应与周围建筑协调。新建建筑外立面建议采用以下传统元素：坡屋顶、木封檐板、木门窗、带线脚的柱身柱础。立面建议采用以下材料：木、青砖、浅色抹灰。应积极利用巷道和建筑内部的天井提供通风采光。

#### 3.2.3.4 传统院落式建筑控制

维护传统院落式建筑的传统风貌，禁止对传统建筑任意拆除、改建。对风貌较好的传统院落式建筑进行加固和修复，对风貌一般和较差的传统院落式建筑进行整饰和改造。加固和修复应考虑历史原真性及维修的可读性与可逆性。

整饰和改造应在历史原真性的基础上，积极运用传统元素和材质。新建建筑的高度不超过15米，正立面宽度不超过20米，宜采用竖向线条划分开间和虚实，建筑的体量与尺度应与周围建筑协调。新建建筑外立面建议采用以下传统元素：平坡屋顶、山花、水平檐板、木门窗、带线脚的柱身柱础、西洋装饰或彩画。立面建议采用以下材料：木、青砖、抹灰和石米。应积极利用巷道和建筑内部的天井提供通风采光。

### 3.2.4 产业及人口结构调整

分析现有商业形态，调查市民的消费需求，升级和优化商业形态，引进代表地方传统与特色的商业，通过同类集聚形成传统墟市和特色专业街。适当引入新型的产业，为街区的发展提供可持续的动力。更新规划旨在通过调整产业结构、改善生活环境、更新公共设施等手段吸引更多的年轻人在此街区消费和生活，从而逐步调整历史街区的人口年龄结构，减缓和改变街区由于老龄化而导致逐步衰落的问题。规划力图通过调整商业业态和对商业进行升级、改善消费环境等方式吸引潜在的消费人群，从而让本街区的商业得到良性发展，整体提升街区的环境品质与内涵，提高在五邑地区的影响力，让整个历史街区成为江门一个具有独特魅力的城市吸引点。

artistic, architectural and cultural values. While for land blocks surrounded by the above-mentioned key roads, despite the unique external walls of the buildings featuring western and eastern styles, the value of the land block is seriously decreased by unlicensed construction and illegal building projects.

#### 3.2.3.3 Protection and Renewing of Traditional Buildings with a Courtyard in the Middle

Historical features in traditional buildings with a courtyard in the middle should be preserved, while any arbitrary dismantling and rebuilding are prohibited. Well preserved building with a courtyard in the middle should be maintained and repaired, while poorly kept ones should be regenerated. Authenticity, readability and reversibility in the repairing and maintenance project should also be stressed. Traditional elements and materials are preferred in order to keep buildings' authenticity.

For poorly built and presented buildings and land blocks, new buildings no higher than 15 meters and no wider than 20 meters and well matched in size and scale with its surroundings can be built, after dismantling the uncoordinated style ones. Following elements are suggested to apply on decoration of external walls: pitched roofs, wooden curtain plate, wooden windows and doors, pillars with lines and corners and western style paintings or ornaments, while materials for external walls include wood, plain brick and plastering layer. The alley as well as the courtyard in the middle of the building should be fully utilized to ventilation and natural lighting.

#### 3.2.3.4 Protection of Ancient Courtyard Buildings

Historical features in ancient courtyard buildings should be preserved, while any arbitrary dismantling and rebuilding are prohibited. Well preserved courtyard building should be maintained and repaired, while poorly kept ones should be regenerated. Authenticity, readability and reversibility in the repairing and maintenance project should also be stressed.

Traditional elements and materials are preferred in order to keep buildings' authenticity. New buildings no higher than 15 meters and no wider than 20 meters and well matched in size and scale with its surroundings can be built. Following elements are suggested to apply on decoration of external walls: flat roofs, pediments, flat curtain plate, wooden windows and doors, pillars with lines and corners, western style paintings or ornaments, while materials for external walls include wood, plain brick, plastering layer and chicken girts. The alley as well as the courtyard in the middle of the building should be fully utilized to provide ventilation and natural lighting.

### 3.2.4 Industry and Population Restructuring

The planning suggests the analysis of existing business forms, the citizen's consumption needs and the upgrading of business forms as well as the introduction of businesses with local traditions and characteristics. When the same form of businesses is gathered together,

图3-2-15　堤中路
PICTURE 3-2-15　DIZHONG ROAD

图3-2-16　上步路
PICTURE 3-2-16　SHANGBU ROAD

图3-2-17　墟顶街社区活动中心内景
PICTURE 3-2-17　XUDING ROAD COMMUNITY CENTER'S INTERIOR

### 3.2.4.1 改善滨水环境、商业购物环境与交通环境，吸引本地与外来居民

重点改善滨水环境和商业氛围，提升街区整体活力，强化用地在仓后街道以及区域中的商业服务功能，加强规划区的商业集聚效应，增强商业区域流动的吸引力。这将对街区内以及整个区域的经济、社会建设起到促进作用。

良好的交通区位条件是使一个地区发展和吸引人流的重要条件。对于传统街区而言，要使人口集中，必须提高区域整体的基础设施条件。在全市范围来看，要加强对外的公共交通联系。区域内主要的交通问题则是公共交通不足，道路建设滞后，道路分级、管理混乱，这对于历史街区复兴产生了制约和影响，不利于商业的发展。

通过商业类型与产业结构的调整，改变街区现有老龄化的人口结构，吸引更多元的人口来此居住与生活。

### 3.2.4.2 充分发挥区内优秀学校对外来人口的吸引力

规划区内现有一间中学、两间小学，这些学校是规划区文化教育发展的主要力量，在更新保护规划中应充分利用这些资源发挥老城教育优势。

江门是一个侨乡，无论是在历史上还是当下，对教育事业都非常重视。据报道，改革开放以来，祖籍江门的华侨、华人和港澳台同胞为家乡捐资捐物已达数十亿港币，其中大部分被用于教育事业的发展，这将有可能成为旧城更新的重要推动力。

### 3.2.4.3 改善老城居住区环境

随着城市化进程的加快和城市人口的增加，城市建设步伐不断加快，江门城市也得到了很多发展机遇。然而长堤历史街区居住环境已明显不适应城市现代生活发展的需要，尤其是还有相当一部分老城区居民的居住条件相对较差，这不仅对外地人吸引力弱，连本地人也有外迁趋势。改善居住环境，对于传统街区人口现状的改善，将发挥最大的作用。

### 3.2.4.4 积极地推进第三产业的发展

随着产业结构的调整和劳动生产率的日益提高，农村剩余劳动力会向第三产业转移，我国第三产业就业人员逐年上升。在历史街区内发展第三产业能有效地为城市吸纳更多人力资源，并为区内服务水平和环境质量的提高提供更多的支持。强化第三产业，a special commercial street will be in place. It's also suggested that the new business are brought in to provide sustainable impetus for development. The re-development plan aims to adjust the industrial structure, improve the living environment and public facilities to attract potential consumers. The goal of the planning is the healthy development of the region, the improvement of the environmental quality and raise influence in the region. The whole historical neighborhood will become an attraction with unique charm in the entire city.

### 3.2.4.1 Better Waterfront and Better Environment for Business and Transport to Attract More Residents

Most efforts will be made to improve the waterfront and business environment and make the whole neighbourhood more vibrant. The neighborhood will play a bigger role in business services and attracting more businesses and the attraction of the commercial district should be strengthen. This will contribute to the socio-economic development of the district and the entire region.

Good transport location is important for regional development and the influx of people. For the district, the overall infrastructure needs to be improved to attract more people. At the city level, external public transport links need to be more extensive. Currently the major traffic problems are the lack of public transportation, poor road construction and confusing road classification and management. These problems constrain the renovation of the district and are not conducive to the development of commerce.

Therefore the adjustment of business types and industrial structure will attract a more diverse population to settle down and change the ageing population structure.

### 3.2.4.2 Attract People from Outside by Quality Schools

Currently there are one middle school and two primary schools, which are essential for the cultural development in the region. Such advantages should be given full play in the renovation planning.

Jiangmen is a town of Overseas Chinese. Historically it attached importance to education and it does so today. It is reported that since the reform and opening up, the Overseas Chinese and Hong Kong, Macau and Taiwan patriots who were originally from Jiangmen have donated six billion HKD to their hometown and most of the donations financed education. This can be an important driving force of the re-development of the old town.

### 3.2.4.3 Improve the Living Conditions in the Old Town

As the urbanization speeds up and the population grows, the city construction is getting faster with many development opportunities. Yet the living conditions in Changdi Historical Neighborhood can't meet the demands of the modern urban development. The living conditions of quite a few residents in the old town are very bad. It is

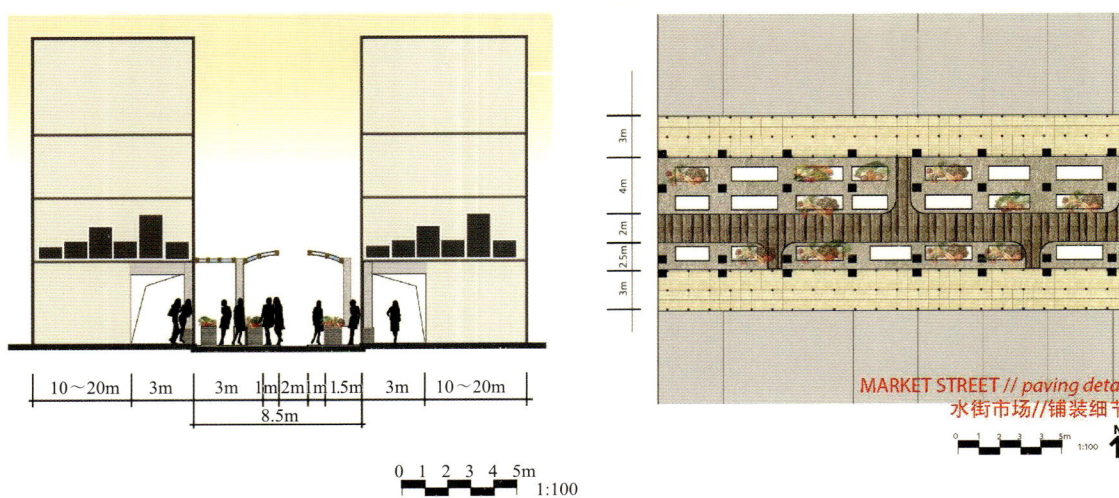

MARKET STREET // paving detail
水街市场//铺装细节

图3-2-18 水街农贸市场改造示意图
PICTURE 3-2-18 TRANSFORMATION OF SHUIJIE FARMERS MARKET

图3-2-19 水街农贸市场
PICTURE 3-2-19 SHUIJIE FARMERS MARKET

图3-2-20 水街农贸市场
PICTURE 3-2-20 SHUIJIE FARMERS MARKET

特别是能够提高生活质量的教育、健康、环保、文化、家政等新型服务业，可推进城镇化进程，使城镇化与农村劳动力转移和服务业的发展相互促进，充分发挥其吸纳就业的巨大潜力。重点塑造文化旅游吸引物和多元产业吸引物，吸引多样化的、多年龄层次的市民，扭转街区衰败的趋势，提升街区的人口吸引力。

对历史街区商业进行调整，结合该区域特色发展特色商业，如传统手工艺和地方美食等；历史街区的商业在服务城市低收入人群的同时，部分可以从低档零售批发升级到中高档的商业，吸引更多不同的消费人群，通过适度混合保障本地区经济的可持续发展。历史街区在上层次规划中的定位是历史文化旅游区域，发展中应充分利用该历史街区的历史文化资源，如五邑侨乡文化等，以及片区的山水格局和蓬江两岸的骑楼风貌发展相关的旅游产业。利用历史街区中丰富的历史文化资源，参考类似的城市案例并结合相关的调查研究，选择在历史街区植入相关的文化创意产业，丰富街区的产业结构，带动旅游、教育等相关产业的发展。

unattractive to outsiders and the local people have the intention to move out. If the living conditions can be improved the population in historical neighborhood can be optimized.

#### 3.2.4.4 Promote the Development of the Tertiary Industry

As the industrial structure adjusts and the labor productivity increases, a large number of rural surplus labor forces will be transferred to the third industry. China's tertiary industry employment rate has increased year by year. The development of the third industry will attract more human resources to the city and provides more support for the level of service and the quality of the environment. A stronger tertiary industry will improve the quality of education, health, environmental protection, culture, economics and new services and promote urbanization. The urban and rural labor transfer and the development of services will promote each other and tap the potential of human resources. Focus should be put on attracting tourists and multi industries as well as diverse and multi-age people. In this way the neighborhoods will stop declining and the become more attractive for people.

The commercial historical neighborhoods need to be adjusted in connection with the business with regional characteristics such as traditional crafts and local food. While the region remains attractive for the low-income people, some low-level businesses can be upgraded to high-end retail and wholesale businesses to attract different consumer groups to achieve economic sustainable development. In the planning, the Historical Neighborhood is designated as the historical and cultural tourism area. So the tourism development should take full advantage of the historic and cultural resources, such as Wuyi culture, and landscape pattern and the Qilou streets. Cultural and creative industries can be developed using the rich historical and cultural resources and referencing similar cases from research in other cities. When industrial structure gets more diverse, tourism, education and other related industries can be boosted as well.

图3-2-21 水街农贸市场
PICTURE 3-2-21 SHUIJIE FARMERS MARKET

图3-2-22 石湾直街
PICTURE 3-2-22 SHIWANZHI STREET

图3-2-23 堤中路
PICTURE 3-2-23 DIZHONG ROAD

图3-2-24 堤中路
PICTURE 3-2-24 DIZHONG ROAD

图3-2-25 历史街区活动
PICTURE 3-2-25 ACTIVITY IN THE HISTORICAL DISTRICT

perspective of open space:
（公共空间透视）

图3-2-26　建筑空间改造意向
PICTURE 3-2-26　OBJECTIVE OF ARCHITECTURE TRANSFORMATION

图3-2-27　历史街区活动
PICTURE 3-2-27　ACTIVITY IN THE HISTORICAL DISTRICT

223

图3-3-1 常安路
PICTURE 3-3-1 CHANG'AN ROAD

图3-3-2 莲平路
PICTURE 3-3-2 LIANPING ROAD

图3-3-3 历史街区鸟瞰图
PICTURE 3-3-3 BIRD-VIEW OF THE HISTORICAL NEIGHBORHOOD

# 3.3 旧城复兴项目策划
## 3.3 OLD TOWN RESTORATION PLAN

江门长堤历史街区的保护更新项目包括保护项目、植入项目和更新与升级项目。在历史街区的开发和再利用的过程中，需要对这些项目的更新时序做出合理安排。

### 3.3.1 保护项目

需要保护的传统街巷包括墟顶片区墟顶街，包括东南盛街和京果街、石湾直街片区的石湾直街、骑楼片区现有主要的骑楼街道。

需要保护的建筑项目包括了市级文物保护单位和有价值的历史风貌建筑或建筑群。市级文物保护单位包括中山纪念堂、永安按当铺、宝和按当铺和陈白沙钓台；特色建筑群有启明里建筑群、余庆里建筑群和骑楼商业街区。

常安路步行街目前是江门市唯一一条以服饰为主的商业步行街，在市民心中有较高的认知度，其商业业态规划应予以保护。莲平路五金家装特色项目目前是江门市知名的以小五金为主的专营性商业街，江门主城区市民及附近的镇区都会来此地进货或购买小五金及家装材料，其商业业态在规划中应予以保护。在江门市区，提起买手机，几乎所有的市民都会在第一时间想起蓬莱路电讯街，为鼓励、引导与该行业相关的商家入街经营，并适度为该行业提供配套服务，2003年11月，蓬江区政府正式命名仓后街道办事处辖区的蓬莱路为"蓬莱电讯器材街"。该街道全长450米的路段有商铺149家。

### 3.3.2 更新与升级项目

在历史街区中，存在一些具有历史意义并且风貌良好的场所，但它们在适应现代化社会的发展方面具有不相适应的地方，因此规划建议对其进行更新和升级。这些项目包括中山公园的扩建、墟顶传统住宅群自主更新、启明里和南芬里住宅群自主更新、青年广场改建。对于骑楼街，应提升骑楼街部分低档次商业经营模式，逐步使长堤风貌街的商业类型置换为休闲餐饮娱乐商业。

The restoration for the Jiangmen Changdi Historical Neighborhood includes conservation projects, implantation projects and re-development projects and upgrades. In the development and reuse process, it is important to make reasonable arrangements for the restoration projects.

### 3.3.1 Conservation Projects

The traditional streets that need to be protected include Xuding Street at Xuding, Dongnansheng Street and Jingguo Street, Shiwanzhi Street at Shiwanzhi and most of the Qilou buildings.

The municipal listed architectural projects and valuable historical buildings need to be preserved. The listed buildings include Sun Yat-sen Memorial Hall, Yongan Pawnshop, Baohe Pawnshop and Chen Baisha Stool. The special architectural projects include the buildings at Qiming Lane, Yuqing Lane and the Qilou Commercial Street.

As the only commercial pedestrian street selling costumes in Jiangmen, Chang'an Pedestrian Street is quite famous among the residents. Its commercial activities should be protected. The Lianping Road is famous for its specialisation in hardware; the Jiangmen citizens and even the residents from nearby would come here to purchase hardware and home improvement materials. Its commercial activities should be protected too. And most people will go to the Telecommunications street at Penglai Road if they plan to buy a new cell phone. Supporting services need to be provided to this area to attract more industry-related business. In November 2003, the Pengjiang District government officially named Penglai Road as Penglai Telecommunications Equipment Street. The 450-meter road have 149 shops.

### 3.3.2 The Regeneration and Updating Projects

In the historical neighborhoods, some places are of historic value and in good shape yet they can't adapt to modern society. It is therefore suggested that those projects be re-developed. The projects include the expansion of Sun Yat-sen park, the restoration of traditional residential buildings at Xuding and Qiming Lane and Nanfen Lane as well as the Youth Square. As for the Qilou streets, the low level business model needs to be wiped out and makes room for casual dining and entertainment business that fits the historical neighbourhood.

# PHASING 阶段与进度

PRESERVATION AND REVITALIZATION OF JIANGMEN DISTRICT SHALL BE CARRIED OUT IN THREE PHASES. FIRST TWO PHASES SHALL COVER THE CAPITAL IMPROVEMENT WORKS TO BE DONE BY THE GOVERNMENT AGENCIES. THIS WILL INCLUDE WATERFRONT DEVELOPMENT, CREATING ACCESSES AND INFRASTRUCTURE CORRIDORS, ACQUISITION FOR THE DEVELOPMENT WORK, LAYING OF THE SERVICES INFRASTRUCTURE, DEVELOPMENT OF VACANT SPACES AND RETROFITTING OF HISTORICALLY SIGNIFICANT BUILDINGS. THIRD PHASE SHALL INCLUDE RENEWAL OF ALL STATE OWNED PROPERTIES.

THE INCREMENTAL RENEWAL OF INDIVIDUAL PROPERTIES SHALL RUN PARALLEL TO ALL THESE PHASES.

江门的旧城区的保护与修复将分成三个阶段来完成：
前两个阶段涵盖由政府主导完成的最主要的修复改善工程。其中包括沿河的建设工程、疏散通道和输排水管线廊道的增加、为建设工作开展的产权收购工作、管线铺设的铺垫工程、空置空间的建设以及对历史建筑的改造翻新；第三阶段包括对所有公有产权建筑的更新工程。

对独立产权建筑的增值更新会与这三个阶段同时进行。

图3-3-4 历史街区修复进程示意
PICTURE 3-3-4 RENOVATION PHASES OF THE HISTORICAL DISTRICT

### 3.3.3 植入项目

在墟顶片区和石湾直街片区，沿着东南盛街、京果街和石湾直街，建议依次植入余庆里创意文化商业及工作室、墟市主题广场、城市论坛、江门华侨文化体验馆、江门名人文化教育馆和江门历史博物馆。规划还打算在这两个片区分别植入民俗特色传统小商业街和古玩街。考虑到墟顶片区自古以来拥有的小吃文化，规划打算在该片区植入土特产经营项目。骑楼街片区可植入侨乡特色商业。

### 3.3.4 环境设施改善

#### 3.3.4.1 居住条件的改善

历史街区部分建筑环境破败，居民以老年人群和低收入者为主。而骑楼街区首层以上空间，大部分也已失去原有的居住功能。这种居住环境下，生活质量得不到改善，从而使大量居民外迁，历史街区也逐渐失去原有的生活气息与活力。

针对历史街区居住条件改善所遇到的问题，其改善策略不应仅仅停留在建筑本身，而应更多地在街区的保护与更新中满足原居民的生活需求。具体策略如下：

（1）在满足建筑保护要求下保留原居民生活

居住条件的更新应该以尊重原居民生活作为首要任务，最大程度保留原居民的生活，在解决居住问题的同时保护街区生活风貌。

（2）街道社区及原居民共同参与方案设计

在政府的引导管理下鼓励居民的参与，并将街道社区组织作为双向运行的中介。居民在自身利益驱动下，能积极参与改造工程，同时居民间的相互制约的作用，也能避免以往在政府单方面主导下引起的分配不公。

（3）资金来源倡导政府投入与居民自助、社会参与相结合

为了保护居住性历史街区的生活真实性，切实改善居民生活水平，对于该类街区的改造采取政府投入与居民自助、社会参与相结合的方式。

#### 3.3.4.2 公共环境的改善

历史街区公共环境的改善，应以延续城市肌理、改善街区活力为目标。公共环境的改善策略具体为：

### 3.3.3 The Implant Projects

In Xuding and Shiwanzhi, it is recommended to add the Creative and Cultural Business Studio, Xushi Plaza, City Forum, Jiangmen Overseas Chinese Culture Experience Center, Jiangmen Celebrity Gallery and Jiangmen History Museum along the Dongnansheng Street, Jingguo Street and Shiwanzhi Street. The planning also intends to add traditional folklore street and antique street. Considering the snack culture in this region the specialty products businesses will be brought in. The Qilou-style region will have special business as a town for overseas Chinese.

### 3.3.4 Improving the Environment

#### 3.3.4.1 Better Living Conditions

Part of the historical neighborhoods are dilapidated and most of the residents are the elderly and low-income people. Most space above the arcade are no longer liveable. The quality of life can not be improved in such context; so a large number of original residents transferred to other areas and the historical neighborhoods lost its original vitality.

In response to the problems in the living conditions, the improvement strategy should not only focus on the building itself, but do more to meet the needs of the inhabitants in the preservation and upgrading. The specific strategies are as follows:

(1) Stick to the original lifestyle while preserving the buildings

It is important to respect the residents first when updating the living conditions. The original lifestyle should be kept to the largest extent. The housing problems should be solved while keeping the original flavour.

(2) The community and original residents should be involved in the design

The government will encourage the residents to provide their input and use the communities as intermediaries. Driven by self-interests, the residents have the incentive to take part in reconstruction projects. In addition, the residents can restrain each other and avoid unfair distribution caused by the government's unilateral actions.

(3) Advocacy financial resources funded by the government combined with the residents and social participation.

The strategy needs to preserve the authenticity of the historic district and improve the living standards. It should be advocated that finanical resources funded by the government combined with the residents and social participation and commercial development in pursuit of economic interests should be avoided.

#### 3.3.4.2 Improve The Public Environment

Environment improvement actions in the historical neighborhoods should keep the essence of the area and add the vitality. The improvement strategies should be the following.

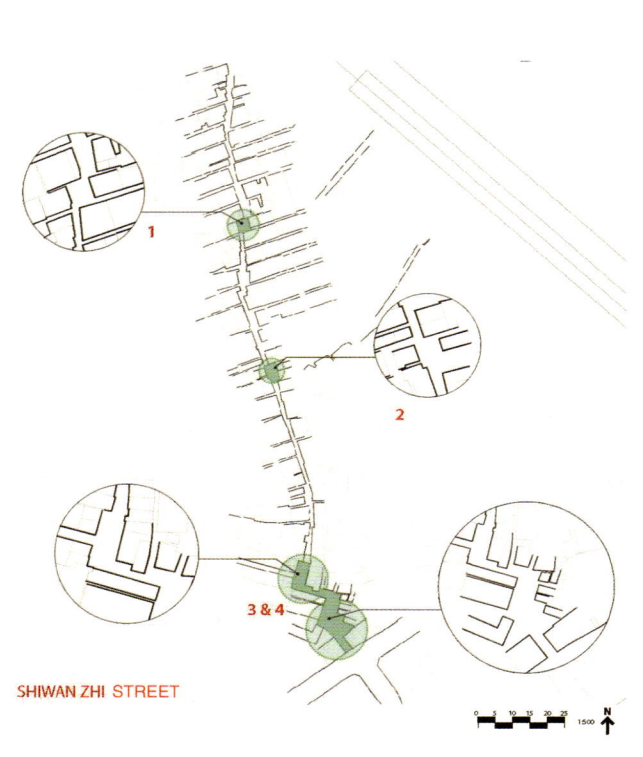

SHIWAN ZHI STREET

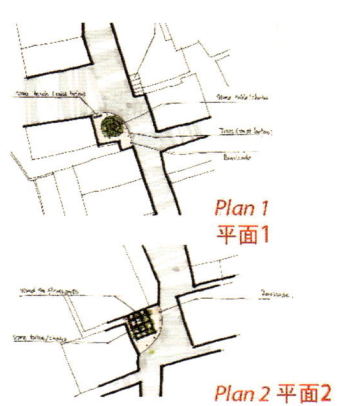

Plan 1
平面1

Plan 2 平面2

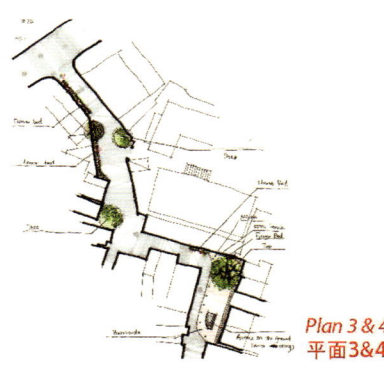

Plan 3 & 4
平面3&4

Perspective 1
透视1

Perspective 2
透视2

Perspective 3
透视3

Perspective 4
透视4

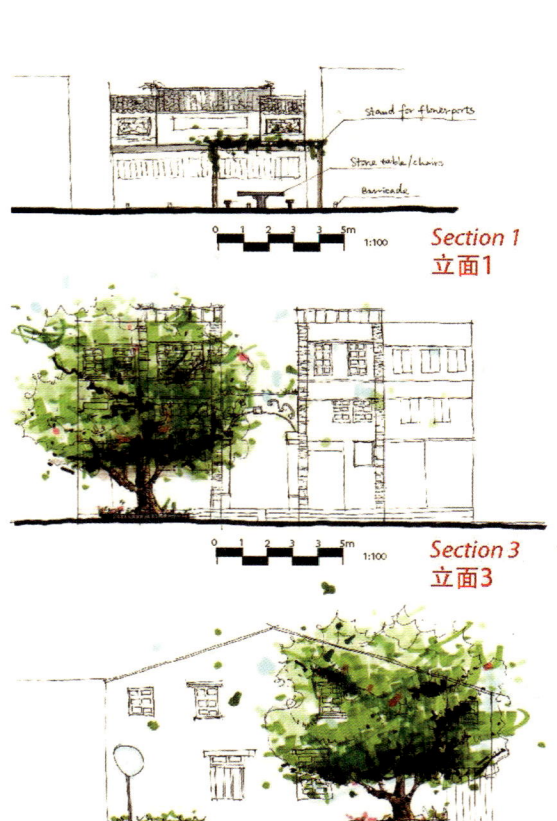

Section 1
立面1

Section 3
立面3

Section 4
立面4

图3-3-5 公共空间节点设计示意图
PICTURE 3-3-5 NODE DESIGN OF THE PUBLIC SPACE

（1）景观环境：历史街区内环境品质较差。绿化应结合公共空间布置，重点改善生活条件，通过室外活动场所的改善，整活街区环境。提倡各种形式的花坛和盆栽绿化，以适应街巷的狭小空间。有选择性地清除地块内个别建筑质量差、价值低的建筑，将腾出的空地结合景观绿化布置为社区居民活动空间。公共活动空间中适合种植乔木，留出树下活动空间，以高效利用有限的公共空间。

（2）街道景观：骑楼街区骑楼空间下，对首层商业进行整治，保证骑楼步行空间的连续性。同时建筑立面风格应与周边相协调，整治乱搭乱建。

### 3.3.4.3 基础设施的改善

历史街区基础设施建设较为滞后，但设施的改善必须以适应历史格局、保护历史原真性为前提，以改善居民生活、延续历史街区生命力为目标，不能简单地套用一般的城市标准进行规划设计和建设。必须在全面深刻地理解和掌握街区内在价值的基础上，根据历史街区的现状和实际需要，选择和综合运用各种有效的、具备适应性的改善措施。

(1) Landscape Environment: The neighborhood has poor environmental quality. The public space layout needs to combine more green elements and the living conditions need to be improved. The improved outdoor activities area will raise the level of environmental quality. Flower beds and bonsais are encouraged because the street area is quite small. Poor-quality and low-value buildings should be demolished and make room for community residents. Tree planting is encouraged in the outdoor space. The space under the tree can be used. In this way the limited public space can be utilized.

(2) Street Views: The ground floor commercial shops need to be remedied and the Qilou pedestrian street need to have continuity. The building facade should match the surroundings and illegal buildings need to be demolished.

### 3.3.4.3 Improvement of Infrastructure

The infrastructure is in poor condition. Yet the improvements need to consider the historical layout and authenticity, try to improve the resident's lives and revitalize the region. A standardized planning and design should be avoided. The adopted measures should be effective and adaptive, drawing from thorough research and understanding of the internal values and the status quo.

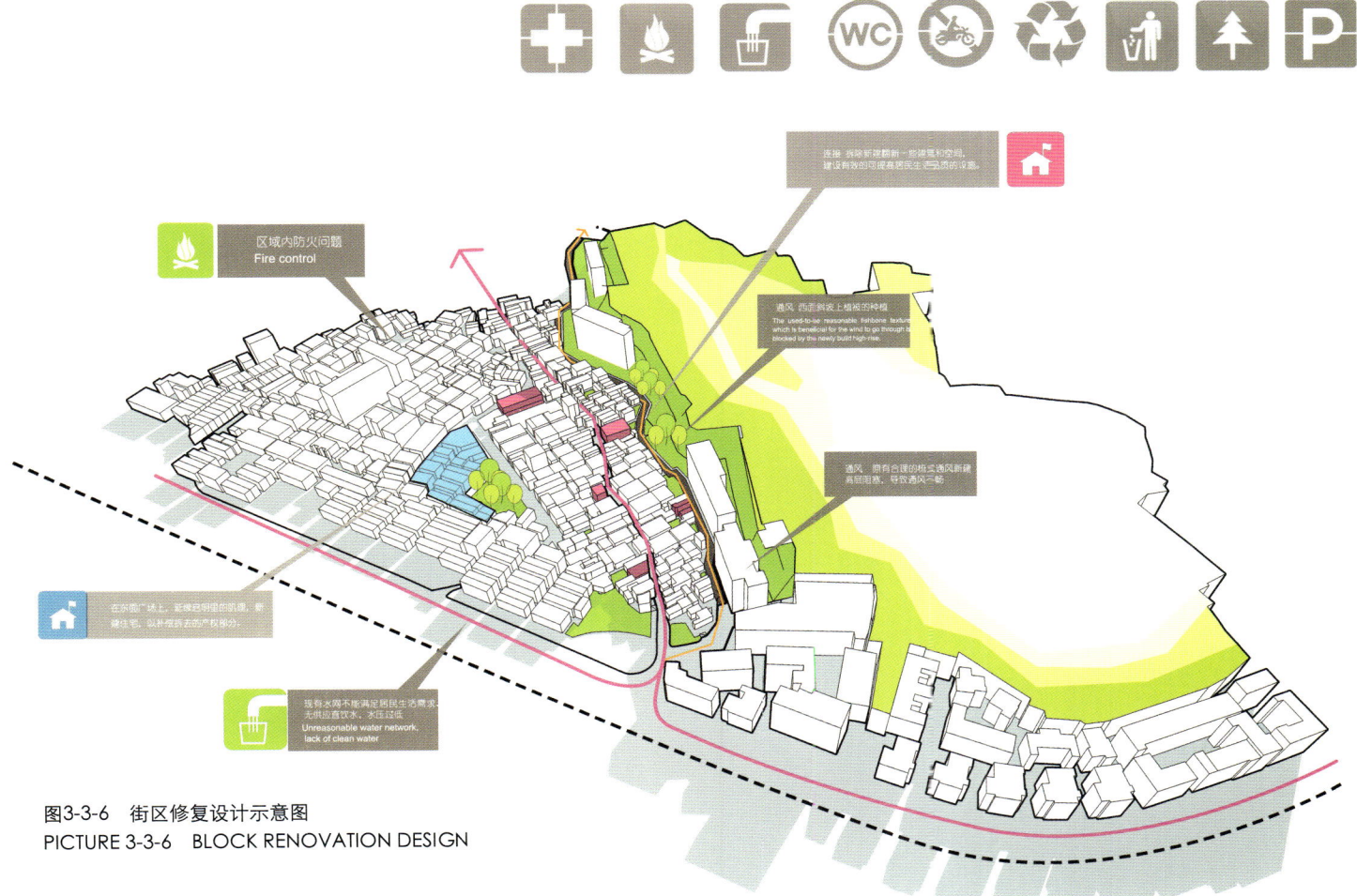

图3-3-6　街区修复设计示意图
PICTURE 3-3-6　BLOCK RENOVATION DESIGN

图3-3-7 历史街区鸟瞰图
PICTURE 3-3-7 BIRD-VIEW OF HISTORICAL NEIGHBORHOOD

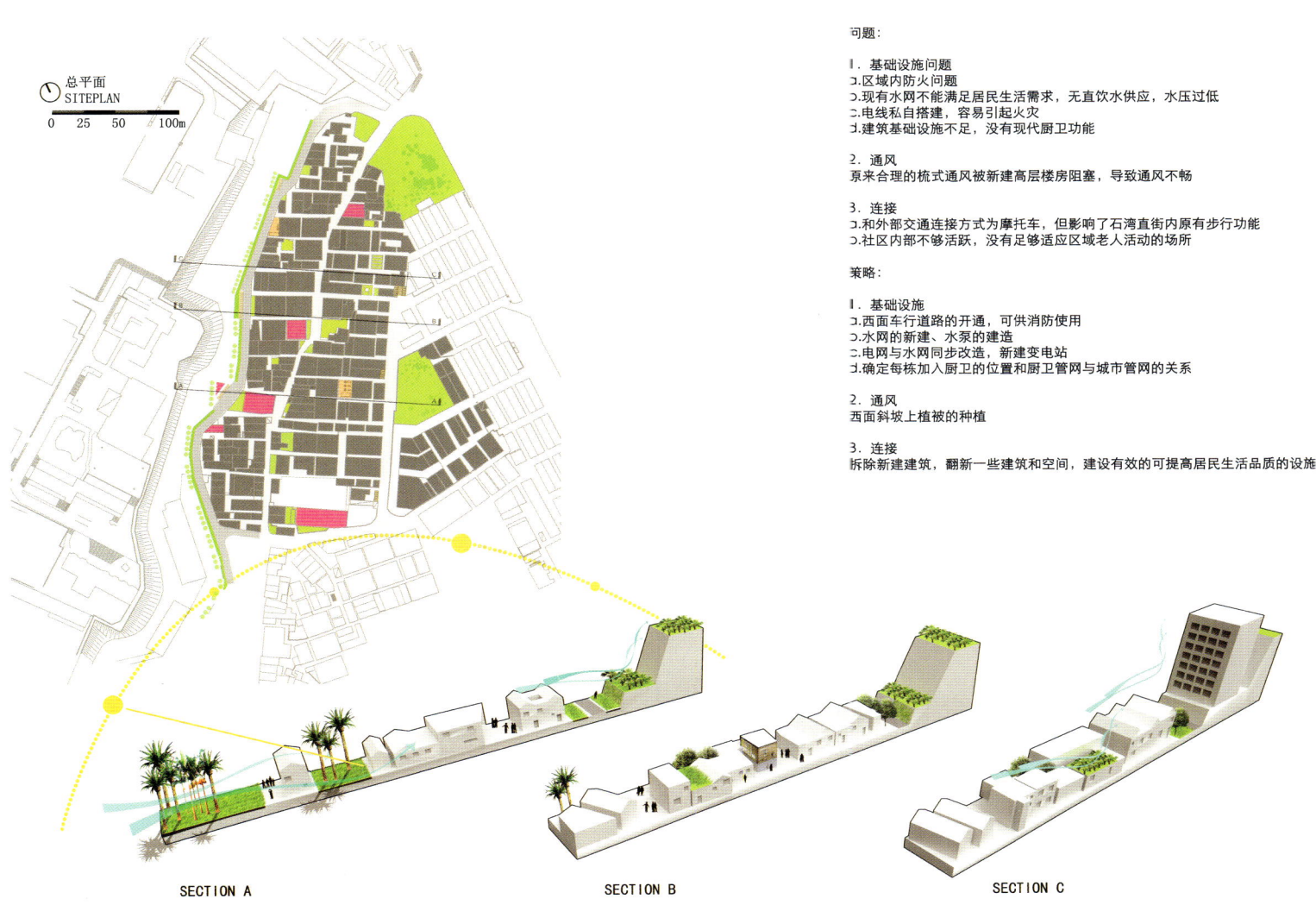

问题：

1. 基础设施问题
   a. 区域内防火问题
   b. 现有水网不能满足居民生活需求，无直饮水供应，水压过低
   c. 电线私自搭建，容易引起火灾
   d. 建筑基础设施不足，没有现代厨卫功能

2. 通风
   原来合理的梳式通风被新建高层楼房阻塞，导致通风不畅

3. 连接
   a. 和外部交通连接方式为摩托车，但影响了石湾直街内原有步行功能
   b. 社区内部不够活跃，没有足够适应区域老人活动的场所

策略：

1. 基础设施
   a. 西面车行道路的开通，可供消防使用
   b. 水网的新建、水泵的建造
   c. 电网与水网同步改造，新建变电站
   d. 确定每栋加入厨卫的位置和厨卫管网与城市管网的关系

2. 通风
   西面斜坡上植被的种植

3. 连接
   拆除新建建筑，翻新一些建筑和空间，建设有效的可提高居民生活品质的设施

图3-3-8 街区断面研究
PICTURE 3-3-8 BLOCK SECTION RESEARCH

# 附录：江门长堤历史街区重要历史建筑名录
Apendix

| 建筑编号 | 路名 | 门牌号码 | 建筑名称 | 是否有骑楼 | 建筑分级 | 建筑性质 | 混合方式 | 建筑年代 | 建筑层数 | 产权情况 | 建筑质量 | 建筑外观质量 | 结构类型 | 建筑风貌 |
|---|---|---|---|---|---|---|---|---|---|---|---|---|---|---|
| A-J055 | 启明里 | 9 | | | 一类 | 居住 | | 清末民初 | 2 | 私房 | | 中等 | 砖木结构 | 好 |
| A-J056 | 启明里 | 8 | | | 一类 | 居住 | | 清末民初 | 2 | 私房 | | 中等 | 砖木结构 | 好 |
| A-J059 | 启明里 | 4? | | | 一类 | 居住 | | 清末民初 | 2 | 私房 | | 中等 | 混合结构 | 好 |
| A-J060 | 启明里 | 5 | | | 一类 | 居住 | | 清末民初 | 2 | 私房 | | 中等 | 混合结构 | 好 |
| A-J075 | 启明里 | 17 | | | 一类 | 居住 | | 清末民初 | 2 | 私房 | | 中等 | 砖木结构 | 好 |
| A-J076 | 启明里 | 16 | | | 一类 | 居住 | | 清末民初 | 2 | 私房 | | 中等 | 砖木结构 | 好 |
| A-J077 | 启明里 | 15 | | | 一类 | 居住 | | 清末民初 | 2 | 私房 | | 中等 | 砖木结构 | 好 |
| A-J078 | 启明里 | 14 | | | 一类 | 居住 | | 清末民初 | 2 | 私房 | | 中等 | 砖木结构 | 好 |
| A-J079 | 启明里 | 13 | | | 一类 | 居住 | | 清末民初 | 2 | 私房 | | 良好 | 砖木结构 | 好 |
| A-J080 | 启明里 | 12 | | | 一类 | 居住 | | 清末民初 | 2 | 私房 | | 良好 | 砖木结构 | 好 |
| A-J101 | 启明里 | 23 | | | 一类 | 居住 | | 清末民初 | 2 | 私房 | | 中等 | 砖木结构 | 好 |
| A-J102 | 启明里 | 22 | | | 一类 | 居住 | | 清末民初 | 2 | 私房 | | 中等 | 砖木结构 | 好 |
| A-J103 | 启明里 | 21 | | | 一类 | 居住 | | 清末民初 | 2 | 私房 | | 中等 | 砖木结构 | 好 |
| A-J104 | 启明里 | 20 | | | 一类 | 居住 | | 清末民初 | 2 | 私房 | | 中等 | 砖木结构 | 好 |
| A-J112 | 新第里 | 15 | | | 一类 | 居住 | | 清末民初 | 1 | 私房 | | 中等 | 砖木结构 | 好 |
| A-J171 | 长庆里 | 25 | | | 一类 | 居住 | | 民国时期 | 3 | 私房 | | 中等 | 砖木结构 | 好 |
| A-J181 | 新第里 | 3 | | | 一类 | 居住 | | 清末民初 | 3 | 私房 | | 良好 | 砖木结构 | 好 |
| A-J182 | 新第里 | 2 | | | 一类 | 居住 | | 清末民初 | 3 | 私房 | | 良好 | 砖木结构 | 好 |
| A-J183 | 新第里 | 1 | | | 一类 | 居住 | | 清末民初 | 3 | 私房 | | 良好 | 砖木结构 | 好 |
| A-J216 | 启明里 | 42 | | | 一类 | 居住 | | 民国时期 | 3 | 私房 | | 中等 | 砖木结构 | 好 |
| A-J217 | 启明里 | 41 | | | 一类 | 居住 | | 民国时期 | 3 | 私房 | | 中等 | 砖木结构 | 好 |
| A-J219 | 启明里 | 40 | | | 一类 | 居住 | | 民国时期 | 3 | 私房 | | 中等 | 砖木结构 | 好 |
| A-J220 | 启明里 | 39 | | | 一类 | 居住 | | 民国时期 | 3 | 私房 | | 中等 | 砖木结构 | 好 |
| A-J233 | 龙聚里 | 5 | | | 一类 | 居住 | | 民国初期 | 2 | 私房 | | 中等 | 砖木结构 | 好 |
| A-J238 | 龙聚里 | 3 | | | 一类 | 居住 | | 民国初期 | 2 | 私房 | | 良好 | 砖木结构 | 好 |
| A-J241 | 启明里 | 61 | | | 一类 | 居住 | | 民国时期 | 2 | 私房 | | 中等 | 砖木结构 | 好 |
| A-J242 | 启明里 | 60 | | | 一类 | 居住 | | 民国时期 | 2 | 私房 | | 中等 | 砖木结构 | 好 |
| A-J253 | 南芬里 | 46? | | | | 居住 | | 清末民初 | 2 | 私房 | | 中等 | 砖木结构 | 好 |
| A-J255 | 启明里 | 70 | | | 一类 | 居住 | | 民国时期 | 2 | 私房 | | 良好 | 砖木结构 | 好 |
| A-J256 | 启明里 | 69 | | | 一类 | 居住 | | 民国时期 | 2 | 私房 | | 良好 | 砖木结构 | 好 |
| A-J257 | 启明里 | 68 | | | 一类 | 居住 | | 清末民初 | 2 | 私房 | | 良好 | 砖木结构 | 好 |
| A-J258 | 启明里 | 67 | | | 一类 | 居住 | | 清末民初 | 2 | 私房 | | 良好 | 砖木结构 | 好 |
| A-J259 | 南芬里 | 76 | | | 一类 | 居住 | | 清末民初 | 2 | 私房 | | 中等 | 砖木结构 | 好 |
| A-J264 | 南芬里 | 34 | | | 一类 | 闲置 | | 民国初期 | 2 | 私房 | | 良好 | 砖木结构 | 好 |
| A-J265 | 南芬里 | 30 | | | 一类 | 居住 | | 民国初期 | 2 | 私房 | | 良好 | 砖木结构 | 好 |
| A-J274 | 南芬里 | 17 | | | 一类 | 居住 | | 清末民初 | 2 | 私房 | | 中等 | 砖木结构 | 好 |
| A-J277 | 南芬里 | 16 | | | 一类 | 闲置 | | 清末民初 | 2 | 私房 | | 中等 | 混合结构 | 好 |
| A-J280 | 南芬里 | 40 | | | 一类 | 居住 | | 清末民初 | 2 | 私房 | | 良好 | 砖木结构 | 好 |
| A-J285 | 南芬里 | 未知 | | | 一类 | 居住 | | 清末民初 | 2 | 私房 | | 中等 | 砖木结构 | 好 |
| A-J290 | 南芬里 | 25 | | | 一类 | 居住 | | 民国初期 | 2 | 私房 | | 良好 | 砖木结构 | 好 |
| A-J291 | 南芬里 | 24 | | | | 居住 | | 民国初期 | 2 | 私房 | | 一般 | 砖木结构 | 差 |
| A-J292 | 南芬里 | 12 | | | 一类 | 混合 | 下商上居 | 清末民初 | 2 | 私房 | | 中等 | 砖木结构 | 好 |
| A-J293 | 南芬里 | 11 | | | 一类 | 混合 | 下商上居 | 民国初期 | 2 | 私房 | | 良好 | 砖木结构 | 好 |
| A-J294 | 南芬里 | 10 | | | 一类 | 居住 | | 民国初期 | 2 | 私房 | | 良好 | 砖木结构 | 好 |
| B-J054 | 龙聚里 | 35 | | | 一类 | 居住 | | 民国时期 | 2 | 私房 | | 一般 | 砖木结构 | 中 |
| B-J094 | 龙聚里 | 36 | | | 一类 | 居住 | | 民国时期 | 3 | 私房 | | 中等 | 砖木结构 | 中 |
| B-J351 | 未知 | 72 | | 是 | 一类 | 混合 | 下商上居 | 清末民初 | 3 | 私房 | | 一般 | 砖混结构 | 好 |
| B-J366 | 未知 | 44 | | 是 | 一类 | 混合 | 下商上居 | 清末民初 | 3 | 私房 | | 中等 | 砖混结构 | 好 |
| B-J437 | 未知 | 未知 | 宝和当铺 | | 文保 | 公共 | | 民国时期 | 5 | 私房 | | 中等 | 砖木结构 | 好 |
| C-J239 | 太平路 | 27 | | 是 | 一类 | 混合 | 下商上居 | 清末民初 | 3 | 私房 | | 一般 | 砖木结构 | 好 |
| C-J254 | 太平路 | 57 | | 是 | 一类 | 混合 | 下商上居 | 清末民初 | 3 | 私房 | | 中等 | 砖木结构 | 好 |

续表

| 建筑编号 | 路名 | 门牌号码 | 建筑名称 | 是否有骑楼 | 建筑分级 | 建筑性质 | 混合方式 | 建筑年代 | 建筑层数 | 产权情况 | 建筑质量 | 建筑外观质量 | 结构类型 | 建筑风貌 |
|---|---|---|---|---|---|---|---|---|---|---|---|---|---|---|
| C-J285 | 新椰路 | | | 是 | 一类 | 居住 | | 清末民初 | 3 | 私房 | | 一般 | 砖木结构 | 好 |
| D-J022 | 镇东路 | 未知 | | | | 混合 | 下商上居 | 清末民初 | 3 | 私房 | | 良好 | 砖木结构 | 好 |
| D-J028 | 钓台路 | 未知 | | 是 | 一类 | 混合 | 下商上居 | 清末民初 | 4 | 私房 | | 一般 | 砖木结构 | 好 |
| D-J145 | 书院路 | 未知 | | 是 | | 混合 | 下商上居 | 民国时期 | 3 | 私房 | | 良好 | 砖木结构 | 中 |
| D-J308 | 堤中路 | 未知 | | 是 | 一类 | 混合 | 下商上居 | 清末民初 | 3 | 私房 | | 良好 | 砖木结构 | 好 |
| D-J309 | 堤中路 | 未知 | | | | 混合 | 下商上居 | 清末民初 | 3 | 私房 | | 良好 | 砖木结构 | 好 |
| D-J347 | 堤中路 | 未知 | | 是 | 一类 | 混合 | 下商上居 | 清末民初 | 2 | 私房 | | 良好 | 砖木结构 | 好 |
| D-J361 | 镇东路 | 未知 | | 是 | 一类 | 混合 | 下商上居 | 清末民初 | 3 | 私房 | | 中等 | 砖木结构 | 好 |
| D-J374 | 钓台路 | 未知 | 钓台故居 | 是 | 文保 | 公共 | | 清代 | 2 | 自有 | | 中等 | 砖木结构 | 好 |
| E-J038 | 莲塘南路 | 19? | 莲塘南当铺 | 是 | 一类 | 未知 | | 民国时期 | 5 | 未知 | | 良好 | 混合结构 | 好 |
| E-J075 | 新华路 | 15 | | 是 | 一类 | 混合 | 下商上住 | 清末民初 | 4 | 未知 | | 中等 | 混合结构 | 好 |
| E-J139 | 仓后路 | 未知 | | 是 | 一类 | 混合 | 下商上住 | 清末民初 | 3 | 未知 | | 良好 | 混合结构 | 好 |
| E-J184 | 常安路 | 未知 | 粤中专员总署 | | 一类 | 商业 | | 清末民初 | 6 | 未知 | | 良好 | 框架结构 | 好 |
| E-J237 | 仓后路 | 44 | | 是 | 二类 | 商业 | | 清末民初 | 3 | 公房 | 有危险点 | | 框架结构 | 好 |
| E-J240 | 仓后路 | 38 | | | | 商业 | | 清末民初 | 3 | 公房 | 基本完好 | | 混合结构 | 好 |
| E-J365 | 兴宁路 | 69 | | 是 | 一类 | 商业 | | 清末民初 | 3 | 未知 | | 中等 | 框架结构 | 好 |
| E-J376 | 兴宁路 | 63 | | 是 | 一类 | 混合 | 下商上住 | 清末民初 | 3 | 未知 | | 中等 | 框架结构 | 好 |
| E-J403 | 新市路 | 36 | | 是 | 一类 | 商业 | | 清末民初 | 3 | 未知 | | 中等 | 混合结构 | 好 |
| E-J443 | 兴宁路 | 23 | | 是 | 一类 | 商业 | | 清末民初 | 3 | 公房 | 基本完好 | | 混合结构 | 好 |
| F-J195 | 余庆里 | 21 | | | 一类 | 居住 | | 民国初期 | 2 | | | 良好 | 混合 | 好 |
| F-J196 | 余庆里 | 28 | | | | 居住 | | 民国初期 | 2 | | | 良好 | 混合 | 好 |
| F-J197 | 余庆里 | 20 | | | | 居住 | | 民国初期 | 2 | | | 良好 | 混合 | 好 |
| F-J198 | 余庆里 | 29 | | | | 居住 | | 民国初期 | 2 | | | 良好 | 混合 | 好 |
| F-J199 | 余庆里 | 19 | | | | 居住 | | 民国初期 | 2 | | | 良好 | 混合 | 好 |
| F-J200 | 余庆里 | 31 | | | | 居住 | | 民国初期 | 2 | | | 良好 | 混合 | 好 |
| F-J201 | 余庆里 | 18 | | | | 居住 | | 民国初期 | 2 | | | 良好 | 混合 | 好 |
| F-J202 | 余庆里 | 32 | | | | 居住 | | 民国初期 | 2 | | | 良好 | 混合 | 好 |
| F-J203 | 余庆里 | 17 | | | | 居住 | | 民国初期 | 2 | | | 良好 | 混合 | 好 |
| F-J204 | 余庆里 | 33 | | | | 居住 | | 民国初期 | 2 | | | 良好 | 砖木 | 好 |
| F-J205 | 余庆里 | 16 | | | | 居住 | | 民国初期 | 2 | | | 良好 | 砖木 | 好 |
| F-J206 | 余庆里 | 34 | | | | 居住 | | 民国初期 | 2 | | | 良好 | 混合 | 好 |
| F-J207 | 余庆里 | 15 | | | | 居住 | | 民国初期 | 2 | 政府 | | 良好 | 混合 | 好 |
| F-J208 | 余庆里 | 36 | | | | 居住 | | 民国初期 | 2 | | | 良好 | 砖木 | 好 |
| F-J209 | 余庆里 | 14 | | | | 居住 | | 民国初期 | 2 | | | 良好 | 混合 | 好 |
| F-J210 | 余庆里 | 37 | | | | 居住 | | 民国初期 | 2 | | | 良好 | 砖木 | 好 |
| F-J219 | 余庆里 | 10 | | | | 居住 | | 民国初期 | 2 | | | 良好 | 砖木 | 好 |
| F-J221 | 余庆里 | 9 | | | | 居住 | | 民国初期 | 2 | | | 良好 | 混合 | 好 |
| F-J223 | 余庆里 | 8 | | | | 居住 | | 民国初期 | 2 | | | 良好 | 混合 | 好 |
| F-J225 | 余庆里 | 7 | | | | 居住 | | 民国初期 | 2 | | | 中等 | 混合 | 好 |
| F-J227 | 余庆里 | 6 | | | | 居住 | | 民国初期 | 2 | | | 中等 | 混合 | 好 |
| F-J228 | 余庆里 | 5 | | | | 居住 | | 民国初期 | 2 | | | 中等 | 混合 | 好 |
| F-J229 | 余庆里 | 4 | | | 一类 | 居住 | | 民国初期 | 2 | | | 中等 | 混合 | 好 |
| G-J113 | 东南胜街 | 未知 | 永安按当铺遗址 | | 文保 | 历史遗迹 | | 民国时期 | 3 | 私房 | | 良好 | 混合结构 | 好 |
| G-J361 | 莲平后街 | 8 | | | 一类 | 住宅 | | 清末民初 | 3 | 私房 | | 中等 | 混合结构 | 好 |
| H-J249 | 堤中路 | 73 | | 是 | 一类 | 商业 | | 清末民初 | 4 | 公房 | 基本完好 | | 框架结构 | 好 |
| H-J260 | 堤中路 | 79 | | 是 | 一类 | 商业 | | 清末民初 | 3 | 未知 | | 良好 | 混合结构 | 好 |
| H-J271 | 堤中路 | 85 | | 是 | 一类 | 混合 | 下商上居、商业办公混合 | 清末民初 | 6 | 未知 | | 良好 | 框架结构 | 好 |
| H-J272 | 堤中路 | 86 | 中华酒店 | 是 | 一类 | 混合 | 酒店、快餐店混合 | 民国时期 | 3 | 公房 | 一般损坏 | | 框架结构 | 好 |

注释：根据华南理工大学建筑设计研究院编制的《江门历史街区保护与更新规划》（2013）对历史建筑风貌及质量进行的综合价值评估，建议上述99座历史建筑为重点保护建筑。

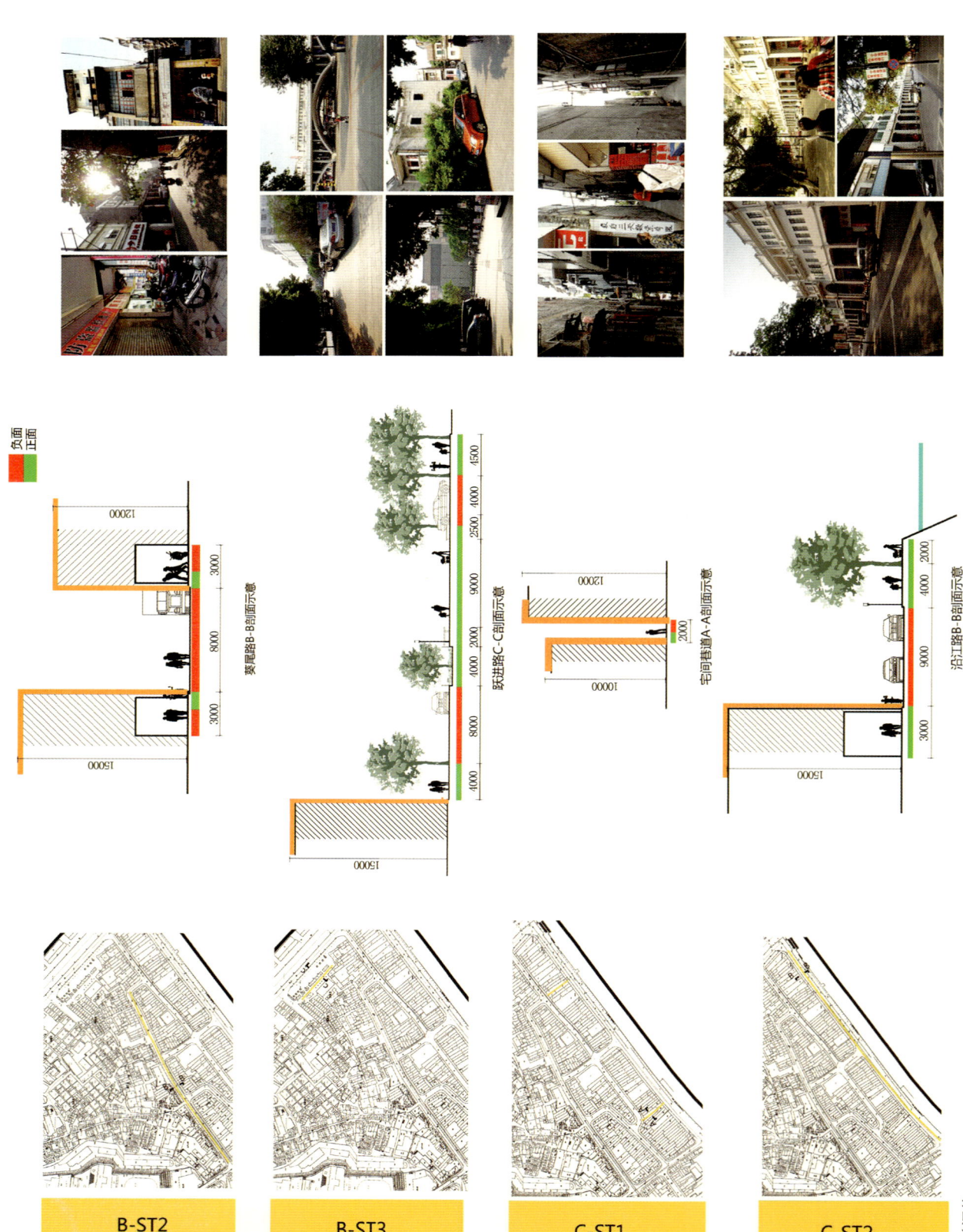

街道评价：

B-ST2评价：骑楼架空，人行道宽高比约为3:4，空间尺度良好，但摩托车乱停乱放阻碍通行情况严重。街道与建筑的宽高比约为2:3，人车混行。

B-ST3评价：跃进路与建筑群区域以广场相间。广场内车行通道与一侧建筑的宽高比为4:5。宽度能满足一般人车混行，但常被停车占据空间。广场地面无高差，满足无障碍通行。

C-ST1评价：以树荫为界面形成明暗分区，满足休憩与活动需求。

C-ST2评价：作为连接大道的支巷，尺度宜人，宽高比为1:5，有冷巷效应。

C-ST2评价：街道与一侧建筑的宽高比为3:5，高峰时期容易交通堵塞。

附图1-1 街道评价
FIGURE 1-1 STREET EVALUATION

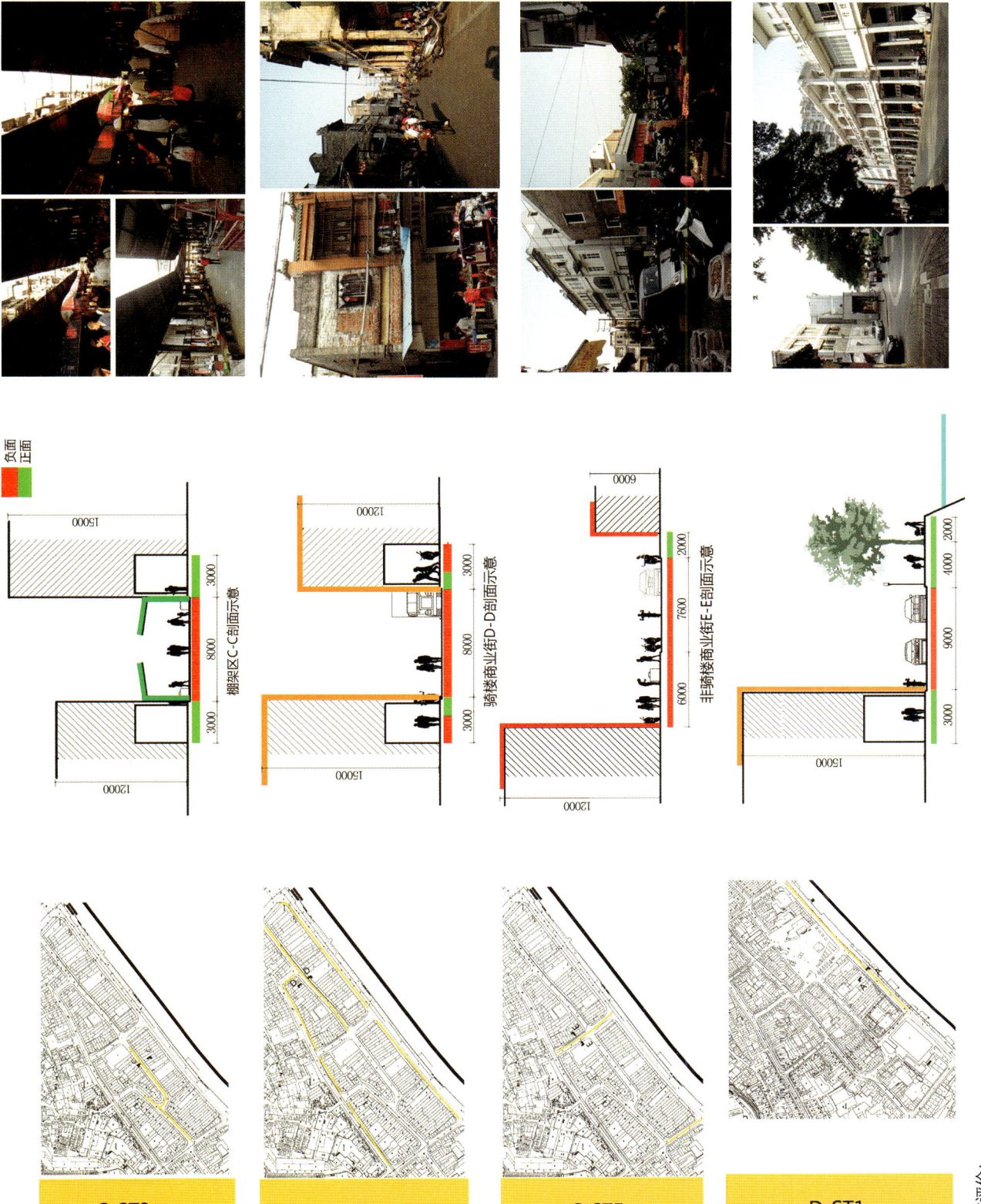

街道评价：

C-ST3评价：街道与建筑宽高比约为8:15，满足使用要求，卫生条件需改善。

C-ST4评价：街道与建筑宽高比为7:15，人车混行，两边多被小贩占据。

C-ST5评价：道路与建筑的高宽比为12.7~1:1，步行道路虽然有6米宽，但是被摩托车和临时摊档大面积占用，行走不顺畅。

D-ST1评价：街道与一侧建筑的宽高比为3:5，高峰时期容易交通堵塞。

附图 1-2　街道评价

FIGURE 1-2　STREET EVALUATION

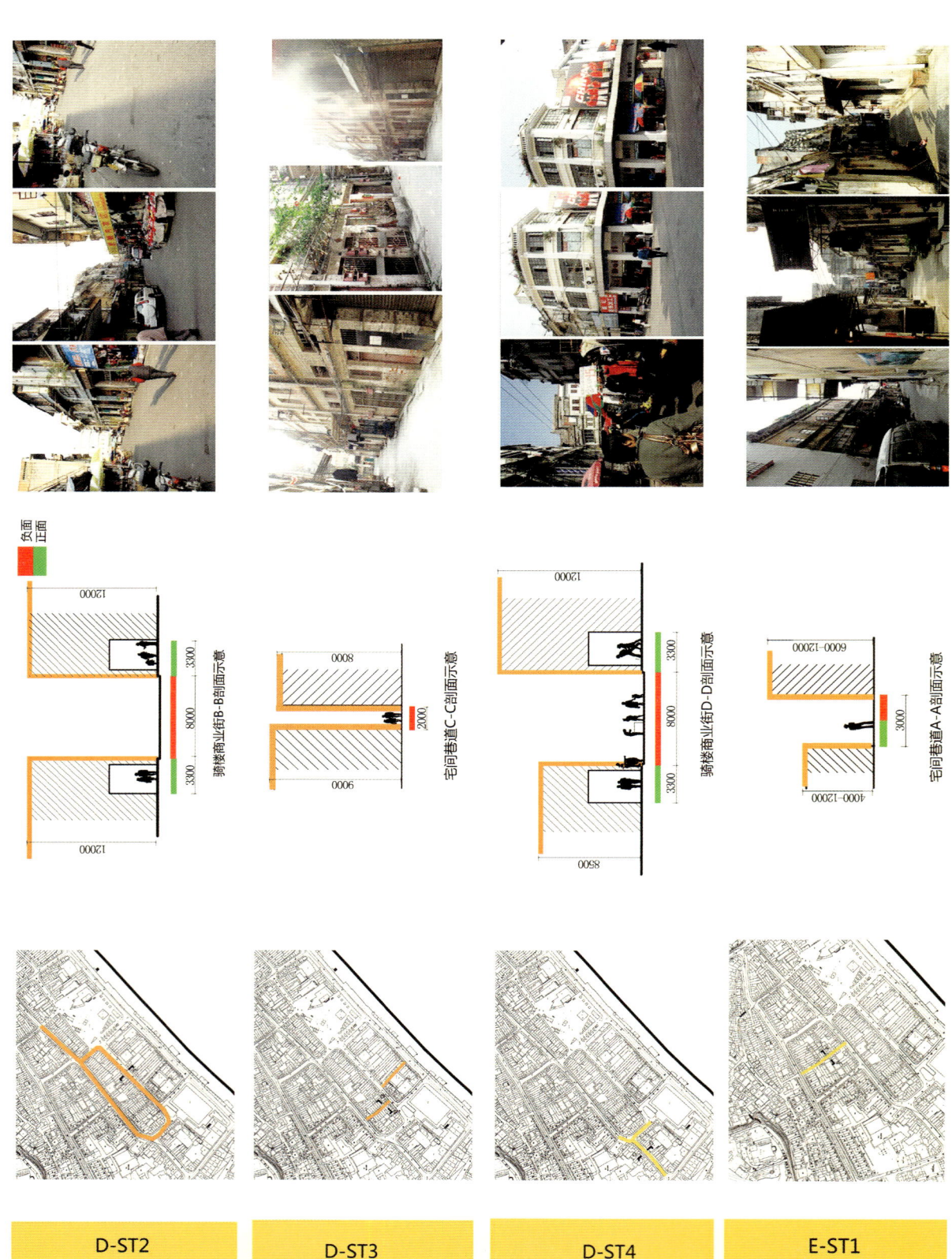

附图 1-3 街道评价
FIGURE 1-3 STREET EVALUATION

附图1-4 街道评价
FIGURE 1-4 STREET EVALUATION

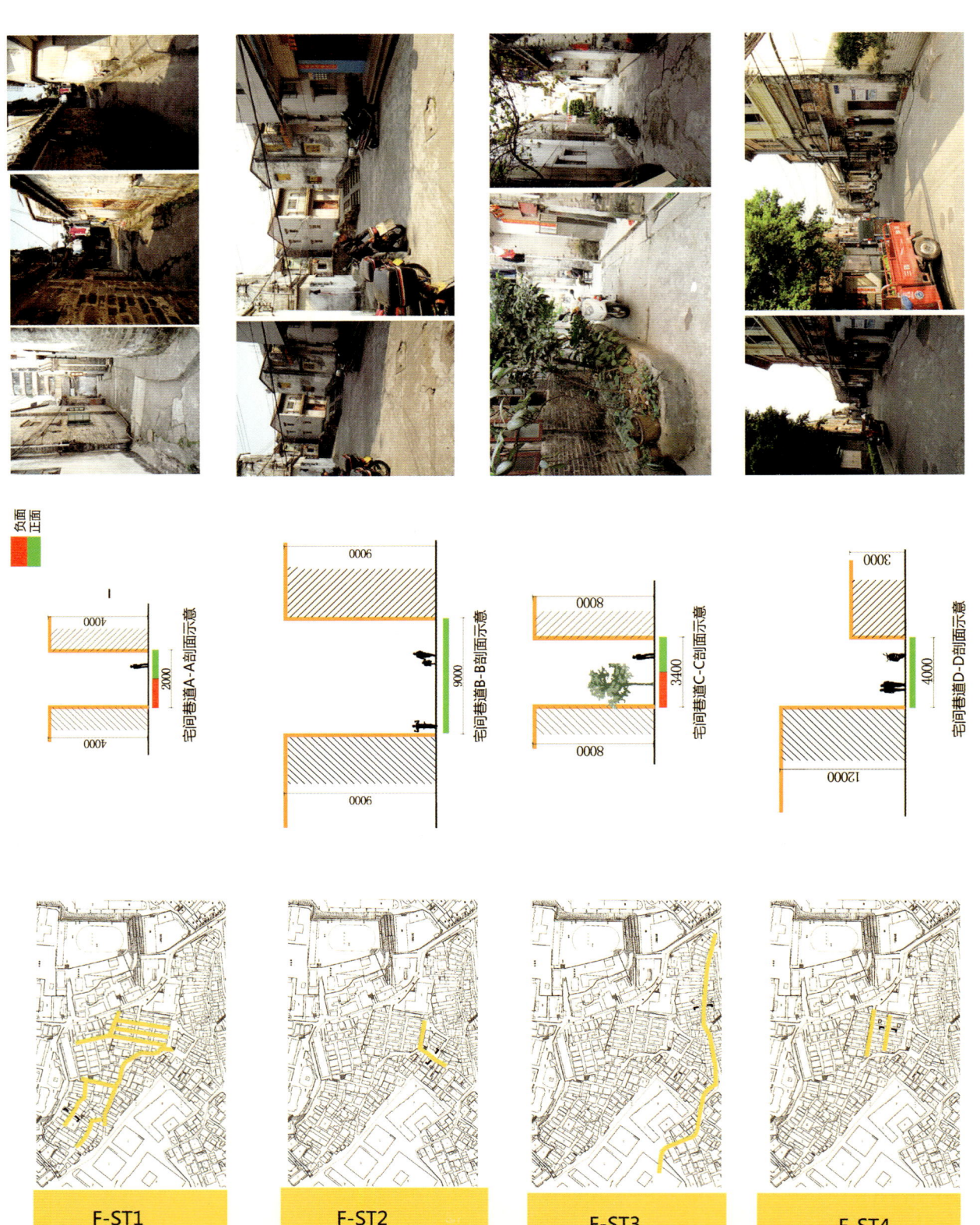

附图 1-5 街道评价
FIGURE 1-5 STREET EVALUATION

街道评价：

F-ST1评价：这是民居中比较典型的巷道形式，尺度宽高比约为1:2，道路比较曲折，一侧为民居的正面，一侧多为民居的背面。

F-ST2评价：此处为周边较大的空地，宽高比为1:1，空间较为舒适。

F-ST3评价：联排民居之间的巷道，尺度宽高比约为1:2.35，并有一定的绿化，适宜居民休憩。

F-ST4评价：街道与建筑宽高比约为1:3，道路人车混行。

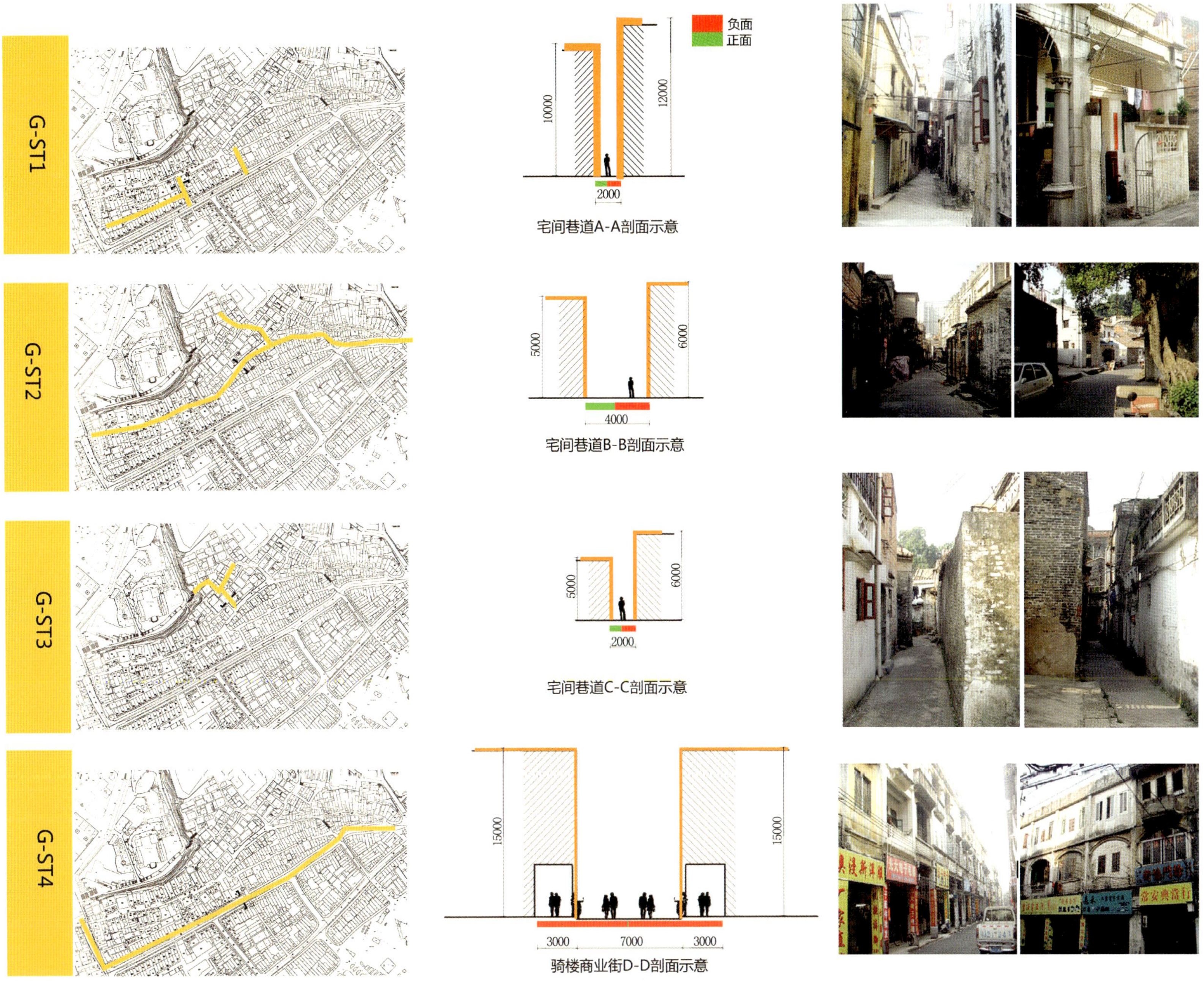

街道评价：

G-ST1评价：小巷为连接大道的捷径，尺度宜人，宽高比为1:5，有冷巷效应。
G-ST2评价：街道与建筑宽高比为1:1~2:1，可容纳较多的活动。
G-ST3评价：街道与建筑宽高比为2:1~3:1，尺度宜人，弯道多，对于非当地住户，其路径比较难以寻找。
G-ST4评价：人行道多被占用，用作停车和摆放杂物。

附图 1-6 街道评价

FIGURE 1-6 STREET EVALUATION

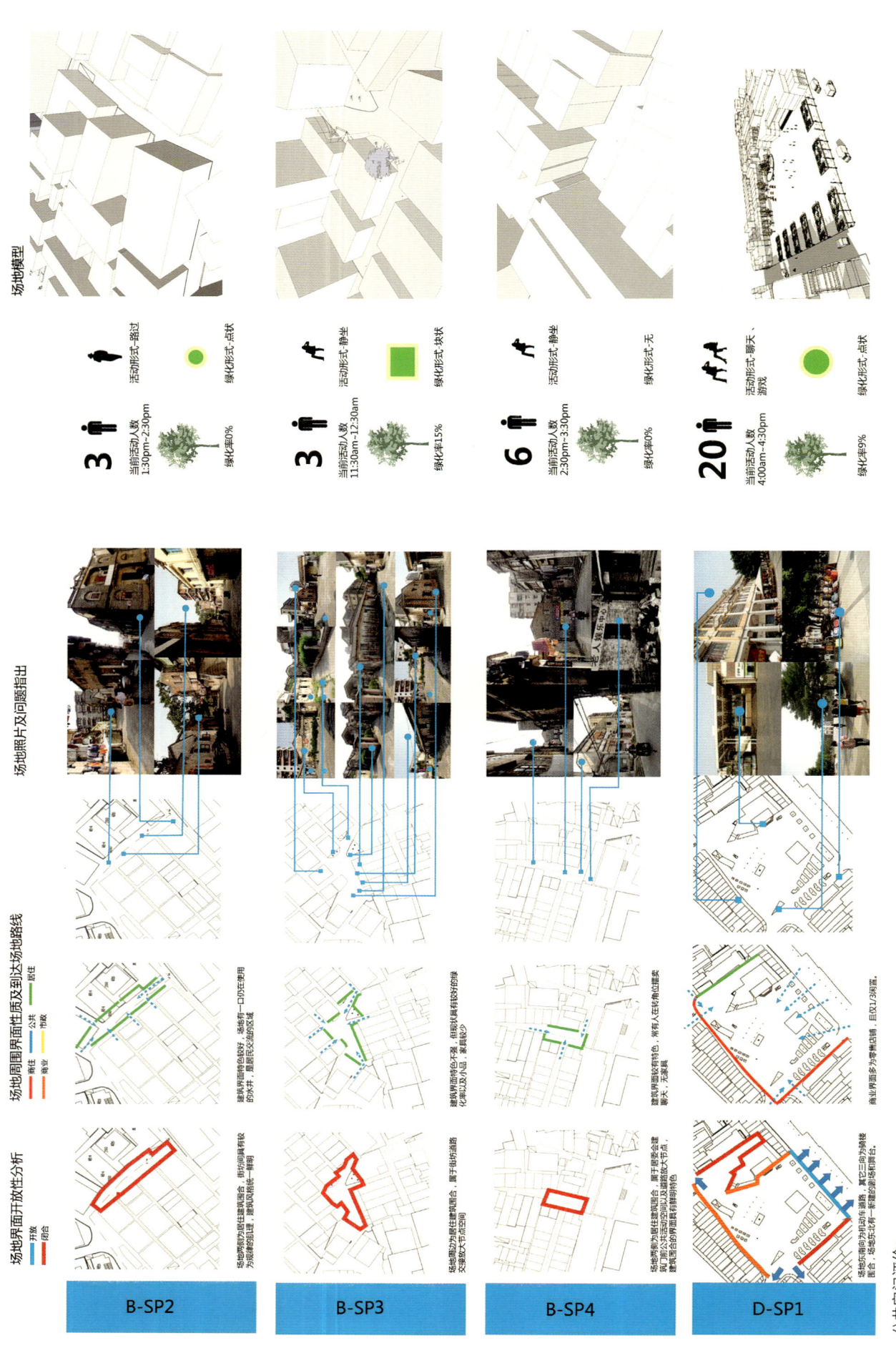

附图 1-7 公共空间评价 FIGURE 1-7 PUBLIC SPACE EVALUATION

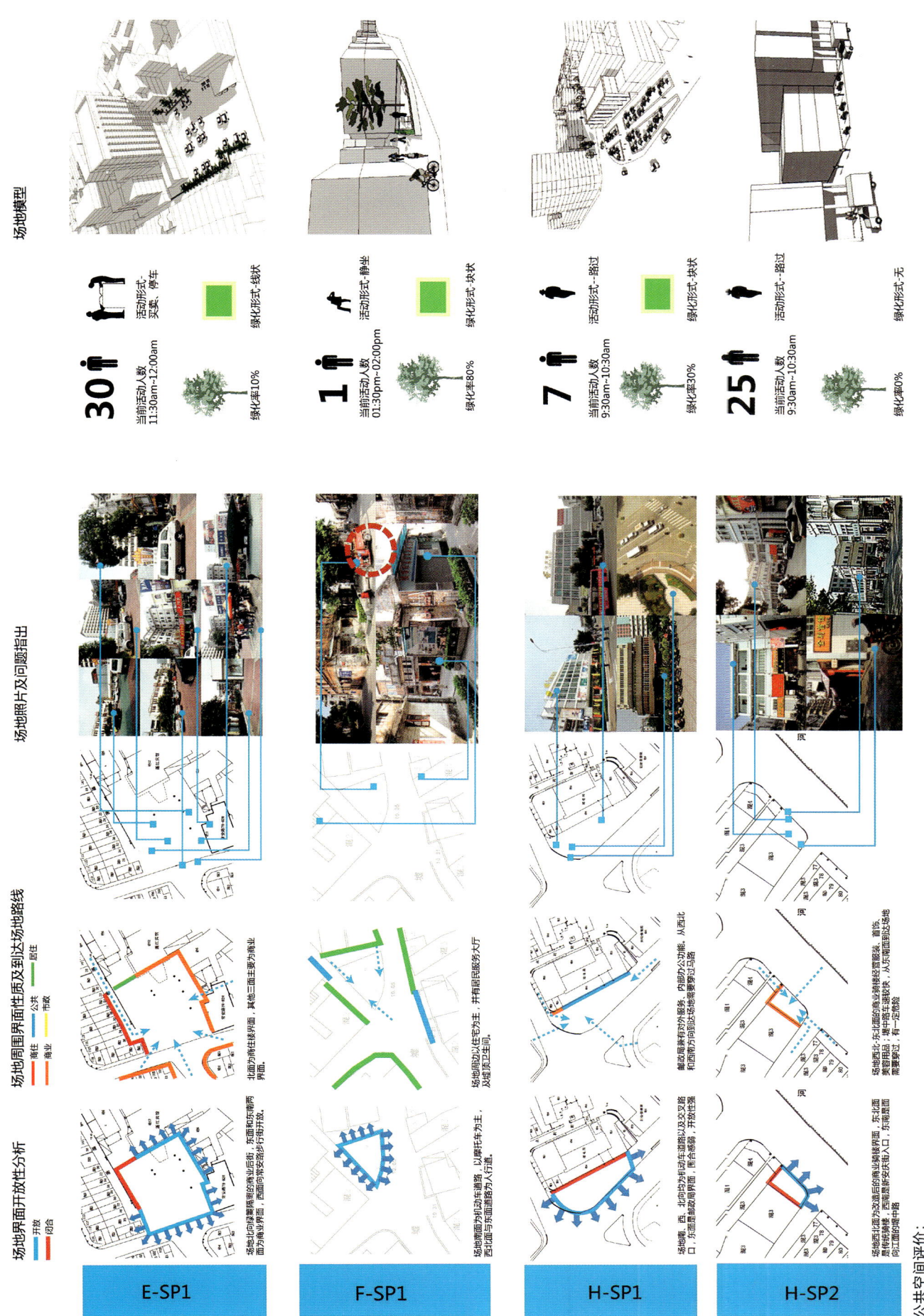

附图1-8 公共空间评价

FIGURE 1-8 PUBLIC SPACE EVALUATION

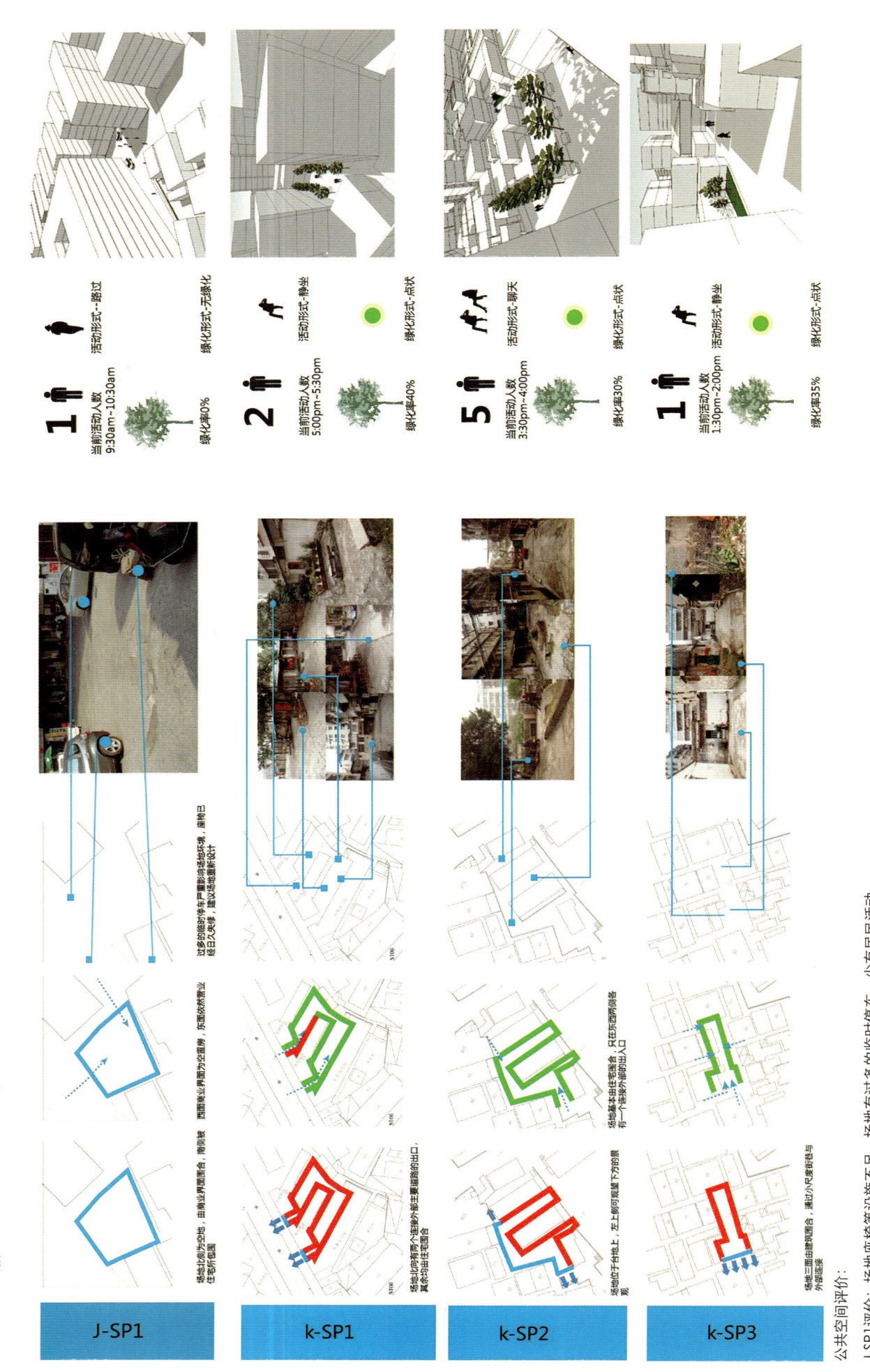

附图 1-9 PUBLIC SPACE EVALUATION

附图 1-10　中山公园
FIGURE 1-10　ZHONGSHAN PARK

附图 1-11　启明里广场
FIGURE 1-11　THE QIMING LANE SQUARE

附图 1-12 蓬江沿岸历史照片
FIGURE 1-12 HISTORICAL PICTURE OF PENGJIANG COAST

附图 1-13 蓬江沿岸历史照片
FIGURE 1-13 HISTORICAL PICTURE OF PENGJIANG COAST

附图 1-14　蓬江沿岸历史照片
FIGURE 1-14　HISTORICAL PICTURE OF PENGJIANG COAST

附图 1-15　长堤路历史照片
FIGURE 1-15　HISTORICAL PICTURE OF CHANGDI ROAD

附图 1-16　长堤路历史照片
FIGURE 1-16　HISTORICAL PICTURE OF CHANGDI ROAD

附图 1-17　长堤路历史照片
FIGURE 1-17　HISTORICAL PICTURE OF CHANGDI ROAD

附图 1-18 长堤路历史照片
FIGURE 1-18 HISTORICAL PICTURE OF CHANGDI ROAD

# 主要参考文献

[1] 江门市地方志编纂委员会．江门市志（上下册）[M]．广州：广东人民出版社，1998．
[2] 江门市地名委员会，江门市国土局．江门市地名志 [M]．广州：广东省地图出版社，1991．
[3] 江门市蓬江区地方志编纂委员会．蓬江区志：1984—2004[M]．北京：方志出版社，2012．
[4] 江门市水利志编纂委员会．江门市水利志 [M]．水利水电出版社，2008．
[5] 江门市档案局，江门市地方志办公室．江门之最（第一辑）[M]．2004．
[6] 何福海．光绪新宁县志 [M]．广东江门台山：清光绪 19 年．
[7] 佟世男．康熙恩平县志 [M]．广东江门恩平．
[8] 余棨谋．民国开平县志 [M]．广东江门开平．民国 22 年．
[9] 《江门日报》[N]．2005-12-16．
[10] 张春阳，孙一民，苏平．传统街区保护与更新的地域文化战略 [J]．建筑与文化，2011(09)．
[11] 苏平．黄埔临港商务区国际联合城市设计工作坊回顾 [J]．南方建筑，2010(01)．
[12] 丛艳国．江门市城市空间结构演变研究 [D]．广州：华南师范大学，2002．
[13] 杨谢华．江门老城区地名浅析 [J]．五邑大学学报（社会科学版）．2006(08)．
[14] 吴宏岐，胡乐伟．近代江门的侨资房地产业及其对城市建筑景观的影响 (1862-1949 年 )[J]．华侨华人历史研究，2010(2)．
[15] 张国雄．五邑文化刍议 [J]．五邑大学学报（社会科学版），1999(04)．
[16] 李龙潜．明清时期广东墟市的类型及其特点 [J]．学术研究，1982(06)．

# MAIN REFERENCE

[1] Jiangmen Local Records Compilation Committee. The history of Jiangmen, Guangdong People Press, 1988.
[2] Jiangmen Gazetteer Compilation Committee, Jiangmen City Land Bureau, Jiangmen gazetteer, Guangdong Map Publishing House, 1991.
[3] Jiangmen Local Records Compilation Committee, The history of Pengjiang district:1984-2004, Fangzhi Press, 2012.
[4] Jiangmen Local Records Compilation Committee, Water conservation of Jiangmen, Water Power Press, 2008.
[5] Jiangmen City Archives, Jiangmen Local Records offie, Jiangmen the most (First Edition), 2004.
[6] He FH, 1893, The history of Xinning in Guangxu years (Taishan, Jiangmen, Guangdong).
[7] Tong SN, The history of Enping in Kangxi years( Enping, Jiangmen,Guangdong).
[8] Yu QM,1933, The history of Kaiping in Mingguo years( Kaiping, Jiangmen, Guangdong).
[9] Jiangmen Daily,2005.12.16.
[10] Chong CY, Sun YM, Su P. Local culture strategy of protection and renewal in Traditional Blocks. Architecture & Culture,2011(09).
[11] Su P. Review of SCUT-UC Berkeley Whampoa Harbor Workshop. South Architecture, 2010(01).
[12] Chong YG. A study on development of urban spatial structure in Jiangmen. Master Degree Thesis, South China Normal University.
[13] Yang XH. An analysis of the old place names in Jiangmen old urban area. Journal of Wuyi University(Social Science Edition), 2006(08).
[14] Wu HQ,Hu LW. Investment of overseas Chinese in the real estate of modern Jiangmen and Its Impact on the Architecture Landscape 1862-1949. Overseas Chinese History Studies, 2010(06).
[15] Zhang GX. Study of Wuyi culture, Journal of Wuyi university(Social Science Edition), 1999(04).
[16] Li LQ. The Type and feature of Guangdong market in Ming and Qing Dynasty. Academic Research, 1982(06).

# 图片来源

江门市城乡规划局提供：
图 0-1、图 1-1-3、图 1-1-4、图 1-1-5、图 1-1-12、图 1-1-17、图 1-2-2、图 1-2-4、图 1-2-5、图 1-2-6、图 1-2-7、图 2-0-3、图 2-0-4、附图 1-12、附图 1-13、附图 1-14、附图 1-15、附图 1-16、附图 1-17、附图 1-18

来源自《江门市志》（上下册）[M]，江门市地方志编纂委员会，广东人民出版社，1998 年 11 月版：
图 1-1-6、图 1-1-7、图 1-1-8

来源自华南理工大学建筑设计研究院编制的《江门历史街区保护与更新规划》（2013）：
图 1-2-1、图 1-2-3、图 1-2-8、图 1-2-10、图 1-2-12、图 1-2-19、图 1-2-20、图 1-2-23、图 1-2-25、图 1-2-26、图 3-1-1、图 3-1-2、图 3-1-17、图 3-1-18、图 3-1-19、图 3-1-20、图 3-1-21、图 3-1-22、图 3-1-23、图 3-1-24、图 3-2-3、图 3-2-10、附图 1-1、附图 1-2、附图 1-3、附图 1-4、附图 1-5、附图 1-6、附图 1-7、附图 1-8、附图 1-9

来源自"华南理工大学 - 加州大学伯克利校区江门历史街区国际联合城市设计工作坊（2011）"：
图 3-1-3、图 3-1-4、图 3-1-5、图 3-1-15、图 3-1-16、图 3-1-25、图 3-2-5、图 3-2-7、图 3-2-9、图 3-2-11、图 3-2-18、图 3-2-26、图 3-3-4、图 3-3-5、图 3-3-6、图 3-3-7、图 3-3-8

其余照片均为骆乐、李昕旻和谢光源拍摄，技术图纸由何善思、蔡宁、赵杰、吴振兴等 2014 年度城市设计专门化课程班同学绘制。

## IMAGES SOURCE

PROVIDED BY THE PLANNING BUREAUCRACY OF JIANGMEN:
PICTURE0-1, PICTURE1-1-3, PICTURE1-1-4, PICTURE1-1-5, PICTURE1-1-12, PICTURE1-1-17, PICTURE1-2-2,PICTURE1-2-4,PICTURE1-2-5,PICTURE1-2-6,PICTURE1-2-7,PICTURE2-0-3,PICTURE2-0-4,FIGURE1-12,FIGURE1-13,FIGURE1-14,FIGURE1-15,FIGURE1-16,FIGURE1-17,FIGURE1-18

SOURCE FROM JIANGMEN LOCAL RECORDS COMPILATION COMMITTEE, 1988, THE HISTORY OF JIANGMEN, GUANGDONG PEOPLE PRESS :
PICTURE1-1-6,PICTURE1-1-7,PICTURE1-1-8

SOURCE FROM CONSERVATION AND RENEWAL OF HISTORIC DISTRICT IN JIANGMEN:
PICTURE1-2-1 ,PICTURE1-2-3 ,PICTURE1-2-8,PICTURE1-2-10,PICTURE1-2-12,PICTURE1-2-19,PICTURE1-2-20,PICTURE1-2-23,PICTURE1-2-25,PICTURE1-2-26,PICTURE3-1-1 ,PICTURE3-1-2,PICTURE3-1-17,PICTURE3-1-18,PICTURE3-1-19,PICTURE3-1-20,PICTURE3-1-21 ,PICTURE3-1-22,PICTURE3-1-23,PICTURE3-1-24,PICTURE3-2-3,PICTURE3-2-10,FIGURE1-1 ,FIGURE1-2,FIGURE1-3,FIGURE1-4,FIGURE1-5,FIGURE1-6,FIGURE1-7,FIGURE1-8,FIGURE1-9

SOURCE FROM THE INTERNATIONAL JOINT URBAN DESIGN WORKSHOP OF SOUTH CHINA UNIVERSITY OF TECHNOLOGY AND UNIVERSITY OF CALIFORNIA BERKELEY(2011):
PICTURE3-1-3 ,PICTURE3-1-4,PICTURE3-1-5,PICTURE3-1-15,PICTURE3-1-16,PICTURE3-1-25,PICTURE3-2-5,PICTURE3-2-7,PICTURE3-2-9,PICTURE3-2-11 ,PICTURE3-2-18,PICTURE3-2-26,PICTURE3-3-4,PICTURE3-3-5,PICTURE3-3-6,PICTURE3-3-7,PICTURE3-3-8

THE PHOTOS ARE PHOTOGRAPHED BY LUO LE, LI XINMIN AND XIEGUANGYUAN AND DRAWN BY HE SHANSI, CAI NING, ZHAO JIE, WU ZHENXING AND URBAN DESIGN FOR THE 2014 CLASS.

# 后记

　　江门长堤历史街区较为完整地体现了江门城市形态数百年发展演变的历史脉络，保留着以清代和民国时期为代表的建筑群体和街巷空间，以及充满地域特色的社区环境和人文气氛。长堤历史街区传统风貌保存的完整性在珠三角地区表现突出，同时作为历史名人、传统文化、自然环境有机结合的代表地区，是蕴涵着较高价值的重要历史文化遗产。在江门市人民政府的大力支持和江门市城乡规划局以及相关职能部门的充分配合下，华南理工大学建筑学院在近几年对历史街区开展了持续的研究，从具体项目的规划编制到联合毕业设计、国际工作坊的学术交流等各个方面进行多层面的工作。在此过程中，江门各界给予大力的支持与帮助，衷心感谢江门市城乡规划局、蓬江区政府、仓后街道办及下属各居委会等部门的大力支持，特别感谢江门市城乡规划局李荣彬副局长、曾宪谋总工程师、容瑞钊副局长、方刘伟等给予的鼎力支持与帮助。

　　历史街区未来可持续发展的关键在于正确处理保护与利用的关系，包括编者在内的华南理工大学建筑学院部分师生结合教学与科研在这方面进行了初步的研究。在 2011 年初，由编者组织参与，成立了华南理工大学 - 加州大学伯克利校区江门历史街区国际联合城市设计工作坊，多次的教学与科研活动都从风貌保护区、街巷空间形态、建筑单体以及社区环境等各个层面对江门长堤历史街区的发展策略进行了分析研究并提出了相应的设计建议。衷心感谢加州大学伯克利校区教授 Peter Bosselmann，学　生 Richard Crocket、Sarah Moos、Se Woong Kim、Kelly Janes、Leo Hammond、Brain Chambers、Karlene Gullone、Hugo Corro、Deepak、Mahammad Momin、Qinbo Liu；衷心感谢参与教学与科研活动的华南理工大学师生，教师有王成芳、李敏稚、周毅刚、徐好好、董慰等，学生有彭竞、刘卉妍、朱建春、艾雪、何英杰、黄慕贞、许琳莉、雷霄雁、林梓丹、简宇祺、冯志丰、王国斌、李知浩、黄文英、苏癸捷、罗婕、杨忆东、杨倩茜、殷晴、黄文耀、李璐颖、易照墅、胡熙、徐靖、李海全、余月鏻、刘珊、朱怡晨、陈靖敏、王寅、傅静怡、蔡宁、陈泽弘、林桂鹏等。

　　历史街区的保护与更新是城市化进程快速发展的今天不容忽视的议题，希望通过我们的研究整理，让更多的人感受到江门长堤历史街区的独特魅力，也希望能为研究江门长堤历史街区的后来者提供一些参考，共同努力以期让江门悠久的历史文脉在更远的将来可以得到良好的继承和延续。与此同时，编者也期待社会各界在进一步了解江门长堤历史街区的过程中，成为推动街区发展的参与者，集思广益，共同为历史街区的研究和保护贡献力量。

　　最后，衷心感谢为本书的最终排版做出贡献的华南理工大学建筑学院研究生蔡宁、何善思、赵杰。衷心感谢参与历史街区历史建筑摄影的骆乐和李昕旻。

编者

# EPILOGUE

The Jiangmen Historical Neighborhood reflects a complete story line of the historical development of Jiangmen city for hundreds of years. It also presents the buildings and streets in the Qing Dynasty and the Republic of China as well as the local environment and cultural characteristics of the community. The preservation of historical elements in Jiangmen Historical Neighborhood was quite outstanding in the Pearl River Delta region. Meanwhile as an example of combining historical figures, traditional culture and natural environment, it is an important historical and cultural heritage with important values. With the support of the Jiangmen City Government, the Urban and Rural Planning Bureau and other government departments, the School of Architecture of South China University of Technology conducted a consistent study in the region for several years and carried out a series of work from project planning to joint graduation project and academic exchanges as international workshops. In this process, all sectors of Jiangmen community gave strong support and help. We'd like to thank the Jiangmen Planning Bureau, Pengjiang District Government, Canghou Street Office and the subordinated community administration committees and other departments. Our heartfelt thanks also go to the deputy director general Li Rongbin,,chief engineer Zeng Xianmou, deputy director general Rong Ruizhao and Fang Liuwei from Jiangmen Planning Bureau who have given us great support and help.

The sustainable development of historical neighborhoods lies in a proper relationship between protection and utilization. The editors and students from the School of Architecture of South China University of Technology conducted the initial study. In the early 2011, the SCUT-UC Berkeley Jiangmen Historical Neighborhood International Joint Urban Planning Workshop was organized and participated by editors. The many teaching and research activities we conducted have all analyzed and provided designing plans for the development of the historical neighborhood in terms of its preservation area, streets and lanes layout, individual buildings and community environment. We'd like to thank Professor Peter Bosselmann and his students including Richard Crocket, Sarah Moos, Se Woong Kim, Kelly Janes, Leo Hammond, Brain Chambers, Karlene Gullone, Hugo Corro, Deepak, Mahammad Momin, Qinbo Liu from UC Berkeley. We'd also like to thank all the SCUT teachers and students who are involved in the research and teaching. The teachers include Wang Chengfang, Li Minzhi, Zhou Yigang, Xu Haohao and Dong Wei, etc. The students include Peng Jing, Liu Huiyan, Zhu Jianchun, Ai Xue, He Yingjie, Huang Muzhen, Xu Linli, Lei Xiaoyan, Lin Zidan, Jian Yuqi, Feng Zhifeng, Wang Guobin, Li Zhihao, Huang Wenying, Su Yanjie, Luo Jie, Yang Yidong, Yang Qianqian, Yin Qing, Huang Wenyao, Li Luying, Yi Zhaozhao, Hu Xi, Xu Jing, Li Haiquan, Yu Yuelin,, Liu Jin, Zhu Yichen, Chen Jingmin, Wang Yin, Fu Jingyi,Cai Ning,Chen Zehong and Lin Guipeng, etc.

The protection and renewal of the historical neighborhood is a subject that can not be ignored during the rapid development of urbanization. We hope that our research findings can give readers more knowledge about the unique charm of the Changdi Historical Neighborhood and provide some references for future academic research. Let's work together to protect and sustain Jiangmen's long history. Meanwhile, we hope that everybody can participate in the community development after they get a better understanding of the Historical Neighborhood. We hope they can brainstorm and contribute to the research and preservation of historical neighborhoods.

Finally, we wish to thank Cai Ning, He Shansi, and Zhao Jie, graduate students from the School of Architecture who contributed to the editing of this book. Our heartfelt thanks also go to Luo Le and Li Xinmin, our photographers for the historical neighborhoods.

**Authors**

#### 图书在版编目（CIP）数据

江门长堤历史街区 / 孙一民，张春阳，林健生等编著. —广州：华南理工大学出版社，2016.10
ISBN 978-7-5623-4964-8

Ⅰ.①江… Ⅱ.①孙… ②张… ③林… Ⅲ.①商业街-介绍-江门 Ⅳ.①F727.653

中国版本图书馆CIP数据核字(2016)第110437号

### 江门长堤历史街区

孙一民　张春阳　林健生　苏　平　骆　乐　编著

出 版 人：卢家明
出版发行：华南理工大学出版社
　　　　　（广州五山华南理工大学17号楼，邮编510640）
　　　　　http://www.scutpress.com.cn　E-mail: scutc13@scut.edu.cn
　　　　　营销部电话：020-87113487　87111048（传真）
策划编辑：赖淑华
责任编辑：刘　锋　江肖莹
印 刷 者：深圳市福威智印刷有限公司
开　　本：635mm×965mm　1/8　印张：34　字数：410千
成品尺寸：230mm×300mm
版　　次：2016年10月第1版　2016年10月第1次印刷
定　　价：268.00元

版权所有　盗版必究　　印装差错　负责调换